Imageless Truths

Shelley's Poetic Fictions

Karen A. Weisman

University of Pennsylvania Press

Philadelphia

Library of Congress Cataloging-in-Publication Data

Weisman, Karen A
     Imageless truths : Shelley's poetic fictions / Karen A. Weisman.
          p.   cm.
     Includes bibliographical references and index.
     ISBN 0-8122-3222-4
     1. Shelley, Percy Bysshe, 1792–1822—Criticism and interpretation.
I. Title.
PR5438.W44   1994
821'.7—dc20   93-41982
                                                                      CIP

For My Parents,
Harvey and Sandra Weisman

—If the Abysm
Could vomit forth its secrets:—but a voice
Is wanting, the deep truth is imageless;
For what would it avail to bid thee gaze
On the revolving world?

Contents

Acknowledgments

I could not possibly record all the debts of gratitude owed to individuals who have helped me begin to understand the language of poetry, the genre of literary criticism, and the relevance of Romantic discourse; however, it is a distinct pleasure to make at least some effort. My first professors receive my first thanks, especially Professors D.B. Jewison, A.G. Bedford, and C.H. Wyke. From a later period, and in relation to this specific project, I have benefited from the support, instruction, or advice of the following individuals, to whom I am deeply grateful: Professors John Baird, Alan Bewell, Brian Corman, Stuart Curran, the late Vincent A. De Luca, Mark Houlahan, J.R. de J. Jackson, Michael Henry Scrivener, and Milton Wilson. To Stuart Curran in particular I should like to inscribe my thanks for his enormous intellectual generosity, criticism and unfailing kindness. His work on Shelley and the Romantics provides the model I hope one day to be able to emulate. My greatest debt is to Milton Wilson, who supervised this work in its earliest stage as a doctoral thesis, and whose great wisdom, generosity, patience, and support meant—and mean—more to me than he could possibly know.

I am honoured to acknowledge that the earliest version of this book was the recipient of the 1990–91 A.S.P. Woodhouse Prize at the University of Toronto.

A portion of Chapter Five appeared in an earlier version in "Shelley's Triumph of Life over Fiction,"*Philological Quarterly* 71,3 (1992): 337–60, and is reprinted by permission.

Permission is acknowledged to reprint material from published sources as follows:

George Gordon, Lord Byron, *Childe Harold's Pilgrimage*, ed. Jerome J. McGann. Oxford: Clarendon Press, 1980. Copyright © and reprinted by permission of Oxford University Press.

William Cowper, *Poetical Works*, ed. H. S. Milford, 4th ed. rev. Norma Russell. London: Oxford University Press, 1967. Copyright © and reprinted by permission of Oxford University Press.

The Poetical Works of Leigh Hunt, ed. H. S. Milford. London: Oxford University Press, 1923. Copyright © and reprinted by permission of Oxford University Press.

John Keats, *Complete Poems*, ed. Jack Stillinger. Cambridge, MA: Belknap Press of Harvard University Press, 1982. Copyright © 1978, 1982 by the President and Fellows of Harvard College.

John Locke, *An Essay Concerning Human Understanding*, ed. Peter H. Nidditch. Oxford: Clarendon Press, 1979. Copyright © and reprinted by permission of Oxford University Press.

John Milton, *Complete Poems and Major Prose*, ed. Merritt Y. Hughes. Indianapolis: Odyssey-Bobbs-Merrill, 1957. Copyright © 1985 by Macmillan College Publishing Company. Reprinted by permission of Macmillan College Publishing Company, Inc.

The Letters of Percy Bysshe Shelley, ed. F. L. Jones. 2 vols. Oxford: Clarendon Press, 1964. Copyright © and reprinted by permission of Oxford University Press.

Shelley's Poetical Works, ed. Thomas Hutchinson, corrected G. M. Matthews. Oxford: Oxford University Press, 1983. Copyright © and reprinted by permission of Oxford University Press.

Shelley's Poetry and Prose, ed. Donald H. Reiman and Sharon Powers. New York: Norton, 1977. Copyright © 1977 by Donald H. Reiman and Sharon B. Powers. Reprinted by permission of W. W. Norton and Company, Inc.

Shelley's Prose: or The Trumpet of a Prophecy, ed. David Lee Clark. New York: New Amsterdam Press, 1988. Copyright © 1988 by Fourth Estate Ltd. Reprinted by permission.

The Poetical Works of William Wordsworth, ed. F. de Selincourt and Helen Darbishire, rev. Helen Darbishire. Oxford: Oxford University Press, 1952–59. Copyright © and reprinted by permission of Oxford University Press.

Note on Texts

I cite the Reiman/Powers Norton Critical edition of Shelley's poetry and prose wherever possible. Poems not in the Norton edition (notably *The Revolt of Islam*) are quoted from the Oxford Standard Authors edition, edited by Hutchinson and corrected by Matthews. I cite *A Defence of Poetry*, "On Life," and "On Love" from the Norton edition; all other prose references are to David Lee Clark's edition.

Introduction: With Phantoms an Unprofitable Strife

thou didst say thou knewest
A Jew, whose spirit is a chronicle
Of strange and secret and forgotten things.
I bade thee summon him—'tis said his tribe
Dream, and are wise interpreters of dreams.

(Shelley, Hellas 132–36)

O that our dreamings all of sleep or wake
Would all their colours from the sunset take:
From something of material sublime,
Rather than shadow our own soul's daytime
In the dark void of night. For in the world
We jostle—. . . .

(Keats, "Dear Reynolds, as Last Night I Lay in Bed" 67–72)

Peace, peace! he is not dead, he doth not sleep—
He hath awakened from the dream of life—
'Tis we, who lost in stormy visions, keep
With phantoms an unprofitable strife,
And in mad trance, strike with our spirit's knife
Invulnerable nothings.

(Shelley, Adonais 343–48)

This book offers a new reading of the Shelley canon in the context of the poet's evolving constructions of—and self-consciousness with respect to—poetic fictions.[1] Shelley's understanding of language in general, and of fictions and their rhetorical tropes in particular, underwent perpetual modification and transformation throughout his entire career; I claim that it is in his self-consciousness over those chronic transformations that the primary motivating factor in his philosophical and literary development can be found. This inverts the normative paradigm of mainstream Shelley criticism, then, since I study the inherent problematics of fictionality as the very ground of his motivating anxieties. I therefore read the Shelley canon as a developing quest for a mode of fiction-making which is sensitive to the poet's ill-defined belief in a metaphysical ultimate (a belief which is itself a controversial assumption in Shelley studies), but also to his anxiety over the ominous implications of poetic fiction-making with respect to the quotidian world. It is this implicit, vexed attention to the quotidian which forms one of the central foci of my study.

There are, of course, many "Shelley"s current on the present critical scene; my own Shelley reverts to a distrust of imagination that had long been waning among English theorists, even in such skeptical philosophers as David Hume.[2] For Shelley, the "dream," or (often ill-formed) desire, is a motivating force in poetic creation, but it also yields poetic creation as "invulnerable nothing" which potentially attenuates the value, and obviates perception, of the empirical world in which we jostle. To be a wise interpreter of a dream, or of an aesthetic rendering of desire, then, would also be to recognize the dream-like quality of dreams; more to the point, it would be to recognize the pre-symbolic being of those objects in the quotidian world which form the ground of symbol and of fiction-making.

Shelley did come gradually to distrust the very notion of such a "ground," of an unmediated external reality; by 1819, in the fragmentary essay "On Life," he goes so far as to assert that "the difference is merely nominal between those two classes of thought which are vulgarly distinguished by the names of ideas and of external objects" ("On Life" 477). But to problematize reality is not to dismiss the obtrusive fact of the quotidian, the daily life of ill health and financial unease and domestic trauma. Indeed, however much he came to appreciate the reciprocity between perceptual mediation and external reality, and between philology and epistemology, the pressures of dailiness never eluded Shelley. He could experience considerable anxiety over his troping of the world without oversimplifying the philosophical cruxes pertaining to the ontology of reality. His peculiar feat, then, was to struggle at once with both the actual and its problematizations.

Shelley's search for a mode of fiction-making that would protect the integrity of his philosophical musings, as well as the "external reality" from which his metaphors are appropriated, at once places him within, and sets him apart from, the received orthodoxy about the "expressive theory" of Romanticism. Though I respect, within various qualifications, M. H. Abrams's historical context—which is still our received *critical* orthodoxy, even in the midst of an age of new historicism—I claim that Shelley's resistance to any form of complacency is of a piece with his anxiety over the commonly available modes of poetic thinking. Abrams famously characterizes "the expressive theory of art" as one "in which the artist himself becomes the major element generating both the artistic product and the criteria by which it is to be judged" (*Mirror and Lamp* 22). Negotiating the value terms of any age, however, is an immensely vexed, and vexing, issue, and grave implications attend upon the determination of a wholly self-generated artistic criterion. David Simpson, in *Irony and Authority in Romantic Poetry* and in *Wordsworth and the Figurings of the Real*, has offered some of the most important recent discussions of the problematics of Romantic guilt over metaphor; I cite an example from *Irony and Authority* which is consonant with my own claims for the problematics of Shelley's poetic fictions: "The problem becomes almost theological; if the creation of objects from the mind alone is a false or demonic creation, then the reduction of the many to the one, even when a part of a process of reapproaching that oneness (which always involves modification), is a misuse of what has been created already" (152). It is in such contexts, which recall Abrams even as they qualify him, that Simpson interprets the Romantic poetic canon. Speaking of the Lucy poems, for example, he clarifies: "The narrator of 'A Slumber Did my Spirit Seal' learns too late that he has mistaken metaphor for reality and consequently failed to apprehend that living reality" (151). My claims for Shelley have much in common with Simpson's assumptions about Wordsworth, but I also hold to some important differences. In my view, Shelley's evolving guilt over the poetic attenuation of the value of the quotidian is related to, indeed proceeds from, the necessary inefficacy of his tropes for the transcendent. I further claim that he did indeed hold to some form of faith in the existence of a metaphysical absolute, albeit ill-defined, highly ambiguous, and often tormented. But the epistemological problems attendant on leaps of faith are for Shelley only the beginning; the limits of understanding are related to the limits of articulation, of course, but the very quest to resolve such difficulties is partly responsible for the limitations in our capacity to appreciate the external, empirical, quotidian world. Ultimately, his attempt to answer for the implications of his fiction-making becomes the fulcrum on which his development turns.

Philosophical and literary speculation about the limits of language, and the limits and implications of fictions, has a long progeny, and Shelley was a voracious reader in many diverse traditions. But while he assimilated, altered, and rejected many of the views of many of his predecessors and contemporaries, he never wholly appropriated a single tradition in which he could rest assured in the comforts of philosophic or literary sanction. Shelley took what he could and then went on to write poetry, always angst-ridden, rarely consistent by the strictures of conventional logic. For Shelley worries over the possibilities of negotiating Romantic "expressiveness" without diluting the value of actual objects in the world, but also without reverting to what has come down to us as the eighteenth-century aesthetic of imitation. There are, to be sure, many eighteenth-century views on the constitutive function of language and of metaphor, but Shelley would also have been responding to the conventional wisdom of, for example, Samuel Johnson, whose Imlac warns in *Rasselas* that "To indulge the power of fictions and send imagination out upon the wing is often the sport of those who delight too much in silent speculation. . . . He who has nothing external that can divert him, must find pleasure in his own thoughts, and must conceive himself what he is not" (*Rasselas* 114).

Fear of solipsism, of the kind hinted at in *Rasselas*, is one of Shelley's great fears, but finally he comes to suspect that it is the inherent inefficacy of language itself which leads to his particular poetic forms of solipsism. Resonating in the background of his struggle with poetic fictions, then, are such Neoclassical precursor texts as Pope's *An Essay on Criticism*. Witness especially lines 297–327, which exploit the importance of "dress" to character in eighteenth-century thought in ways that bear on an idea of language that Shelley also troubles over. Here there is false eloquence (clothes that show off but do not fit), and true expression, which is truly "suitable":

> Others for *Language* all their Care express,
> And value *Books*, as Women *Men*, for *Dress*:
> Their Praise is still—*The Stile is excellent*:
> The *Sense*, they humbly take upon Content.
> *Words* are like *Leaves*; and where they most abound,
> Much *Fruit* of *Sense* beneath is rarely found.
> *False eloquence*, like the *Prismatic Glass*,
> Its gawdy Colours spreads on *ev'ry place*;
> The Face of Nature we no more Survey,
> All glares *alike*, without *Distinction* gay:
> But true *Expression*, like th'unchanging *Sun*,
> *Clears*, and *improves* whate'er it shines upon,
> It *gilds* all Objects, but it *alters* none.
> Expression is the *Dress* of *Thought*, and still
> Appears more *decent* as more *suitable*;
> A vile conceit in pompous Words exprest,
> Is like a Clown in regal Purple drest. . . . (305–21)

We have a variation, then, on one of the more conservative eighteenth-century permutations of language as the dress of thought, one which Shelley inherited with all of its ambiguities and muted anxieties: Pope compares true expression to the sun, which paradoxically gilds and improves without altering. And it is particularly interesting that Pope's "dress" here acts like the sun, which *reveals* objects by shining on them. Having assimilated such possibilities as part of his received starting point, Shelley will eventually move towards the recasting of such hints into the realization that in a dualistic universe, the process of poetic covering and unveiling amount to the same thing.

I therefore claim that Shelley, unlike Berkeley but like Locke and his successors such as Lord Monboddo, seems finally to have regarded all words as human fictions, rather than separating fictional words from real Adamic ones instituted by God. This is an important background issue, although I always maintain that Shelley's primary concern is with poetic practice, with the implications of poetic craft. Ultimately he is a poet, not a metaphysician, not a linguist. I therefore invoke Shelley's philosophical context, but do not make it a primary consideration in the book. Hans Aarsleff, James Engell, M. H. Abrams, and others have extensively analyzed the intricate history of debate over language that forms the large canvas on which the Romantics drew their fictional worlds.[3] I shall cite, therefore, only representative assertions, by way of briefly indicating the presuppositions Shelley was both formed by and straining against.

We could indeed begin with Plato—certainly, as my chapters make clear, an important source for Shelley—but Plato's disjunction between the realm of Ideal Forms and the mutable world would have been viewed by Shelley through a vista of British skepticism. Locke's *An Essay Concerning Human Understanding* is most helpful in orienting us to the received problem of articulation in its commerce with abstract notions:

> It may also lead us a little towards the Original of all our Notions and Knowledge, if we remark, how great a dependence our *Words* have on common sensible *Ideas*; and how those, which are made use of to stand for Actions and Notions quite removed from sense, *have their rise from thence, and from obvious sensible* Ideas *are transferred to more abstruse significations*, and made to stand for Ideas that come not under the cognizance of our senses; v.g. to *Imagine, Apprehend, Comprehend, Adhere, Conceive, Instil, Disgust, Disturbance, Tranquility*, etc. are all Words taken from the Operations of sensible Things, and applied to certain Modes of Thinking. (*Essay Concerning Human Understanding* 403)

For Locke, the study of language presupposes the study of the human mind, and also suggests another familiar problem: we cannot univocally predicate tangible attributes of that which by its very nature is abstract. I return to this notion at greater length in the course of this study; for our present purposes, it is sufficient to realize that metaphoric predication is the immediate problem in linguistic explorations, for both the idealists and the skeptics. Rousseau too, coming from a different tradition, in *Essay on the Origin of Languages* holds that the original impetus for speech related to the passions, so that language in its initial stages consisted of rhetorical figures.

We may see, then, that the problem of trope as ornament versus trope as epistemological necessity is one mark of virtually all serious speculation on the nature of language; returning again to the British skeptics, it is evident that even Hume's work on cause-and-effect relationship is related in crucial ways to the problem of imagination in its linguistic manifestations. Discussing, in *A Treatise of Human Nature*, our desire to apprehend "cause," Hume explains:

> And how must we be disappointed, when we learn, that this connexion, tie, or energy lies merely in ourselves, and is nothing but that determination of the mind, which is acquir'd by custom, and causes us to make a transition from an object to its usual attendant, and from the impression of one to the lively idea of the other? Such a discovery not only cuts off all hope of ever attaining satisfaction, but even prevents our very wishes; since it appears, that when we say we desire to know the ultimate and operating principle, as something, which resides in the external object, we either contradict ourselves, or talk without a meaning. . . .
>
> For if we assent to every trivial suggestion of the fancy; beside that these suggestions are often contrary to each other; they lead us into such errors, absurdities, and obscurities, that we must at last become asham'd of our credulity. Nothing is more dangerous to reason than the flights of the imagination, and nothing has been the occasion of more mistakes among philosophers. Men of bright fancies may in this respect be compar'd to those angels, whom the scripture represents as covering their eyes with their wings. (266–67)

Shelley finally seizes on such warnings not only in his anxiety over the representation of the abstract and the transcendent, but also in his anxiety over the covering of his eyes, as it were, to the quotidian.

Such warnings, though, form part of a background which also offers great sanction to the creative imagination, to the creative, poetically conceived "heterocosm" — to appropriate Sir Philip Sidney's familiar formulation—which holds out the promise of a truth which is aesthetically pleasing, and ultimately of greater worth than the normative, quotidian apprehension of mundane truth in nature. Joseph Addison's essays on "The Pleasures of the Imagination" (1712) pay particular attention to the value of visual images for the imagination, and at one point Addison goes so far as to insist that words used well are such "that a Description often gives us more lively Ideas than the Sight of Things themselves" (*Spectator 416* 3: 292). He then further clarifies: "In this Case the Poet seems to get the better of Nature; he takes, indeed, the Landskip after her, but gives it more vigorous Touches, heightens its Beauty, and so enlivens the whole Piece, that the Images which flow from the Objects themselves appear weak and faint, in Comparison of those that come from the Expressions." Later, Wordsworth and Coleridge (and many others) sanctioned the poetic rendering of reality, even as they tried to guard against an overly self-centered approach to the world. Coleridge, in the *Biographia Literaria*, complains about the facile position which would reduce the conceivable merely to what can be pictured; but he then goes on, of course, in the famous Chapter 13, to describe the "secondary imagination" in ways that would have alerted Shelley to the potentially ominous implications of Coleridgean aesthetics:

> Every system, which is under the necessity of using terms not familiarized by the metaphysics in fashion, will be described as written in an unintelligible style, and the author must expect the charge of having substituted learned jargon for clear conception; while, according to the creed of our modern philosophers, nothing is deemed a clear conception, but what is representable by a distinct image.   (*Biographia Literaria* Chapter 12; 1: 287–88)

> [the secondary imagination] dissolves, diffuses, dissipates, in order to re-create; or where this process is rendered impossible, yet still at all events it struggles to idealize and to unify. It is essentially *vital*, even as all objects (as objects) are essentially fixed and dead.   (Chapter 13; 1: 304)

To be sure, Coleridge's claim about the value of objects *as* objects is the twin of his reflections on the place of perception within that very world of objects; even so, it is the very casual nature in which objects qua objects can still be dismissed—in the work of his contemporaries and in his own endeavors—to which Shelley finally begins responding. If objects shorn of imaginative perception are fixed and dead, then the leap of imaginative fiction-making is severely burdened where matters of the ineffable are concerned, especially the ineffable transcendent. Beyond even that, however, is also Shelley's anxiety over the integrity of the quotidian—a quotidian which is itself relentlessly elusive—and how a poetic practice can be reconciled to it.

Similar potential trouble spots—from a Shelleyan perspective—are rife in Wordsworth's critical prose as well. In the Preface to *Lyrical Ballads*, Wordsworth does remind us that in describing the language and habits of ordinary men, the poet will fall short of his initial model: "However exalted a notion we would wish to cherish of the character of a Poet, it is obvious, that while he describes and imitates passions, his situation is altogether slavish and mechanical, compared with the freedom and power of real and substantial action and suffering" (*Poetical Works* 1: 138).[4] But in the Preface to *Poems, 1815*, this is not ultimately joined to a full recognition of the dangers of the usurping powers of poetic perception. There he clarifies that imaginative apprehension is the precondition to freedom from subjugation to external matter; commenting on the power to describe things "as they are in themselves," he cautions that "This power, though indispensable to a Poet, is one which he employs only in submission to necessity, and never for a continuance of time: as its exercise supposes all the higher qualities of the mind to be passive, and in a state of subjection to external objects, much in the same way as the Translator or Engraver ought to be to his Original" (*Poetical Works* 3: 26).

Such is the climate of critical taste in which Shelley takes his place. The presuppositions of his age conditioned a profound response to the problematic of poetic fiction-making, even when—and especially when—those issues which were problematic for Shelley were being regarded by some of his contemporaries as the standard and assumed prerequisites of poetic and imaginative success. Still, we may detect such uneasiness throughout the period: Keats's concern, in "Ode to a Nightingale," that his fancy may be a "deceiving elf"; Coleridge's realization (albeit in an entirely different context), in "Dejection: An Ode," that individuals can be also the "shroud" of nature; Byron's insistence, in Canto Three of *Childe Harold's Pilgrimage*, that Rousseau's rendering of Clarens within his fiction (in *La Nouvelle Héloïse*), serves reality first: " 'Twas not for fiction chose Rousseau this spot, / Peopling it with affections; but he found / It was the scene which passion must allot / To the mind's purified beings" (*Childe Harold's Pilgrimage* 3.104).

What distinguishes Shelley's contribution is his persistent, double-edged anxiety over his own use of fictions, an anxiety which impels every aspect of his intellectual development, and which finally leads to an obsessive self-consciousness over his comportment to the quotidian. If this sounds somewhat akin to a deconstructionist perspective, that is because deconstruction also immersed itself, at least for a time, in Shelley's struggles with the limitations of language. But the deconstructionist Shelley denies the presence of an extra-textual absolute, and is interested in the quotidian only within narrowly defined limits. I argue that the instability of poetic fictions was eventually perceived as a "given" by Shelley, as the beginning premise which he acknowledged and then tried to move beyond. That attempt to acknowledge and move beyond inefficacy—with the least possible damage to the integrity of the materials and the objects of poetry—forms the subject matter of this book.

1. To Spread a Charm Around the Spot

Queen Mab

> Hark! whence that rushing sound? (*Queen Mab* 1.45)
>
> Behold the chariot of the Fairy Queen!
> Celestial coursers paw the unyielding air;
> Their filmy pennons at her word they furl,
> And stop obedient to the reins of light:
> These the Queen of spells drew in,
> She spread a charm around the spot,
> And leaning graceful from the etherial car,
> Long did she gaze, and silently,
> Upon the slumbering maid. (1.59–67)

To begin with *Queen Mab* is to begin with scrutiny of a youthful confidence and presumption which only barely mask a taut undercurrent of anxiety. But it is also to begin with glimmers of poetic and philosophic doubt which open up, in Shelley's final years, into the fierce compulsions of an angst-ridden—though highly qualified—skepticism, one which seeks always to answer for its own prior efforts at figuring the world. To begin with *Queen Mab*, then, is to begin at the most vulnerable point in the dialectic of Shelley's career, but one no less important, perhaps, for its immaturity. For the description of the descent of Mab's celestial car, in search of the disembodied soul of a young woman who is to be schooled in the Shelleyan basics of philosophy and politics, is paradigmatic of his most persistent concern: in the narrator's insistence that "'twas not an earthly pageant" (1.84), that "not the visioned poet in his dreams" (1.68) had ever witnessed "so bright, so fair, so wild a shape" (1.74), Shelley signals his already overdeveloped desire to describe the ineffable, to figure conceptualizations whose integrity is held to be violated by the very act of figuration. Later in the poem we learn that his ostensible purpose in introducing an unearthly pageant is in the service of a professed love of the quotidian: Mab herself exclaims, "O happy Earth! Reality of heaven" (9.1), and proceeds to describe an earthly future filled with very earthy joys. Even at this early date, then,[1] Shelley is beginning to manifest a dilemma of which he is not yet fully conscious—how to lay bare the naked truth of existence, shorn of its embellishing fictions, without resorting to a new set of fictions. *Queen Mab* is still too early, perhaps too unseasoned in tone to be able fully to concede that its fictions are suspect; but it is his own attempt to make rather large truth claims, in this highly ornamental poem (and its copious discursive notes), which soon alerts him to this most basic of poetic self-contradictions.

Indeed, the poem follows close on the heels of such explicitly political writings as *An Address to the Irish People* and *Proposals For an Association of Philanthropists*. The first of Shelley's elaborate poetic fictions undertaken during his adult years, then, coincides with his most strident efforts to effect substantial and concrete improvement in the living conditions of the general masses. Furthermore, his failure to realize significant change in his Irish expedition of 1812, for which the latter pamphlets had been prepared, had left him angry, perhaps disillusioned with the very objects of his reformer's zeal (he had conceded to Godwin, "I shall address myself no more to the illiterate" [18 March 1812; *Letters* 1: 277]), but ostensibly no less committed to the cause of effecting concrete, visible improvement in the condition of his society. It is entirely consistent with this commitment, then, that when he resumed the writing of poetry he chose for his subject the past and present ills of human society, and their amelioration in a perfectly harmonious future. But in writing *Queen Mab* Shelley was also introduced to the seductive possibilities of poetic fiction-making, to the lyric allure of narrative whose immediate and superficial integrity—whose story, as it were—requires neither apology nor rigorous philosophic sanction; the very allure of lyric narrative, though, was conceived by the Shelley of *Queen Mab* as a means to an end, as an opportunity to create purely conceptual worlds and situations in the service of communicating what he believed to be significant truths about an objective reality.[2] The time was ripe: Southey and Scott (to name only two), both well-loved by him at the time, had been receiving the highest critical praise for their own ventures into extravagantly imaginative metrical narrative, and in a letter to Hogg, he even cited Southey's *Thalaba* as one of his authoritative precedents for employing free verse (7 February 1813; *Letters* 1: 352). Furthermore, moral allegory, such as Thomson's *Castle of Indolence*, had been especially popular in the eighteenth century and had still not entirely lost its appeal by the beginning of the nineteenth.[3] This would not have been lost on Shelley, who above all wanted *Queen Mab* to be a forum for the instruction of humankind.[4] In launching into such an attempt, though, he just begins to realize the paradoxical nature of poetic license as well as the embellishment to which all language is inevitably susceptible.

In a letter of 29 July 1812, a mere two months after he had begun work on *Queen Mab*, Shelley responds to William Godwin's suggestion that he study the classical languages, protesting that there are other endeavors of greater importance. After all, he insists, "we only want one distinct sign for one idea; — do you not think that there is much more danger of our wanting ideas for the signs of them already made, than our wanting these signs for inexpressible ideas" (29 July 1812; *Letters* 1: 317). And later in the letter, he makes the most telling assertion: ". . . the science of things is superior to the science of words" (*Letters* 1: 318). It is not until later in his career that Shelley implicitly ponders the possibility that the science of things and the science of ideas might potentially be equated with the science of words; for now, though, in his youthful enthusiasm to write a poem which will contribute to nothing less than the salvation of humanity, which will survey human history and provide a glimpse of humanity's future, he wants to convey clearly and precisely "things" which are empirically given and truths which are philosophically demonstrable. In fact, fully one year before work on *Queen Mab* had even begun, he had written to Elizabeth Hitchener that "all poetical beauty ought to be subordinate to the inculcated moral—that metaphorical language ought to be a pleasing vehicle for useful & momentous instruction" (5 June 1811; *Letters* 1: 98).

At this point in his development, then, Shelley is uncertainly poised between his youthful assumptions about the merely ornamental function of figurative language, and the emerging notion—forged variously and within various qualifications—that the language of imagination participates in a reciprocal relationship with the life of truth.[5] Furthermore, concomitant with Shelley's early political involvement is his obsession with language as a theory, as an idea; again, this is a somewhat curious concern for a youth professedly convinced that language had best be effectively mastered so that one can get on with the business simply of using it. It is important, certainly, to separate language theory in general from the distrust of tropes in particular; however, Shelley's consideration of language contributed to his evolving sense that both words (normatively construed) and tropes may be distortions of reality.[6] As early as 1812 he is ordering—in addition to a host of works by Enlightenment authors who influenced the shape of his passion for reform—such works as Lord Monboddo's *Of the*

Origin and Progress of Language and Sir William Drummond's *Essay on a Punic Inscription*. He is also beginning to familiarize himself with the British empiricists, and the notes to *Queen Mab* indicate familiarity with Rousseau's *Second Discourse* (the popular name for *A Discourse on the Origin of Inequality Among Men*). Plato had been read at college, and is picked up sporadically throughout the rest of Shelley's career. Now I am not trying to reduce the philosophical and ideological views of so disparate a group of thinkers to any convenient heuristic or single common denominator; I am interested, however, in pointing out that whatever their respective claims about language, they all provide warnings about specifically figurative language. From Plato's famous criminalizations of the mimetic function of art, to Locke's warning that the confounding of metaphor with concrete reality is a form of insanity, and on to Rousseau's correlations of societal corruption with the sophistication of language skills, all these views about language and figurative speech would seem to render impossible, for any poet acquainted with them, the adoption of a complacent attitude with respect to his art.

The problem is, of course, that Shelley has not yet resolved on a definitive stance with respect to his own art, and so his early poetry sometimes displays a slightly naïve attitude toward language and metaphor, coupled with a latent suspicion that he is doing something amiss. Even the title character, Queen Mab—a favorite subject of storytelling to children—had been chosen partly because he hoped that the aristocrats would be deceived into purchasing what appeared to be a harmless child's tale.[7] The Queen Mab described by Mercutio in Shakespeare's *Romeo and Juliet* is a rather frivolous and playful figure who, as a bringer of dreams, infects youths with adolescent forms of desire. In Shelley's poem, however, her only function is to narrate the important "facts" of the poem. Since these involve a revelation of the future, she is necessarily and qualitatively distinct in kind from human beings and even from what human beings are supposed to aspire to be, indeed a figure who arrives in what was "not an earthly pageant" (1.984) from a celestial "Hall of Spells." The point is that Shelley comes to the poem with a desire to convey certain ideas he has already attempted in prose.[8] He needs a narrator and he needs a title: Queen Mab, associated with children's tales on the one hand and dream visions on the other, would do. Never again in Shelley's career does this happen: Asia, the Witch of Atlas, Emily, *Alastor*'s visionary questor, Laon and Cythna—all his significant personae bear tremendous connotative and metaphorical resonances in ways that are completely foreign to the conception of Queen

Mab.[9] Here, then, is a virtually insignificant abstraction who yet insists, "to me 'tis given / The wonders of the human world to keep" (*Queen Mab* 1.167–68), and whom we, along with Ianthe's miraculously disembodied soul, are asked to believe. We shall see, then, that whatever Shelley's desire to employ Mab simply as a convenient mouthpiece, her status becomes problematical in ways he is not mature enough yet to cope with.

Here is naïve fiction, but it becomes especially troubling when we realize that this embodiment of nothing-in-particular is celebrated precisely because of her unearthliness, even though it is a heaven on earth which the poem professedly yearns toward. The lights from her chariot that streak the sky "are such as may not find / Comparison on earth" (1.57–58), and when Mab and Ianthe's soul reach Mab's celestial dwelling place which "mocks all human grandeur" (2.58), they look down upon the earth, where "The thronging thousands, to a passing view, / Seemed like an anthill's citizens" (2.100–101).[10]

It is not enough to say that once they reach the place where matter, space, and time cease to act they can survey the temporal world fairly (because wholly), for as soon as the catalogue of historical evils and the philosophy lesson about religion and Necessity are over, Mab's exclamations point more clearly to an undercurrent which runs throughout the poem—that is, its movement towards obliteration of the present reality, and indeed of the recognizable particular:

> The present now is past,
> And those events that desolate the earth
> Have faded from the memory of Time,
> Who dares not give reality to that
> Whose being I annul. (8.44–48)

Like the angel Michael providing Adam with a vision of history-to-be in the latter books of *Paradise Lost*, she then proceeds to present a vision of the future, but hers is a futuristic world of ever ripe fruit and beings engaging in mutual acts of benevolence, one so gratuitously sentimental that it hardly deserves its resonance of Milton:

> Those desarts of immeasurable sand,
> Whose age-collected fervors scarce allowed
> A bird to live, a blade of grass to spring,

Where the shrill chirp of the green lizard's love
Broke on the sultry silentness alone,
Now teem with countless rills and shady woods,
Corn-fields and pastures and white cottages. . . .   (8.70–76)

Here now the human being stands adorning
This loveliest earth with taintless body and mind;
Blest from his birth with all bland impulses,
Which gently in his noble bosom wake
All kindly passions and all pure desires.
Him, still from hope to hope the bliss pursuing
Which from the exhaustless lore of human weal
Dawns on the virtuous mind, the thoughts that rise
In time-destroying infiniteness, gift
With self-enshrined eternity, that mocks
The unprevailing hoariness of age. . . .   (8.198–208)

Here, Shelley's vision of the perfected future is a sentimental fantasy, a realistic (and therefore oxymoronic) utopia: human beings actually do sink quietly to the grave (9.57–61), and ruins of outmoded forms of rule, such as palaces, are converted: "To happier shapes were moulded" (9.132). Where Michael in *Paradise Lost* had promised salvation for religious sacrifice, Shelley here substitutes a secular betterment of humanity, although he has not yet learned to resist making prophecies out of jingo-like platitudes: "Peace cheers the mind, health renovates the frame; / Disease and pleasure cease to mingle here, / Reason and passion cease to combat there" (8.229–31).

In fact, so insistent is Shelley on emphasizing the non-fictional possibilities of his imaginative projection, that in his notes he qualifies the meaning of those lines which might appear, superficially, as mere forms of fancy; for example, he glosses the phrase "time-destroying infiniteness" with the caveat, "I do not hence infer that the actual space between the birth and death of a man will ever be prolonged; but that his sensibility is perfectible, and that the number of ideas which his mind is capable of receiving is indefinite" (*Poetical Works* 825).[11] The 1812 essay, *Proposals for an Association of Philanthropists*, provides yet another useful gloss to his own qualification: here he asserts the importance of "plain truth, without the confusion and ornament of metaphor" (65). If Shelley is not yet fully attuned to all the ominous implications of metaphor, he is still wary of its superfluous use, and his apologetic caveat about the metaphorical use of "time-destroying infiniteness" at least confirms that he does not want to conflate the rhetorical substitutions of metaphor with the concreteness of empirical reality. The problem thus consists in demarcating a boundary between them.

From the example of Erasmus Darwin, whose *The Botanic Garden* (1791) greatly influenced the structure of *Queen Mab*,[12] Shelley learned that one could, as Darwin claims in his "Advertisement," "inlist Imagination under the banner of Science" (Section 2, page v) without obviously compromising the truth claims of science. Indeed, in Part Two of the work, "The Loves of the Plants," Darwin presents extensive scholarly explanations to the metaphoric amours of plants, and intersperses the cantos with literary critical dialogues. But Darwin's chief interest in mythologizing the plants is to entertain, to make his scientific researches pleasurable; that is, his fiction-making does not betray an epistemological uncertainty. Shelley's appendage of lengthy discursive notes, which give scholarly explanations of their various poetic renderings, betrays a latent uneasiness with his fictions,[13] not so much because he opposes ornament per se, but because he wants to ensure that the "plain truth" is kept distinct from its embellishment. The poetry of *Queen Mab*, though, attempts to describe and to contextualize concepts which for Shelley proceed, at least in part, from moments of intuitive or projected insight. But he has not yet reconciled himself to the possibility that some concepts—possibly all concepts—are not reducible to literal paraphrase.[14]

Mab's apostrophe to a suddenly anthropomorphized "Necessity" as the "mother of the world" is typical in this regard. First the poem exults in her complete egalitarianism; the notes clarify and expand on this idea, but cautiously omit virtually all figurative expressions. The first sentence of the note will serve as example: "He who asserts the doctrine of Necessity means that, contemplating the events which compose the moral and material universe, he beholds only an immense and uninterrupted chain of causes and effects, no one of which could occupy any other place than it does occupy, or act in any other place than it does act" (*Poetical Works* 809). The poetry, he hopes, has already attracted an audience, and so now the "facts" themselves can be addressed. In the notes, he therefore presumes to explain the discursive "meaning" of his poetic devices, because in the final analysis, fiction cannot be entirely trusted. The Shelley of *Queen Mab* simply wants figurative language to be purely ornamental, to help him make what he urgently believes to be a literal point. He is young and for the most part confident in his convictions, at least in apparent posture; the radical fiction of the poem bears upon the world of empirical experience, he insists, its dross no less insistent for its perusal by an extra-terrestrial figment of a post-adolescent imagination.

Queen Mab in particular, however, has often been noted for its philosophical inconsistencies,[15] and Shelley's poetry in general has always been vulnerable to the charge that it wavers uneasily between aspiration to a transcendent otherness, where all mortal anxiety and torment are resolved, and a conflicting desire for a condition of perfection within the temporal world itself. Even Earl Wasserman finally throws up his hands, as it were, and remarks that "perfection in either realm renders the other pointless" (*Critical Reading* 94). I would suggest that as early as *Queen Mab*, Shelley endures repressed anxieties that absolute faith in either realm would amount to subjugation to the very fictions which—as he would prefer to view them—are meant to clarify such faith; that is, he wants to believe that his professed faith does not amount to a conflation of metaphor with reality. I further maintain that the logical inconsistencies of *Queen Mab* are directly related to this condition.

First, when Shelley sets out in *Queen Mab* to describe the past and the present—inescapable and obtrusive realities—he employs concrete, tactile images, most of which possess easily identifiable tenors. This is of course not the case in the later poems, but at this early stage his concern for readability—of the kind which facilitates translation into prose statement—is paramount.[16] Here is a sampling of "figured" assertions, all of which present themselves unobtrusively, almost self-effacingly, and certainly with the least possible difficulty in construal:

The thronging thousands, to a passing view,
Seemed like an anthill's citizens. (2.100–101)

Where Athens, Rome, and Sparta stood,
There is a moral desart now. (2.162–63)

                    Now to the meal
Of silence, grandeur, and excess, he drags
His palled unwilling appetite. (3.44–46)

These are highly figurative descriptions, but they are employed in the easy service of "facts" about the world; they may not yield the same transparent, clear understanding that simplified prose offers, but they can still serve their modest purpose. At this early stage, Shelley's self-conscious apprehensions about metaphor are largely confined to those which are overly mellifluent, and to those which masquerade as imposing, anthropomorphic deities. But *Queen Mab* also offers praise to Nature and Necessity, and betrays an unsophisticated amalgam of the diverse philosophical claims of Godwin, d'Holbach, and Rousseau, of pantheism and panpsychism, all of which is supposed to connect with the notion of an amoral Necessity which impels all things irrevocably towards their final effects. The ultimate apotheosis of such constructs, as we shall soon see, yields poetry that confuses more than it clarifies. In rebelling against institutional Christianity and conventional orthodoxies, Shelley presents a poetical alternative, but he neglects to consider its debt to his fiction-making habits. And this is the omission which subtly—even unconsciously—haunts him, and which will become an explicit focal concern in his later years.

Indeed, the poem's vision of the future is premised on humanity's obliteration of those evil inclinations which impede progress, but Shelley does not sufficiently explain the difference between the individual's freedom to actualize his or her own potential for perfection, and the determinism which is the necessary concomitant of the doctrine of Necessity.[17] It would appear, then, that Necessity is conceived of as an elegant concession to the sorry actualities of the present, but a concession nonetheless to his strained acceptance that what exists without obvious cause still serves its place in terms of a comprehensible, secular scheme. To ascribe so many unknowns to the conscious will of a deity would necessarily require the resources of perhaps too much metaphor, of the kind he has learned to revile. For Shelley is obsessed with his contempt for those who compensate for theological ignorance with anthropomorphic fictions: "but human pride / Is skilful to invent most serious names / To hide its ignorance" (7.24–26). What he does not do, however, is explicitly consider the fictionality of his own alternatives, his own skillful inventions.

For the tendons of poetic control in *Queen Mab* are stretched beyond the bounds of complete recovery: Shelley never concedes that he possesses an intense need to save himself from what we would today process as an existential crisis, as the anxiety, that is, attendant on disavowing faith in a sustaining force of the universe. In the notes he reminds us that his pronouncement, "There is no God," applies only to a creative deity: "The hypothesis of a pervading Spirit coeternal with the universe remains unshaken" (*Poetical Works* 812). Shelley's quest for a grand otherness, for a Spirit which pervades existence but which yet is distinguished from it, is the quest of the politically disaffected in fear of spiritual sterility. Pantheistic nature ("Every grain / Is sentient both in unity and part, / And the minutest atom comprehends / A world of loves and hatreds" (4.143–46) and amoral Necessity and the rejuvenated temporal world have their most significant origin in the young Shelley's unacknowledged inability to confront a de-mythologized quotidian existence, one whose ground of value does not exist outside itself.[18] Always in Shelley's poetry there is an otherness lurking, one which he superficially intends to be the consummation of temporally ordered mortal happiness, but which in fact perpetually deflects attention away from the sensual, material world. This otherness is and must always be, if not itself a fiction, then at least conceptualized in terms of human aspirations to, and illusions of, what an otherness might possibly be; faintly glimpsed forums for fully developed human happiness, after all, do not properly belong to the realm of univocal predication.

Thus, when Shelley exclaims, "O happy Earth! reality of Heaven," he is employing the familiar notion of Christian heaven as a metaphor, as a fictional predication of earth's essential significance. He is troping on tropes here, falling into the very same trap of which he accuses Christian dogmatists, for he has described earth in terms of a metaphor (Heaven) whose normative construal he inveighs against. His own discursive notes to "Necessity, thou mother of the world!" (6.198) are again particularly illuminating in this regard:

> It is probable that the word God was originally only an expression denoting the unknown cause of the known events which men perceived in the universe. By the vulgar mistake of a metaphor for a real being, of a word for a thing, it became a man, endowed with human qualities and governing the universe as an earthly monarch governs his kingdom. (*Poetical Works* 812)

But Shelley presents us with a word—Necessity—and an unknown—the future according to Queen Mab—and implicitly asks us to conflate such metaphors with his own constructions of reality, for he has not yet pondered the possibility that they *are* metaphors, and metaphors that have gotten the better of him. For all Shelley's youthful enthusiasm and energetic concern, *Queen Mab* finally fails, but it is the necessary failure which sets him on his anxious way.

From *Queen Mab* to *Alastor*

Shelley began *A Refutation of Deism* just after completing *Queen Mab*, and its design suggests an emerging tendency to thematize the necessary problematics that attend the communication of assumed truths. The intellectual content of the dialogue represents virtually no progress in the development of his ideas on religion per se—Christianity is still presented as a historical evil that inhibits human potential, and atheism is presented as a liberating alternative—but its concessions to the perplexing intricacies of rhetorical persuasion and the uncertainties of competing philosophies form an important bridge to *Alastor's* full-fledged crisis over the significance of existence and the means of its articulation. Loosely following the form of disputation and dialogue established by Plato and continued with renewed vigor by Bishop Berkeley, David Hume, and many others in the eighteenth century,[19] *A Refutation of Deism* outlines the debate between Eusebes, a Christian, and Theosophus, a Deist, each putting forth arguments that are equally persuasive about the merits of the religion to which they respectively subscribe. Since Theosophus admits that he would rather be even a Christian than an atheist, that "monster among men," Eusebes ends the dialogue by offering a powerful and typical early Shelleyan dissertation on the merits of atheism, ostensibly hoping that Theosophus will be convinced, first that Deism cannot compete with atheism, and then that Christianity ought to be adopted.

One could, of course, argue that atheism wins out in the end, and that Shelley is merely manipulating his readers in clever and subtle ways; however, it is important to bear in mind that, in a slight break from the dialogue form familiar in Shelley's predecessors, all three positions are given virtually equal weight, and that no position is finally given definitive authorial approval.[20] Shelley's commitment to his own version of the principal tenets of atheism is not what is immediately at question here. What is noteworthy is his awakening interest in dialectical thought and the necessary doubts and anxieties attendant on it. Three competing world views are in turn promoted and then reviled, each with virtually equal persuasive powers. The simplicity of naïve communication ends, for Shelley, at this point. The "deep truth" is not yet imageless, as will be asserted in *Prometheus Unbound*, but it is something that, at the very least, has to be chosen from myriad equally seductive hypotheses. *A Refutation of Deism* is still implicitly advocating one particular choice, but it is of the utmost importance to note that hypotheses, uncertainties, and rhetorical arguments about religion and about the essential significance of human life are themselves beginning to form the most salient aspects of his treatment of religion and life. The process is a circular one: if rhetoric can be so seductive, then surely he himself may have become seduced by the urgency of his own rhetoric—especially of the highly figurative variety—even while such rhetoric is the issue of his urgency to affirm definitive positions about Truth.

We witness the beginnings, then, of Shelley's life-long fear of solipsism, of the subjectivity that causes projected fictions to take the place of the very objective reality one seeks to define. In *Alastor*, a poet/questor consumes himself into annihilation by over-indulging his desire to transcend the spiritual aridity which, he believes, is the defining feature of the mutable world. By the end of the poem both the solipsistic vision he pursues and the empirical, mutable world become vacant to him, and so the only thing he can do is die. The real crisis begins: neither quotidian life, nor one's fictionalized projections of meaningful otherness, is sufficient. Henceforth Shelley struggles with his growing consciousness of the reciprocity between, and inextricability of, the anxiety of human impoverishment and philosophical premise, of subjective order and human value.

Contemporaneous with the writing of *Alastor* is Shelley's revision of parts of *Queen Mab* into the much shorter *Daemon of the World*, which, along with *Alastor*, starts to respond poetically to his earlier postures. The later poem leaves out the narration of the historical past and present, leaves out the logically inconsistent lessons about Necessity and pseudo-pantheism which by this point Shelley has discarded from his philosophical baggage, and concentrates exclusively on the vision of the future. Now it might appear that virtually plunging into the future without leading up to it in temporal sequence, or preparing for it by way of offering its philosophical underpinnings, yields an even more obtrusive fiction. But that is precisely the point of the revision: the hopeful vision, which in *Queen Mab* is offered as actual prediction, in *Daemon* remains just a hopeful vision. In the revision, the past and present evils of humanity are not paraded again for the reader's condescending scrutiny, because the more mature Shelley becomes the further he realizes that one cannot simply sum up the past and present and then predict a future that will miraculously replace it. And, most important, it is not a royal personage, not as imposing a presence as Queen Mab, who teaches Ianthe, but a daemon, a spirit who serves simply as an intermediary between earth and the assumed spiritual realm.

In *Queen Mab*, when the Fairy's chariot descends, Shelley vigorously insists that no one had ever before witnessed such a sight—not even the "visioned poet in his dreams" (1.68). The paradox seems to be entirely intentional: if not even the visioned poet is privy to such sights as Ianthe sees, then poet Shelley (who after all does see what Ianthe sees) is merely acting as voyeur/eavesdropper to someone else's significant experience. This situation conditions a peculiar and potent suspension of disbelief, one that goes far beyond anything needed for simple storytelling. For the context becomes one of authentic revelation, a kind of trance in which a real event is glimpsed. Not surprisingly, this stanza is omitted entirely in *Daemon*, and though the narrator in the later poem does assert of the daemon that "Human eye hath ne'er beheld / A shape so wild, so bright, so beautiful," the vision's inaccessibility is toned down. It therefore becomes emphatically clear that, for Shelley in 1815, what Ianthe sees is a *poetically* conceived—if fantastic—showcase of virtuous principles and of hopes for human progress. Her superior powers of vision are simply presented, then, in terms of the poet's modest disclaimer:

> For thou hast earned a mighty boon,
>   The truths which wisest poets see
> Dimly, thy mind may make its own,
>   Rewarding its own majesty
>   Entranced in some diviner mood
>   Of self-oblivious solitude. (*Daemon* 84–89)

A poet's construct—the Ianthe of *Daemon of the World*, for example—may be, perhaps, "self-oblivious," but can a poet—especially one in "solitude"—ever be so? Probably not, at least not in the conceptual universe which Shelley gradually comes to inhabit. For in exploring the implications of ascribing value only under the conditions of metaphor's necessary deflections, *Alastor* also evinces Shelley's apprehension that his fictional constructs do not truly correspond to anything, because, worse than taking conventional metaphors for real beings, he himself creates new—but suspect—metaphors. He then not only takes them for real beings but invokes them as higher authorities, ones that are not marred by participation in the dross of temporality.

At the most superficial level, *Alastor* is the story of a poet who dies because he forsakes the temporal world in favor of an abstract vision that he pursues fruitlessly until his death. Ever since Earl Wasserman's ingenious analysis of the poem in *Shelley: A Critical Reading*,[21] it has been generally agreed that the narrator, who opens the poem with a Wordsworthian invocation to Nature, his "Great Parent," is sharply distinguished from the Poet/questor. The latter is the notorious Shelleyan Visionary, who forsakes the love of an Arab maiden and then falls in love with a dream-vision of a veiled maiden, one who in fact appears as the feminized version of the best qualities in himself. Norman Thurston also makes the astute observation that the author of the Preface, who gives a very brief summary and analysis of the situation that is inconsistent with the actual facts presented in the poem, is another one of the dramatis personae ("Author, Narrator, and Hero" 119–31 passim). I grant the validity of the views of Wasserman and his heirs in this regard, but I also see considerable common ground (whatever their different tactics) among narrator, questor, and Preface-writer. As such, my argument departs somewhat from the more dialectical assumptions of Wasserman, even as I recognize the importance of the distinctions that can be made between the dramatis personae.

Indeed, like *A Refutation of Deism*, *Alastor* progresses tentatively, knowing that there is a point to be made but unsure of which one it ought to be. This time, however, Shelley knows that any choice has its dangerous price, as the Preface's discussion of love suggests: "But that Power which strikes the luminaries of the world with sudden darkness and extinction, by awakening them to too exquisite a perception of its influences, dooms to a slow and poisonous decay those meaner spirits that dare to abjure its dominion" (69). This represents a radical departure from the sentiments about human potentiality expressed in *Queen Mab*, *The Daemon of the World*, and indeed even many of the short lyrics written at this period. For in most of the earlier poems Shelley is confident of, if nothing else, human potential to sustain the burden of an improved state of affairs, once an acceptable plateau of progress has been reached. Even in the short lyrics that lament mutability, there is never any uncertainty that, given the chance, the beleaguered personae would rise from their torment with full benevolence and a keen sense of justice. The primary cause of Shelley's turn to doubt lies in his developing understanding of the role that subjective need assumes in the determination of perception.[22] The extent to which we perceive the "Power of the universe" depends on the constitution of our perceptual filters, but also on the decision that such a power actually exists.

In his prefatory invocation, the narrator asks that Nature enable him to "modulate" his own "strain" with "murmurs of the air, / And motions of the forests and the sea" (46–47), so that Nature will "Favour [his] solemn song." Two issues are immediately striking. First, the narrator invokes Nature to help him tell his story, but it is a story in which he tries

to honor a "child of grace and genius" (as he refers to him in the conclusion of the poem), who nonetheless becomes entirely oblivious to the natural world, indeed actively shuns it. Second, the narrator asks that Nature
grant his boon as recompense for his years of love and devotion to Her.
When he proceeds to enumerate the forms of this love, however, it becomes
evident that it is something utterly beyond nature that he has adored:

> I have watched
> Thy shadow, and the darkness of thy steps,
> And my heart ever gazes on the depth
> Of thy deep mysteries. I have made my bed
> In charnels and on coffins, where black death
> Keeps record of the trophies won from thee.
> Hoping to still these obstinate questionings
> Of thee and thine, by forcing some lone ghost,
> Thy messenger, to render up the tale
> Of what we are. . . .
>
> *   *   *   *   *   *   *   *
>
> and, though ne'er yet
> Thou hast unveil'd thy inmost sanctuary,
> Enough from incommunicable dream,
> And twilight phantasms, and deep noonday thought,
> Has shone within me. . . . (20–41)

Enough has shone within him that he may now tell his story of the "incom-
municable dream" of someone else, one who equally fails to "unveil"
nature, the secret of "what we are," or indeed to unveil his veiled maiden.
The narrator goes on, as we have seen, to solicit the aid of the "Great Parent" Nature, but his quest, as he describes it, has absolutely nothing to do
with the natural world. He still clings desperately to his frantic effort to
ascribe ultimate value to nature, though, because transcendental quests
yield no assured answers: "obstinate questionings," for Shelley as for
Wordsworth, are rhetorical questionings.[23]

The narrator has failed because he leaps from natural existence to ultimate reality (by way of some facile, life-denying antics): he wants to believe
that the "tale of what we are" (28–29) is equal to nature revealed,
"unveiled." This may well be naïve, but it is easier to ascribe the source of
ultimate value to something empirically knowable than to an unfamiliar

construct entirely alien to the senses. But the narrator and the questor and even the Preface-writer—who is the only one in the work who acknowledges the potential dangers of poetic powers of insight—all seek something beyond themselves for fulfilment of their spirituality; the nature unveiled which, the narrator believes, will yield a consummation of spiritual striving, is for the Poet something quite different: either impediment to spiritual striving, or symbol for something entirely beyond the natural world. In each case, however, the persona's quest is sustained by his respective fiction.

The construction of these particular fictions is my first concern. The author of the Preface says of the Poet/questor that "So long as it is possible for his desires to point towards objects thus infinite and unmeasured, he is joyous, and tranquil, and self-possessed" (69). But these cease to suffice because "His mind is at length suddenly awakened and thirsts for intercourse with an intelligence similar to itself. He images to himself the Being whom he loves." The poem proper then tells us that the questor's infancy had been nurtured by "solemn vision, and bright silver dream" (67), and when he left his home, he went in search of "strange truths in undiscovered lands" (77). He goes on a tour of "the awful ruins of the days of old" (108), where he pays special attention to "whatsoe'er of strange / Sculptured on alabaster obelisk, / Or jasper tomb, or mutilated sphynx, / Dark Æthiopia in her desert hills / Conceals" (112–16). We have here the beginnings of a romance paradigm, but as Stuart Curran observes in *Poetic Form and British Romanticism*, it is one replete with pointed ironies, for the questor breaches the primary requisites of the romance-hero: "His protagonist spurns love; his only sexuality is involuntary and unproductive; and though he is called a Poet, he never puts pen to paper. He also covers most of the known earth in his compulsive travels and discovers nothing new" (148). Furthermore, the Preface insists that the questor is happy when his desires point to what is infinite, unmeasured; the earth's phenomenal mass is finite and measurable. The author of the Preface, then, appears unwilling to make any unsettling leaps of faith to an intangible unknown, for he believes the infinite is contained within the finite mass which is earth; that is, he seems to equate the questor's various travels to "undiscovered lands" with actual approach to the infinite.

Now the questor obviously is in possession, well before he experiences his dream vision, of infinite longing to satiate his desire for spiritual fulfilment,[24] and his quest is peculiarly poetic in ways that anticipate Shelley's attempt to define poetry, six years later, in the *Defence of Poetry*. In the latter, he counsels that poetry is to "create anew the universe, after it has been annihilated in our minds by the recurrence of impressions blunted by reiteration" (*Defence* 505–6). The questor (who, it is important to remember, is also a "Poet," complete with capital "P") obviates the dangers of recurrent impressions merely by not staying long enough in one place to have impressions recur too often. Even without our privileged position of foresight with respect to the *Defence*, the license for calling the questor a Poet may be clearly observed: he extends his imaginative desire in the service of finding new images that will be answerable to his longing. The problem, of course, is that his longing is ill-defined (in fact, not really defined or focused at all), and he does not discern the difference between discovering hitherto unapprehended truths and discovering objects in nature that are novel enough (and hence mysterious enough) to be regarded as authentic images of truth.

Shelley also deals ironically with the narrator in this respect, for he has him explain that at night, when the questor was gazing on "mysterious halls" that contain, significantly, "*speechless* shapes," he "gazed, till meaning on his vacant mind / Flashed like strong inspiration, and he saw / The thrilling secrets of the birth of time" (*Alastor* 126–28). What these secrets are we are not told, and we may guess that we are not told because the narrator does not know them and the Poet does not articulate them, at least not in this poem. In fact, it would appear that this is at least partly the narrator's own projection, for he too yearns to know "the tale of what we are," and, like the questor, he seems to believe that he will be answered if he witnesses, as he implies in the invocation, images that have not been seen before. The questor does suspect that there is something to be gleaned in life beyond what is immediately perceptible to him, but his initial quest to find it is somewhat naïve: he travels to different lands and sees objects he has not seen before. From these, the narrator tells us, he deduces "meaning," nothing less than the "thrilling secrets of the birth of time." So, either the narrator does not know them, or they are ineffable. Or are the readers— as non-initiates—witnessing an act of intentional concealment of the mysterious secrets of the universe? Shelley, of course, is in control of his confused narrator, indeed is offering an early warning about the dead-end road of reading the world in an exclusively analogical manner.[25]

Indeed, the Poet's presumed moment of epiphany is immediately preceded by his exploration of "ruined temples" and "Stupendous columns," a place where he finds "wild images of more than man" (117–18), where "dead men / Hang their mute thoughts on the mute walls around" (119–20). A new element, therefore, has been introduced: the dead are "mute" and the walls are "mute." The memorials of "the world's youth" are referred to as "speechless shapes" (123). Soon the questor is to experience the vision of the veiled maiden, who tells an "ineffable tale" (168). He may be in search of ultimate truth, but the quest ends in silent images, and in images which are silenced. Both are taken as meaningful experiences of absolute truth. Shelley in 1815 is desperately striving to hold to a representational view of language, but his desire to maintain belief in a transphenomenal, non-discursive reality makes it very difficult for him to do so. If a transcendent reality does exist, then its representation must be beyond the reach of temporal metaphors, if we understand metaphor to be an implicit interaction of two "systems of associated commonplaces"[26]: there are neither stable nor tangible commonplaces of the Unknown to be interacted with. But this is where, for Shelley, the virtual necessity of "believing" in metaphors begins to present itself. Human understanding would seem to require a negotiation between two apparently opposed polarities: a life of perpetual uncertainty or a life of trying to predicate tangible attributes of an intangible, metaphysical ultimate.

But Shelley yearns to experience a world of objects and certain predictions for what can become of them. This is one of the primary reasons that Queen Mab as character proved to be, for him, finally ineffective; eventually he realizes that he cannot get away with having an arbitrary fiction pontificating about the state of human affairs and the ultimate meaning of existence. Shelley begins to consider, then, that he has always been harboring a certain amount of natively given convictions about the transcendentalism of ultimate reality. The question for him now becomes: what are such convictions if not simply the concretization, in language, of his subjective yearning for an existence better than the one in which he irrevocably finds himself? If the communication of his views must rely exclusively on fictions that are arbitrary and vulnerable and hence finally expendable; if knowledge, as he says in "Speculations on Metaphysics,"[27] is bounded by perception; and if, as he reminds us in the notes to *Queen Mab*, the "God of the theologians is invisible," then what is one to make of one's need to realize desires that are beyond perception, beyond communicable knowledge? Indeed, can those convictions about ultimate reality, whose only possible articulation is vulnerable to the kind of fictional collapse that Queen Mab the character had been, be distinguished from desire?

Shelley is so anxious about his speculative vagueness that in "Speculations on Metaphysics" he attempts to excuse their tenuous nature by insisting upon their logical necessity:

> The irresistible laws of thought constrain us to believe that the precise limits of our actual ideas are not the actual limits of possible ideas; the law, according to which these deductions are drawn, is called analogy; and this is the foundation of all our inferences from one idea to another inasmuch as they resemble each other.   ("Speculations on Metaphysics" 184)

Shelley's "laws of thought" sound more like the laws of desire, but in any case analogy in Shelley's day is also commonly understood to be the basis of rhetorical tropes, as they had been defined especially by Aristotle.[28] He would understand by this also, then, that there is a fine line between inference and outright embellishment. For the articulation of an inference of a "possible idea" as opposed to an "actual idea" would (since it is deduced from analogy) necessarily yield a metaphorical utterance. There is, then, great anxiety over the validity of that inferred idea's articulation, of what one can reasonably do with it. Later in the very same essay, Shelley reviles, just as he had reviled them in *Queen Mab*, those who make the "mistake of a name for a thing" (185).[29] To concretize in language one's subjective sense of a "possible idea" is clearly a tricky business, and by 1815 Shelley is just starting to realize it.

We may recall that in *Queen Mab*—for all his superficial insistence on his own atheism—Shelley was still asserting the existence of a pervading (and imageless) "Spirit" of the universe. When Mab and Ianthe surveyed the earth and its history, they did so from a position qualitatively distinct from earth, even physically above the earth and invisible from it, and they did so while Ianthe was disembodied. There is clearly a drive toward a metaphysical dualism operating in the early poem, whatever the youthful Shelley wants to call it; whatever his insistence about earth as the reality of heaven, his desire to believe in a transphenomenal realm that is qualitatively distinct from, indeed better than, earth is stronger than his ill-conceived sentiments about atheism. Mab is naïve fiction and convenient vehicle, yes, but she is also apotheosized in the poem to the point of redundancy, and this is because Shelley takes pleasure in witnessing finally an incarnation of his yearning to apprehend absolute meaning. In *Mab*, the meaning overtly sought is defined as amelioration of life's troubles, but Shelley seems to like Mab's otherworldliness even more than he likes her vision of this world's rejuvenation. We may see more clearly now the proximity of preoccupation between *Queen Mab* and *Alastor*, though *Alastor* responds directly to what in *Queen Mab* is inadvertent: in *Alastor* an unhealthy solipsism necessarily results when the mind, unable to find anything in the external, objective world answerable to its longing for meaning, turns inward and feeds its desire with its own desire, that is, with an overflow of tropes of desire, conceived because the mind must always concretize its contents in some form.

In *Romantic Origins* Leslie Brisman suggests that "The taking of dreams for origins is, throughout Shelley's poetry, a literary taking, a fiction about the workings of consciousness and not a representation of an extrapoetic idealism or belief in a world of spirits" (137). It is precisely this distinction, however—"the workings of consciousness" as opposed to an "extrapoetic idealism"—which is overlooked far too often by critics of Shelley's poetry. Brisman goes on to remark that Yeats "thought spirits brought metaphors for poetry but . . . did not always believe spirits to be themselves metaphors of poetry"; but surely this belief is of the very essence in Shelley, indeed the delineation becomes the raison d'être for the very writing of further poems. Shelley writes *Alastor* because he wants to clarify the difference between consciousness and actual transphenomenal idealism, and he suspects that he is destined to fail in the attempt.

It is therefore entirely appropriate that the questor rejects the love of the Arab maiden. This Poet/questor is attempting to deal in ultimate reality, in apprehension of the infinite; to love a corporeal figure, a real flesh-and-blood woman, would be to transfer his preoccupations from realms only approachable through metaphor and fiction to the concrete and quotidian. The Poet in his frantic travels derives value from that which is mute, dead, unseen by others. His objects of value are objects which can be transmuted into tropes of meaning that have nothing to do with themselves: his travels took him to ruins of the past and the wilds of nature while his "step" was "obedient to high thoughts," that is, obedient to his ability (the only one, as we shall soon observe, that he possesses) to accumulate novel images, ones which can serve as symbols of metaphysical meaning—again: "he gazed, till meaning on his vacant mind / Flashed like strong inspiration, and he saw / The thrilling secrets of the birth of time." It is the perfectly logical stroke of Shelley as controlling poet that after the questor rejects the love of the Arab maiden he falls asleep in a "natural bower" (*Alastor* 147): nature itself, images themselves, indeed even other human beings are "vacant" to him prior to his personal imposition of meaning, prior to his rendering of them as vehicles for his desire to see beyond them, and he experiences a vacancy of the mind until he can fix images as correlatives of his desire.

Having temporarily exhausted his store of such images in the natural world, he has his dream[30]:

> A vision on his sleep
> There came, a dream of hopes that never yet
> Had flushed his cheek. He dreamed a veiled maid
> Sate near him, talking in low solemn tones.
> Her voice was like the voice of his own soul
> Heard in the calm of thought; its music long,
> Like woven sounds of streams and breezes, held
> His inmost sense suspended in its web
> Of many-coloured woof and shifting hues.
> Knowledge and truth and virtue were her theme,
> And lofty hopes of divine liberty,
> Thoughts the most dear to him, and poesy,
> Herself a poet. Soon the solemn mood
> Of her pure mind kindled through all her frame
> A permeating fire: wild numbers then
> She raised, with voice stifled in tremulous sobs
> Subdued by its own pathos: her fair hands
> Were bare alone, sweeping from some strange harp
> Strange symphony, and in their branching veins
> The eloquent blood told an ineffable tale. (149–68)

There has always been a great deal of scholarly discussion about the meaning of all Shelley's veiled maidens, and this one is no exception. I would suggest, however, that her status as symbol is vague—indeed she is veiled partly for this very reason—because her desirability qua symbol is Shelley's primary point of interest: there is no discernable signified. For Shelley, she is a trope of abstract desire recognized as a trope, in all its seductive manifestations, but for the Poet/questor she is an object of desire and veneration, of the kind that Mab as well as Mab's vision of the future had been for the youthful Shelley. The veil itself serves several functions, one of which suggests a kind of defense mechanism. For if the questor could see fully behind it, he would see that he is confronting not an otherness (of any variety), but a formal construal of desire. There would be, not the woman whom he decides is the woman of his dreams, but himself, his own fiction-making capacity that has been called into play because desire must needs finally find an object, if only an illusory one in the end. She does, to be sure, also possess some very sensual qualities; such descriptions as "Her glowing limbs beneath the sinuous veil" (176) and "her parted lips / Outstretched" (179–80), and the questor's very physiological reaction to her, suggest the possibility that he is meeting something less than pure otherness, even in his dreams. But that is precisely one of the defining features of his immaturity. Repressed, he projects a vision overladen with unconcealed sexual connotations, but he does not so much as hesitate before making the vision's sexuality into a trope for an asexual absolute.[31]

The questor's primary difficulty, then, is in determining a locus of objectivity, and so "Her voice was like the voice of his own soul," and her themes are, not surprisingly, the same abstractions for whose sake he has always scorned temporal love: "knowledge, and truth and virtue" and "lofty hopes of divine liberty." We can already see how closely linked the Poet/questor of *Alastor* is with the poet of *Queen Mab*, who also pursues these themes, and who was shown to betray inadvertently a preference for his own fictional projections (Mab herself, Ianthe in her disembodied state, the future as it could never actually be) over the world of often tedious becoming. Shelley is not equating the concept itself of an ultimate Absolute with illusion, but he is pointing up the difficulties of ineffability, of the paradoxical potential to withdraw further into the mind's own fictions precisely when attempting to deal with one's ideas of external otherness. The maiden is thus veiled also because both Shelley and questor prefer mystery to vacancy, at least when mystery can be transformed into a promise of something substantial existing "behind the veil" of their fictions. The problem, of course, is that the questor is entirely unaware of the dynamic his desire for meaning has created (as Shelley himself had been when writing *Queen Mab*), and Shelley is unaware, at least for the purposes of this poem, of any satisfactory alternative.

We have in *Alastor*, then, as William Keach has demonstrated with admirable precision,[32] the first and most prominent use of "reflexive imagery" in the Shelley canon. Keach defines the term "reflexive" in relation to a common verbal pattern in the poetry, in which

> an object or action is compared, implicitly or explicitly, to an aspect of itself, or is said to act upon or under the conditions of an aspect of itself. Such locutions call unusual attention to the act of mind they presuppose in the writer and provoke in the reader, an act of mind in which something is

perceived as both one thing and more than one thing, as both itself and something other than itself. (Keach, *Shelley's Style* 79–80)

The questor's dream-maiden, then, speaks "with voice stifled in tremulous sobs / Subdued by its own pathos," and when the agony of his pursuit is described, he is "Bearing within his life the brooding care / That ever fed on its decaying flame" (*Alastor* 246–47). This is the most prominent use of reflexive imagery in the entire Shelley canon because *Alastor* is his first poetic exploration of the possibility that the form taken by his notion of ultimate reality leads to a particularly narcissistic and dangerous solipsistic vision. Shelley here begins, and now will never abandon, his need to explore the fiction-making capacity necessarily attendant on all quests for meaning; in fact, later in his career he will consider that fictions are constitutive of reality, that the inability to penetrate to a discernable essence distinct from its embellishment is actually further testimony to the manifold possibilities for the generation of meaning. For now, though, he is not as comfortable with his growing suspicion that his affirmations are but subjective projections, and that he has committed the same "mistake of a name for a thing" for which he indicts others.

Reflexive imagery also serves its purpose here because Shelley now toys with the idea that the articulation of his professed beliefs can refer only to itself (that is, to the means of the articulation), that those beliefs may have, finally, no ideal external referent. For the questor's tropes of belief cannot—without considerable difficulty—be exposed as dead-end signs once their creator has decided that their mystery is only further evidence of their ultimate significance. Just as Shelley in *Queen Mab* had created a fictional character, in the image of his own desires, who descends from a mysterious and unknown place to pronounce upon Truth; and just as, in Shelley's understanding of religion, the vulgar take a "name for a thing" and hence believe in a deity which has been narcissistically conceived in the image of man, so here the questor immediately decides that his vision is truth itself—not its symbol, not even its embodiment in a form different from an incorporeal or atemporal origin, but truth itself, the end of all quests:

> Does the dark gate of death
> Conduct to thy mysterious paradise,
> O Sleep? Does the bright arch of rainbow clouds,
> And pendent mountains seen in the calm lake,

Lead only to a black and watery depth,
While death's blue vault, with loathliest vapours hung,
Where every shade which the foul grave exhales
Hides its dead eye from the detested day,
Conduct, O Sleep, to thy delightful realms?
This doubt with sudden tide flowed on his heart,
The insatiate hope which it awakened, stung
His brain even like despair. (211–22)

The questor begins to doubt nature because he now finally considers that the natural world—the "rainbow clouds" and "pendent mountains"—leads only, after all, to the natural world, not to the immutable meaning to which he aspires in his travels. He questions the reflection on the lake, then, in order to hope despairingly for whatever non-natural ideal lies beyond the grave and not below the lake's natural surface.

Indeed, as Ronald Tetreault observes in *The Poetry of Life*, the questor "is a tragic figure who sacrifices his life to vision because he makes the fatal error of remaining unconscious of his own interpretive activity" (57). To decide, by an unconscious act of interpretation, that one's erotic dream is the source of all meaning in the universe is a hyperbolic version of Shelley's fearful apprehension that his own sense of ultimate meaning is predicated solely on the urgency of his desire, with no solid grounding, as it were. The Unknown becomes equated with the Absolute, as is all too easy for it to be, and death is of course the archetype of all unknowns; this is why the questor immediately assumes that "death's blue vault" must lead to the "mysterious paradise" that his sleep has shown him. It is an almost humorous parody of Shelley's earlier morose preoccupations,[33] one that also recalls both the questor's travels to "unknown lands" in the service of seeking truth, and the narrator's earlier explanation that he has kept watch in charnel houses and coffins in an effort to still his "obstinate questionings."

The questor has thus justified the earlier description of his flight: "He eagerly pursues / Beyond the realms of dream that fleeting shade; / He over-leaps the bounds" (205–7), the bounds, that is, of temporality, with its temporally confined, perceptible objects. In his search for the realm of the veiled maiden, he begins another frantic wandering expedition. Now, instead of rejecting only the love of an Arab maiden, the questor neglects all bodily considerations and becomes emaciated, defiantly, like the skylark Shelley is to conceive in four years time, a "scorner of the ground."

As an exposé of the poet's predilection for dead-end fictions, *Alastor* is ruthless, and more so, perhaps, because Shelley himself knows that he remains vulnerable to their comforting appeal; in a letter to Hogg of August 1815 (Shelley was composing *Alastor* by September of 1815), he responds to his friend's story of a persistent missionary who had tried to convert him: "Yet who is there that will not pursue phantoms, spend his choicest hours in hunting after dreams, and wake only to perceive his error and regret that death is so near?" (*Letters* 1: 429–30). Given the questor's—like Shelley's—infinite desire to satiate his infinite longing for communion with some spiritual presence, he has had to withdraw into the mind, where he could project an image of his own desire to be answerable to his longing. Shelley would always be concerned, for the rest of his life, that the inherent task of the poet is too dependent on the active perpetuation of this dilemma, that Plato's warnings about poetry are too well taken. Book Ten of the *Republic* is an important source for the implicit warnings of *Alastor* and for Shelley's letter to Hogg; Socrates offers the following strictures, should poetry fail to defend herself:

> If her defence fails, then, my dear friend, like other persons who are enamoured of something, but put a restraint upon themselves when they think their desires are opposed to their interests, so too must we after the manner of lovers give her up, though not without a struggle. . . .
> At all events we are well aware that poetry, such as we have described, is not to be regarded seriously as attaining to the truth; and he who listens to her, fearing for the safety of the city which is within him, should be on his guard against her seductions and make our words his law. (Plato, *Republic*, X: 484)

Taking a "metaphor for a real being" is bad enough, but taking one's own metaphor for the real being who is going to expose the metaphoricity of other metaphors (what Shelley was bordering on in *Queen Mab*) effectively eliminates the merely ornamental status of metaphor. For we will recall that Shelley had wanted metaphor and fiction to be merely ornamental, to be at the service of an assumed literal truth. Once he comes to realize, however, that there is no possibility of naïve metaphoric predication in matters of invisible spiritual realms, he decides that virtually all his figurative fancies are suspect, and that all his convictions about ultimate meaning are inextricably linked with the irresistibility of his habit of figurative thought.

As the rest of the poem progresses, the Poet's swift descent into death is played against some very beautiful, almost Wordsworthian descriptions of nature, except that Shelley's are more exotically sublime than Wordsworth's:

> The pyramids
> Of the tall cedar overarching, frame
> Most solemn domes within, and far below,
> Like clouds suspended in an emerald sky,
> The ash and the acacia floating hang
> Tremulous and pale. Like restless serpents, clothed
> In rainbow and in fire, the parasites,
> Starred with ten thousand blossoms, flow around
> The grey trunks. . . . (*Alastor* 433–41)

Nature, the very nature which, in the name of his quest, he either forsakes or appropriates to stand for something wholly distinct from it, takes on the appearance of an almost sinister sexuality, as if it were asserting its independent generative existence in a kind of reaction-formation to the Poet's comportment toward it.[34] Nature does not go away just because we want to transcend it. In fact, the Poet enters a boat with the specific intention of meeting death, but he meets first such sublime scenes as the one cited above. The image of a questor frantically trying to appropriate objects of nature to serve as symbol of a presence inimical to nature, is thus suggested yet once more in *Alastor*, but this time, the naïveté of the attempt is made more emphatic. He courts a death *in* nature by allowing nature to die to him, as he cries out, believing he is sure of his vision: "I have beheld / The path of thy departure. Sleep and death / Shall not divide us long!" (367–69). Again, death is the unknown, and so death, he believes, will unite him with what in life had not been fully known to him.

The questor does, however, continue to manifest thwarted potential; the irony of his famous apostrophe to the swan is that he just begins to realize the disjunction between tenor and nature-as-vehicle, but he cannot finally do anything with such latent recognition:

> And what am I that I should linger here,
> With voice far sweeter than thy dying notes,
> Spirit more vast than thine, frame more attuned

> To beauty, wasting these surpassing powers
> In the deaf air, to the blind earth, and heaven
> That echoes not my thoughts? (285–90)

Here he is despairing over the irrevocability of his existential loneliness, because he is bordering on an acknowledgment that the tropes which he has been comfortably appropriating from the visible universe are expendable as tropes: he dismisses the metaphorical value of the swan, and finally betrays an inability to make the naturally mute air, earth and heaven—to be understood, I think, simply as sky—anything other than "blind" and "deaf," that is, anything other than what they are.[35] This draws him closer to the lurking doubt that there is only solipsistic vision behind the veil. He pulls back from sustaining full acknowledgment of this sort, but in the absence of an ability to objectify his identity with reference to the temporal world, he can only reverse the normative process of human-object comparison: compare the above apostrophe to the swan, with the one following, to a rivulet:

> O stream!
> Whose source is inaccessibly profound,
> Whither do thy mysterious waters tend?
> Thou imagest my life. Thy darksome stillness,
> Thy dazzling waves, thy loud and hollow gulphs,
> Thy searchless fountain, and invisible course
> Have each their type in me. . . . (502–8)

It is almost as if he has made *himself* into a "type" of nature, rather than have nature serve as "type," or trope, of his own mind. For after he convinces himself that the rivulet images his life, he claims that *he* serves as a type (line 508) of the various attributes of the stream. It is a feeble attempt: in his search for the veiled maiden, he has resigned all affinity with the organic world. But more important, this type of metaphoric association makes the questor himself into a metaphor. We will meet a fuller exploration of the dangers of rendering human beings *as* metaphors in *Epipsychidion*; in *Alastor*, Shelley is still just hinting at the potential for such a subjugation of human worth. To fragment oneself from unity with the temporal world in favor of a withdrawal into the mind's solipsistic visions is to live in a world of fictions, but it is also to fictionalize the self, to define the self and indeed to ascribe value to the self in the terms of the fictional structure it has projected.

It is in keeping with this withdrawal, then, that while he is still in his boat, with a whirlpool sweeping him upwards toward the top of a cavern, the boat stays in the centre of the water, where it is calm: "'I' the midst was left, / Reflecting, yet distorting every cloud, / A pool of treacherous and tremendous calm" (384–86). The "calm" toward which the questor gravitates is one that "reflects," takes note of, the natural world. But just as the questor, in his earlier travels, had valued the world in the exclusive terms of its malleability, its potential to be rendered as something other than itself, so here the "calm" reflects the clouds only to distort them.

There are no resolutions in *Alastor*. And the narrator's commendation of the questor, who meets a premature death after chasing the heroine of his erotic dream, is pathetic, not inspiring [36]:

> O, that the dream
> Of dark magician in his visioned cave,
> Raking the cinders of a crucible
> For life and power, even when his feeble hand
> Shakes in its last decay, were the true law
> Of this so lovely world! (681–86)

The narrator would still prefer the "lovely world" to be ruled by the visionary "dream." But, as Tilottama Rajan observes, "the Poet's death still has the force not of transcendence but of a double negation: a negation both of the ordinary and of the visionary" (*Supplement of Reading* 301). The magician in a cave seeking life and power, and doing so feebly ("his feeble hand / Shakes in its last decay"), recalls those who, in the myth of the cave in Plato's *Republic*, mistake the shadows of reality on the cave wall for reality itself. It is telling, therefore, that the image also suggests the kind of dynamic to which the poet is prone—a magician seeking vision being the prototype of the visionary poet. Shelley after *Queen Mab* fears the abstractions and displacements of the objective world to which the figurings of imagination lead him. The questor dies because he has metaphorized his own life out of existence, and because such fictional abstractions do not benefit anyone; he is, after all, a Poet, but one without an audience.

Shelley has come a long way from the confident tenor of his adolescent zeal to reform the world. *Queen Mab* suggested a resolute conviction of the concrete good that can come of poetry; now the *Alastor* narrator reminds us of the disjunction between art and the world with which it attempts to communicate, as he insists that when the Poet

> shall live alone
> In the frail pauses of this simple strain,
> Let not high verse, mourning the memory
> Of that which is no more, or painting's woe
> Or sculpture, speak in feeble imagery
> Their own cold powers. Art and eloquence,
> And all the shews o' the world are frail and vain
> To weep a loss that turns their lights to shade.   (705–12)

Shelley throughout his career will struggle to reconcile the contrary claims of imagination (and imagination's manifestations in the necessary fictions of poetry) to the quotidian world from which poetry derives its metaphors and concrete images. The ambiguity with which the poem ends is one which Shelley will never definitively answer to; the narrator seems to privilege an objective, phenomenal world over the limitations of art—"feeble imagery"—but he does so because the particular artist he admires is dead. After the departure of "some surpassing Spirit, / Whose light adorned the world around it" (714–15), nothing of value, he believes, remains:

> But pale despair and cold tranquillity,
> Nature's vast frame, the web of human things,
> Birth and the grave, that are not as they were.   (718–20)

The narrator still believes that the questor is one whose "light adorned the world," because he too seeks answers to the "tale of what we are" by holding close to images of death. But the note on which he ends the poem is unmistakeable: what remains when this poet, indeed when any poet, completes his legacy is still, after all, "birth and the grave." These are "not as they were" when the Poet attempted to transform his world of time and space, because they cannot finally escape "Nature's vast frame." Shelley will spend the rest of his career struggling to comprehend the meaning of these dilemmas.

2. The Awful Shadow of Some Unseen Power

The year 1816 was one of perpetual change for Shelley, more so even than he had come to expect in his already complicated life: a healthy son was born to Mary;[1] the couple visited Switzerland, where Shelley and Lord Byron developed a close intellectual and emotional bond; Mary's half-sister, Fanny, committed suicide in October; Harriet Shelley drowned herself in November; and Percy and Mary formalized their living arrangement by becoming legally married in December. Shelley's reading activity was no less diverse and hectic: he returned to a study of contemporary and skeptical philosophers and renewed his interest in Rousseau and in the major poets of his day. 1816, of course, was also a year of a very poor harvest and of extreme political unrest in England, with insurrections easily—and often brutally—crushed by the government. Amidst such turmoil and activity, Shelley was trying to address the growing crisis of his poetical identity, to reconcile his reliance on poetic fiction-making with his genuine concern for the real-life activities taking place around him. He thus embarked on an attempt to affirm the value of the imagination's activity within the world of time and space; the hymns of 1816 form part of the record of his struggle for such affirmation.

The crisis described in *Alastor*, in which he manifests his uneasiness with his own tropes of desire, remains a pervasive motif during this year. For Shelley is urgently trying to resolve the contradictions that are implicitly acknowledged in the 1815 narrative, and everywhere there is evidence that he feels himself to be treading on precarious ground. Two questions in particular now preoccupy him: first, how to distinguish between ideas of, and tropes for ideas of, the transcendent; and second, how to avoid attenuating the value of the concrete when transmuting objects and experiences into artistic representations of the transphenomenal.

In *Alastor* both the questor and the narrator had been unafraid of death and of images of death (recall the coffins and charnel-houses the narrator kept company with) because their quests had been undertaken in the service of an unknown, and death, I have argued, is the archetype of all unknowns. But Shelley now attends to the disturbing problems posed by such postures; that is, he addresses the naïveté implicit in the common predilection to become so reconciled to the tropes of our desire, that trope comes gradually, inadvertently, but surely and relentlessly to replace the primary object of desire in the inevitable processes of human valuation. Shelley embarks on a quest to remind himself that he is dealing, in most cases of speculative thought, with tropes whose tenors are neither empirically knowable nor recuperable within the available lexicon. All he knows of God, indeed all he knows of true happiness, is that it is, in the language of "The Sunset" (also a lyric of 1816), "more than earth can give." The rhetoric of negation, however, is not the trouble. Rather, the circularity of the relationship between negation and image-appropriation comes to focus his anxieties. For Shelley now begins consciously to grapple with the possibility that it is the world-*as*-trope itself—or, phrased otherwise, the visible world as it appears once the percipient has rendered it as a trope—that has conditioned his very notion of an otherworldliness in the first place.

It is not surprising, then, that the evidence of Shelley's summer trip to Switzerland in 1816 is resonant with his quest for, if not resolution, then at least clarification of the problematics of his craft. During the summer of 1816 he is obsessively reading Rousseau, whom he refers to in a letter to Hogg as the greatest writer since Milton (18 July 1816; *Letters* 1: 357). In the notes to *Queen Mab*, Shelley had made use specifically of Rousseau's *Second Discourse* because, in addition to its digression on language and its exploitation of a "state of nature" fiction, the treatise's treatment of humanity's self-development and infinite potential had been particularly attractive to him. But Shelley continued to read also the Rousseau of, for example, *Reveries of a Solitary Walker*, which, like his earlier *Discourse on the Sciences and the Arts*, treats language and the arts with suspicion and disaffection.[2] It is thus an irony worthy of Rousseau himself that in the summer of 1816, while Shelley is entranced with *La Nouvelle Héloïse*, his immediate interest seems to lie in the author's method of description, in his mastery of literary craft. Indeed, Rousseau's magnificent descriptions of natural landscape effect for Shelley a near "falsification" of actual history, or of the historical attempts to inscribe facts of experience, as he raves to Peacock: "They were created indeed by one mind, but a mind so powerfully bright as to cast a shade of falsehood on the records that are called reality" (12 July 1816; *Letters* 1: 485). Shelley, like Rousseau, knows of the dangers of the heterocosm, but they both know also that it is virtually irresistible; in *La Nouvelle Héloïse* Julie exclaims, "Le pays des chimères est en ce monde le seul digne d'être habité" (2: 340).[3]

The evidence of the external world which is commonly "called reality" had been obliterated for the questor in *Alastor* and for onlookers at the beginning of *Queen Mab*; but in the early poem an otherworldly figure in a chariot from the heavens had effected the change, and in *Alastor* a dream vision masquerading as an otherworldly lover took priority. In Shelley's comment to Peacock about the effects of Rousseau's writings there is something similar at work, but the crucial difference is that now a human being in time and space can write fiction of such mimetic power that it virtually falsifies the real world of time and space. Indeed, here it is a human author whose descriptions, not of celestial halls but of earthly habitations, are all-consuming. Shelley has clearly matured since his youthful insistence that poetic language can be made fully answerable to unadulterated truth; his temporary solution to the dilemma now veers in the direction of celebrating the human mind, which, if it is consigned merely to further embellishing both quotidian existence and ultimate truth, at least does so in a manner powerful enough to create some sort of sustaining force of its own.

Shelley begins, then, to accommodate his poetic spiritual explorations to the fiction-making habits and needs of the human mind. But I argue that he also assimilated—and held as axiomatic—the truism that if a transcendental truth does exist, epistemological doubt will not objectively affect it. Even David Hume, for all his dismantling of the traditional justifications for belief in God, is highly variable on the question of religion, in one essay actually proclaiming, by way of approbation, that Christianity is "founded on *Faith*, not reason" ("Of Miracles" 543).[4] Shelley's newfound attempt at confidence in the human mind, and its irrevocable propensity for metaphoric recreation of all that it meets, suggests an urge to mediate between desire and the Unknown, without the burden of believing that his presentation is unadulterated by his own desires. Indeed, although his full study of skepticism began in the fall of 1813, and though it was an anxiety over his skepticism which had, in a sense, been behind *Alastor*, the full implications of his reading in the skeptical tradition become most apparent in 1816, when he is most clearly struggling with the disturbing implications of articulation, of the complicated relationship between an essential ineffability and poetic representation.[5]

We may thus detect moments in which Shelley, attempting to acknowledge the fictionality of his poetic tropes of belief, begins to confront the guilt of his lying, as it were, his contextualization of intuited truths within the tropes of desire. In *La Nouvelle Héloïse*, Julie's inability to be satisfied by the love of M. de Wolmar results in a strengthening of piety, and the explicitness of the debt of this piety to her earthly impoverishment perhaps struck resonant chords in Shelley: "On dirait que rien de terrestre ne pouvant suffire au besoin d'aimer dont elle est dévorée, cet excès de sensibilité soit forcé de remonter à sa source" (2: 223). Shelley is already more sophisticated than that—even *Alastor*, after all, was a warning against the misapplication of human sensibility, and even there, the questor's dream-maiden was alluring in a very carnal sense—but he does begin trying, finally, to distinguish between a metaphysical "source" of love, and the form taken by his own "excess of sensibility" which leads him to seek that source. Shelley will now openly grapple with the apparent manipulation of human consciousness by abstract and transcendental preoccupations, but taking his lead, perhaps, from Rousseau, he sets himself the task of at least openly recognizing the work of human imagination when he sees it.

"Hymn to Intellectual Beauty"

Surrounded by the magnificence of the scenery in Switzerland, and most especially in view of the great Mont Blanc, Shelley writes his two famous hymns of 1816, the songs of struggle over the mediation between desire and its tropes. The immediate and superficial occasion of "Mont Blanc," however, is the poet's contemplation of an actual object, and one that, qua object, particularly impresses him; in fact, in another letter to Peacock he exclaims, "I never knew I never imagined what mountains were before" (22 July 1816; *Letters* 1: 497). As in his previous letter (cited above), then, we witness the same remarkable concern over the confusion between fiction and ill-defined fact. In order to come to terms with the mountain-as-object, he has had to imagine it; but here he finds an actual mountain—an actual, empirically verifiable object—which is so grand that it chastens even Shelley's confidence in his own imagination. This is a small step, but it is an important one in view of the fact that for Shelley, it is usually imagination, fictionalization, which endangers the integrity of actual objects and experiences. Now, since he is urgently trying to assert the strength and the value of human imagination, he betrays an anxious need to defend it, to remark immediately on the implications for imagination and its domain, when he witnesses an object in nature potentially equal to the mind. "Mont Blanc" proceeds from an actual object, but I shall concentrate on "Hymn to Intellectual Beauty" first, not only because Shelley wrote it first, but because its stark recognition of the relationship between the perceptual concrete and the abstract inaccessible is precisely what lies behind "Mont Blanc" 's peculiar sensitivity to the very actuality of empirical objects.

"Hymn to Intellectual Beauty," according to Mary Shelley's "Note on Poems of 1816," was written while Shelley was voyaging around Lake Geneva with Lord Byron. Yet, despite the manifold beauties of those scenes, Shelley begins the hymn not with a concrete locus in the tangible world, not with an overwhelming sense of the spiritual which is derived from the splendors of nature, but with a bold (and yet vulnerable) desire to articulate immediately his imageless concept: "The awful shadow of some unseen Power / Floats though unseen amongst us." With the exception of "shadow"—which is merely the absence of light, a negative image—virtually every word in the first line of the poem is purely and unapologetically abstract, so much so that the poet's refusal to give the reader an easy entrance into the poem's conception is obtrusively underlined. Shelley here is in direct conflict with the conventional wisdom of, for example, Erasmus Darwin, who had also provided him with a point of departure in his earlier days. In the "Interlude" after Canto One of his "Loves of the Plants," Darwin asserts the primacy, for poetry, of visual images: "Poetry admits of very few words expressive of perfectly abstracted ideas, whereas Prose abounds with them" (*Botanic Garden* 2.41). Joseph Addison, in a similarly typical eighteenth-century assertion, maintains that "We cannot indeed have a single Image in the Fancy that did not make its first Entrance through the Sight" (*Spectator 411*; 3: 277). The first line of "Intellectual Beauty," then, is Shelley's most strident effort so far to qualify the *ut pictura poesis* notions of his poetic forbears.[6] Even as early as 1816 we have the firmly planted seeds of *Prometheus Unbound*'s insistence that "the deep truth is imageless." It remains to be seen, though, if the hymns can sustain this posture of studied obscurity. Indeed, the poet's reversion, at times, to a reliance on images often goes hand in hand with an undertone of guilt over the possibility that he is implicated in the very kind of tropology whose hazards he is struggling to avert.

"Hymn to Intellectual Beauty" begins without prefatory preamble; much in the manner of the eighteenth-century odes to abstract concepts, such as William Collins's odes to Fear, Music, and the Passions, or even the evangelical hymns of Isaac Watts and Charles Wesley, Shelley begins as if he were articulating a common conception that enjoys a general and wide consensus among the reading public.[7] Since he is in fact implicitly challenging the common interpretation of the canonical text (the Bible) which forms, for the general public, the basis for belief in that concept (the meaning of a metaphysical ultimate), it appears that Shelley is in fact warning us about the dangers of common beliefs. Nonetheless, by playing on one of the primary requisites of the traditional hymnic form—a shared, public assumption about the object of its address—he indicates by indirection a certain amount of respect for the very tradition with which he is taking issue.[8]

By 1816 this subtle conservatism goes hand in hand with the poet's radicalism partly because Shelley now acknowledges that, as far as questions about ultimate reality go, he has no reassuring alternatives to offer, that his primary departure from the conventions of Western religion involves a sophisticated acknowledgment of the necessity of skepticism in all attempts at definition, and a grudging—and for now, only partial—acknowledgment of his own reliance on fictions in this regard.[9] Even the bevy of words involved in the quest for definition and clarification must be approached skeptically; as Berkeley warns in *Principles of Human Knowledge*, not every word has a corresponding "thing."[10] The mind itself is still seen as potentially redemptive, but Shelley remains vigilant in his attempt to separate the fictions which the mind produces, from the ultimate reality which it tries to apprehend. Still, the "Essay on Christianity" cautions that "we are not the masters of our own imaginations and moods of mental being"(202).[11] It then goes on to demonstrate the real crux that forms the thematic preoccupation of "Hymn to Intellectual Beauty":

> There is a Power by which we are surrounded, like the atmosphere in which some motionless lyre is suspended, which visits with its breath our silent chords at will. Our most imperial and stupendous qualities—those on which the majesty and the power of humanity is erected—are, relatively to the inferior portion of its mechanism, indeed active and imperial; but they are the passive slaves of some higher and more omnipresent Power. This Power is God. And those who have seen God, have, in the period of their purer and more perfect nature, been harmonized by their own will to so exquisite [a] consentaneity of powers as to give forth divinest melody when the breath of universal being sweeps over their frame. ("Essay on Christianity" 202)

The conviction expressed in this passage is radically different from the world views which are promoted in *Queen Mab* and implicitly suggested in *Alastor*; unlike the former, it consciously acknowledges belief in a metaphysical dualism, and unlike the latter, it explicitly situates human creativity within a metaphysical world view. Shelley reviles institutionalized forms of religion, but his belief in the real presence of a "higher and more omnipresent power" stays with him for the rest of his days.

In *Alastor* the narcissistic foundation of the questor's dream vision had suggested some room for doubt that there exists, for Shelley, a form of transcendent being which is qualitatively distinct from the human mind. Shelley had been coming to terms with the irresistible habits of his fiction-making and his vulnerability to the threat of seduction by his own constructions. Since the "Hymn to Intellectual Beauty" belongs to a more sophisticated period of his development, the first line's profusion of abstractions signals his immediate understanding that poetic images do not bear any objective consonance with their intended transcendent signifieds: the *Alastor* questor's desire to apprehend "Power" had resulted in a visualization—in the form of mistaken fantasy—of a projected form for it; the hymn immediately insists that the "Power" is "unseen," and that what is apprehended at all is its "awful shadow," its teasing reminder of an absented presence.

Shadows are projected *from*; absence, in this instance, is an absence *of*. The rhetoric of "Hymn to Intellectual Beauty" is one of indirect positive assertion, a rhetoric that enables us to confront, if only tentatively, the process of displacement itself—but where displacement is understood as an elision of direct confrontation, not as an effacement of presence. Indeed, no single definitive antecedent to a "that" is given, only clauses which proceed from, and which attempt to qualify, the relative pronouns:

> *Like* moonbeams that behind some piny mountain shower,
> > It visits with inconstant glance
> > Each human heart and countenance;
> *Like* hues and harmonies of evening,—
> > *Like* clouds in starlight widely spread,—
> *Like* memory of music fled,—
> *Like* aught that for its grace may be
> Dear, and yet dearer for its mystery.
> > > ("Intellectual Beauty" 5–12 ; italics mine)

It is a significant index of his growing sophistication that the similes are obtrusively made; they are most emphatically not metaphors, not equivalents, and not naïve projections from the mind of what the unseen Power might actually be. Hence the Power's visitations are "*Like* moonbeams that behind some piny mountain shower." The insistence on simile here is of a piece with an essentially theistic orientation: the Spirit is tentatively *like* the moonbeams, not identical to them, and not of the same order as them. Further, it just hints at his growing concern over the implications of his acts of appropriation—his appropriation, in particular, of the phenomenal world exclusively for the purpose of exalting something of presumed greater value.

It was clear in *Alastor* that the questor had been, in a phrase from that poem, "obedient to the light that shone within his soul." But after being admonished for questing after self-made fictions, is there a context in which we can maintain belief in the existence of a metaphysical ultimate, without being vulnerable to the charge of irresponsibility or philosophical immaturity? In "Hymn to Intellectual Beauty" Shelley is very careful to discriminate tropes from their intended tenors, to insist that the outward forms he employs as rough analogues of his metaphysical speculations are prevented from themselves becoming our objects of allurement. It is for this reason that the anaphoric use of the word "like" in the first stanza is so emphatic: Shelley wants to make the conscious artifice, and the tentativeness of his equations, wholly obtrusive. But once he has exhausted his store of unsuccessful analogues, he finally concedes openly the futility of implicit comparison ("Like *aught* that for its grace may be / Dear"), and then turns to an approbation of the effect of Beauty's inscrutable nature—and of the inscrutability itself—as he gracefully gives up the struggle for definition: "and yet dearer for its *mystery*."

As early as 1812, in a letter to Elizabeth Hitchener of 27 February, Shelley insisted that he would like to extract the "mystery and immorality" that surround the moral sayings of Jesus (*Letters* 1: 265). In his early years, he was of course more interested in obliterating "mystery" for the sake of revealing an unadulterated truth, its lack of ornamentation being tantamount, he believed, to a freedom from mystery. It may initially strike us as paradoxical, though, that as late as 1816 he seems to approve of "mystery," this time in the very midst of a conscious commitment to responsible use of fiction's embellishments. "Intellectual Beauty," however, in fact betrays a more sophisticated understanding of truth's necessary adulteration. "Essay on Christianity" provides the best prose gloss to the hymn's distinctive first stanza:

> Tacitus says, that "the Jews hold God to be something eternal and supreme, neither subject to change nor to decay. Therefore, they permit not statues in

their cities or their temples." The Universal Being can only be described or defined by negatives which deny his subjection to the laws of all inferior existences. Where indefiniteness ends idolatry and anthropomorphism begin. ("Essay on Christianity" 202)

This passage resembles Wordsworth's statement, in his *Preface of 1815*,[12] that "the anthropomorphitism of the Pagan religion subjected the minds of the greatest poets in those countries too much to the bondage of definite form" (*Prose* 2: 34), and that Spenser had been spared such subjection because of his "allegorical spirit, at one time inciting him to create persons out of abstractions; and, at another, by a superior effort of genius, to give the universality and permanence of abstractions to his human beings" (35). The apparent quest for definition of the shadow of the Power in the first stanza of "Hymn to Intellectual Beauty," like Wordsworth's failure to provide assured guidance to the meaning of the "visionary gleam" in the "Immortality Ode," is finally an exposé of its resistance not only to visualization and definition, but also to discursive articulation of intuitive intimation.

The second stanza reinforces this problem, as the poet points to a bevy of abstractions which, though invoked in the service of clarification, are themselves resistant to definitive definition, and therefore resistant to definitive imposition of *attributes*:

> Ask why the sunlight not forever
> Weaves rainbows o'er yon mountain river,
> Why aught should fail and fade that once is shewn,
> Why fear and dream and death and birth
> Cast on the daylight of this earth
> Such gloom,—why man has such a scope
> For love and hate, despondency and hope?
>
> ("Intellectual Beauty" 18–24)

"Sunlight" belongs to the world of empirical phenomena, as do the rainbows cast over "mountain river"; but these are empirical phenomena which are diffuse, which transform themselves into states that are invisible, impenetrable. And sunlight, for all of Shelley's various sporadic associations of it with a life-affirming force, is also employed in subtle ways to suggest the culpability of transforming empirical phenomena into representations precisely of those abstractions which are held to transcend phenomena.[13]

The outlines of Shelley's maturation process, then, are coming into clearer focus. *Alastor*'s alluring image of the dream-maiden had been given the outlines of a particular form; she bore with her the vagueness that such beings necessarily require, but the questor's desires had still drawn to a point—however inadequate—which for him summed up the end of all longing. "Intellectual Beauty" instead reveals a poet who has finally caught himself at his own game of idolatry and inadvertent anthropomorphism (remember the preference betrayed in *Queen Mab* for naïve fictions about celestial creatures); he is one who takes the opportunity of the hymn to reveal his fictions *as* consciously constructed fictions, and his fondness specifically for fictions of otherness as one of the irrevocable facts that force him to acknowledge his erstwhile latent belief in the existence of some transcendent order.

This potential for theological conservatism, however, is qualified by his skepticism and results, for the time being, in a poet who is terrified of making poetic assertions that have the appearance of definitive authority. Indeed, Shelley's new emphasis on his conscious use of artifice can also be read as a defensive response to the Lockean caution against living in terms of one's imaginative misconceptions. According to the reading list Mary kept in her journal, Shelley read *An Essay Concerning Human Understanding* in 1815, and in November and December of 1816, just a few months after he completed the composition of "Mont Blanc," he returned to the work. "Intellectual Beauty"'s implicit struggle to claim that the poet is in full control of his fictions recalls the following passage from *Human Understanding*, in which Locke discusses "mad men":

> For by the violence of their Imaginations, having taken their Fancies for Realities, they make right deductions from them. Thus you shall find a distracted Man fancying himself a King, with a right inference, require suitable Attendance, Respect, and Obedience. . . . Hence it comes to pass, that a Man, who is very sober, and of a right Understanding in all other things, may in one particular be as frantick, as any in Bedlam; if either by any sudden very strong impression or long fixing his Fancy upon one sort of Thoughts, incoherent Ideas have been cemented together so powerfully, as to remain united. (161)

Although Locke does justify the use of mere abstractions, the sort of confusion he describes here bears a certain consonance with the hymn's insistence that its speaker's "fancies" about ultimate reality are not identical to ultimate reality, that whereas the young Shelley had "sought for ghosts" and "called on poisonous *names*" (italics mine), the more reflective man knows that that which is an entirely transcendent, genuine "awful LOVE-LINESS" ("Intellectual Beauty" 71) is what will "give what'er these words cannot express" (72).

The hymn questions its status as a conveyor of ultimate meaning—part of Shelley's departure from one aspect of the hymnic tradition—but it does not necessarily undermine belief in an extra-textual ultimate meaning.[14] In fact, it is his very conviction of metaphysical dualism that conditions, in its initial stages, his anxiety over the inefficacy of language. Shelley would claim that if he insists on the existence of an unknowable, inaccessible presence which cannot be articulated or even fully comprehended, indeed, if he insists on the integrity of a presence whom the more naïve interpreters of theology would garble into tyranny, at least he does so knowing that he too can offer only "Frail spells," but ones which are presented *as* "Frail spells," and which remain distinct from "Thy [the Spirit's] light alone."

The third stanza, then, so often interpreted as uncomplicated evidence of the poet's atheism, is a response to the dangers of common "*records* of endeavour"—including his own—not an assured repudiation of the remnants of faith itself:

No voice from some sublimer world hath ever
    To sage or poet these responses given—
    Therefore the name of God and ghosts and Heaven,
Remain the records of their vain endeavour,
Frail spells—whose uttered charm might not avail to sever,
      From all we hear and all we see,
      Doubt, chance, and mutability. (25–31)

Richard Cronin has suggested that "Shelley's God remains a rhetorical device rather than an embodied emotion, so that Shelley becomes the prophet of a rhetorical figure, a role that the reader is expected to regard with an unacceptable gravity" (230). Cronin has isolated the central problem, but it is one that I would claim is actually being addressed in the hymn, not a mistake which threatens its integrity. An "embodied emotion" is precisely what Shelley does not want to present as the image of truth, in fact would render him guilty of the kind of error committed by the *Alastor* questor. Shelley declared his faith in the first line of the poem ("The awful shadow of some unseen Power"); in the second ("Floats though unseen amongst us") he declared his inability to give it definition in the manner of an eighteenth-century *ut pictura poesis* poem, or of a devotional, fully confident evangelical hymn.[15] Now, in the third stanza, he identifies "voice," speakers ("sage or poet"), "name," "records," "Frail spells," and "uttered charm." These designations are clearly shown to be in direct contradiction with "Thy light alone" of the final lines of the stanza, which "Gives grace and truth to life's unquiet dream." Like the speaker of Coleridge's "Eolian Harp," who had indulged his own private reverie on the meaning of "all of animated nature" and then reminded himself that "never guiltless may I speak of him, / The Incomprehensible," Shelley also recalls that he lacks sanction to name the ineffable, and that this is the burden of guilt which he identifies in those whom he would like to claim as his ideological opponents, not his partners in common crime.

We have here a clear foreshadowing of Shelley's resumption of the study of Plato, which he undertook at Marlow in 1817,[16] shortly after the composition of the hymns. For in 1816 he clearly requires sanction for the fine line he is treading between desire for articulation of the ineffable and his concessions to the limits of language. His task is all the more difficult because such concessions proceed from his acknowledgment of the potential naïveté of metaphoric predication, the latter being the process by which the names of "God and ghosts and Heaven" have been handed down to us. The poet, for Shelley as for Plato, is at two removes from ultimate truth, but whereas Plato insists that this is so because earth is but an imitation of the Forms,[17] Shelley holds that the world of becoming has its own integrity, one whose value does not rely exclusively on its proximity to the transcendent. It is the described beauty of the world, the very recitation of the unsuccessful analogues of Beauty (music, mountain mist, hues and harmonies of evening, and so on), that convinces him in the first place of the Spirit's prodigious worth. The hymn ultimately consigns nothing to the domain of Platonic pathos—that is, its *tropes* of metaphysical otherness compel attention in ways that their referent cannot. Finally, are the mists and hues and harmonies themselves being thrown into relief, or—their ostensible purpose—are they really no more than vehicles in the poem?

Nevertheless, in strictly logical terms, Shelley's metaphysical convictions yield only the affirmations of a negative theology, for the materials of the given world still provide but an unclear idea of the transcendent, and language—the "Frail spells" and "uttered charm"—can only speak in the voice of its temporal circumscription. Shelley is becoming increasingly responsive to his realization that human understanding and human language are circumscribed by time and place. Thus his acknowledgment that the "uttered charm" cannot objectively alter "Doubt, chance, and mutability" paradoxically serves as an appropriate prelude to his own appropriation of the language of mutability:

> Thy light alone—like mist o'er mountains driven,
>   Or music by the night wind sent
>   Through strings of some still instrument,
>   Or moonlight on a midnight stream,
> Gives grace and truth to life's unquiet dream.
>
> ("Intellectual Beauty" 32–36)

As in the first stanza, there is no clear metaphoric predication to describe the Absolute; Shelley again opts for an obtrusive use of simile, and appropriates only those images from the natural world which are unabashedly circumscribed by time ("mist," "music," "moonlight"), precisely because he, like Coleridge, is never guiltless when speaking of the Incomprehensible. Shelley's Incomprehensible Absolute, however, will also make him feel guilty about his appropriation of the wholly accessible.

I have earlier mentioned that Shelley's choice of the hymnic form betrays a latent, highly qualified conservatism, because the eighteenth-century hymn in particular traditionally trades on the shared assumptions of the poet's society. A William Collins, for example, could claim full license to generalize, to assume confidently that his response to the abstract nouns of his address would conform to the contexts of a normative ethos. This is one reason for the abundance of personified abstractions in certain kinds of Neoclassical poetry.[18] Though Shelley is consciously trying to effect a subversion of some of the consequences of status quo generalizations, it is significant that he does so from within the hymnic form itself. And I would like to suggest that he does so, not because he wants to beat his ideological opponents at their own game, but because the tradition of literary exploration of abstract concepts is a legacy he would like to refine, not annihilate.

Indeed, Shelley's decision in 1816 to write hymns, after years of preoccupation with the narrative forms employed for such poems as *Queen Mab* and *Alastor*, is all the more striking when placed in the context of the reading public's predilection for long narratives, for poems (such as Southey's and Scott's) that had actual stories to tell.[19] Shelley's appropriation of the form of hymnody is, I think, part of a maturing recognition of the relevance of at least certain aspects of the theological presuppositions on which such forms are partly premised. Of course, the hymn-like ode had also been employed, in somewhat revised form, by Wordsworth and Coleridge, among others of Shelley's own contemporaries. He could invoke also a modest amount of contemporary license, then, not only from such poems as Wordsworth's "Immortality Ode" (with which "Hymn to Intellectual Beauty" has the most in common), but also from Wordsworth's insistence, in his Preface to the *Lyrical Ballads*, that he has not employed personified abstractions because they are not part of the "language of ordinary men." Shelley would not have failed to notice that the *Lyrical Ballads* are full of personified abstractions, that ordinary men and poets too seem to have a habit of personification that is irresistible, and that that is because human beings tend toward abstract thought. And abstract thought *will* find a means—often through personification—of articulation.

It is with this somewhat disjointed tradition in mind that in the fourth stanza, Shelley refers to "Love, Hope, and Self-esteem." Such personified abstractions yield far less difficulty than does a transcendent absolute, of course, when being described imagistically. But Shelley's anxiety over abstractions of the transcendent issue also in heightened awareness of all abstractions, especially those which he describes in terms of their complete dependence on Intellectual Beauty. "Love, Hope, and Self-esteem," then, receive upper-case first letters, unlike their counterparts in the second stanza, when Shelley wonders "why man has such a scope / For love and hate, despondency and hope?" By the fourth stanza of the poem, he has already shown why he has given up the search for definitive definition or clear imagistic detail, and so he has greater license to indulge in abstractions. But stanza Four also begins to manifest another undertone of anxiety; it begins to hint at Shelley's need to reclaim the value of the quotidian, to protect it from the sort of depreciation that its inadequacy as a trope for transcendence (or even for abstract concepts such as Love and Hope) might give rise to. Earlier I noted that his vision differs from Plato's, because Shelley's delineation of the limits of language also betrays an inherent beauty in the world not reliant upon mere mimesis. Now he even praises the Spirit by way of suggesting that its illumination of earthly experience depends not on causation—causation being the primary unknown of the British skeptics—but on contrast: "Thou—that to human thought art nourishment, / Like darkness to a dying flame!" (44–45).

Shelley began the poem by offering negation as a rhetorical strategy which affirmed belief in a spiritual presence. But here we are reminded that the ground of his negative contrast (that is, earth) is precisely what he does not wish to adumbrate. Stanzas Five and Six continue his double-visioned quest:

> When musing deeply on the lot
> Of life, at that sweet time when winds are wooing
>   All vital things that wake to bring
>   News of buds and blossoming,—
>   Sudden, thy shadow fell on me;
> I shrieked, and clasped my hands in extacy! (55–60)

The epiphanic moment of illumination is not entirely pre-verbal (he *had* been "musing deeply," and he did shriek), but to stop musing and start shrieking, especially "in extacy," is to bring the process of metaphoric substitution to a halt, at least for the immediate moment. If his happiness in the world is a precondition to belief in a beneficent Power, this stanza underlines the source not of the Spirit itself, but of his fugitive pleasures in a world which is his forum for apprehension of it: not the "poisonous *names* with which our youth is fed" (53), but "that sweet time" of "buds and blossoming" gives him a vocabulary for his experience of Intellectual Beauty.

How, then, is one to mediate between such polarities? The speaker in his youth, much like some characters we have met in Shelley's earlier poetry, stayed up all night in homage to the Spirit's supremacy, "in visioned bowers / Of studious zeal or love's delight" (65–66). "Even now" he calls upon the "thousand hours" who have "Outwatched with me the envious night," and so in the penultimate stanza recalls the potential for denigration of the temporal world to which Spirit-worship is prone.

In the concluding stanza, however, while offering this poem's final apotheosis of its own object of address, he indicates that he himself has matured, that his youthful quests for the sublime have been replaced by experiences of the Beautiful, moments of serenity that allow him to become reconciled with his world.[20] He draws attention to the "harmony in autumn" and the "lustre in its sky, / Which through the summer is not heard or seen, / As if it could not be, as if it had not been!" (75–77). Of course, the autumn scenes indeed *could* be and *had* been, just as, Shelley implies, the Spirit's visitations are inevitable. Another problem and another anxiety are being brought to the fore. If the Spirit's visitations are as unconditioned by human desire as is the renewal of autumn—the obvious extension of Shelley's comparison—and if, as his description of his youthful experience suggests, he experiences its beneficence only when he is exulting in the manifold beauties of the natural world, then how can one attest to a Beneficence beyond that of an unconscious, wholesome interaction with nature?

With respect to the problematics of belief, Shelley is almost back at the first stage of his development; the difference now is that he is more responsible and more skeptical. For if he cannot articulate his conviction of the existence of a spiritual presence within a literary form that presupposes its existence, then there is no reason to assume that he can articulate it at all, in discursive form or otherwise. Again, then, within what circular pattern of impoverishment and desire can his convictions be situated? After all Shelley's efforts to exercise caution in his use of fictions, he may well have resigned himself to a necessary enslavement. For the concluding stanza begins in a manner that utterly reverses the pattern established in the first; that is, he begins stanza Seven not with an abstraction, not with an immediate demonstration of his tropological method, not even with a recollection of a happy time spent specifically questing for the Spirit, but with a description of the natural world: "The *day* becomes." When he finally moves on to the point of the comparison, he does so with an assimilation of the concept of the serenity of the autumn noon, to our vague sense of the Spirit:

> Thus let thy power, which like the truth
> Of nature on my passive youth
> Descended, to my onward life supply
> Its calm—to one who worships thee,
> And every form containing thee,
> Whom, SPIRIT fair, thy spells did bind
> To fear himself, and love all human kind. (78–84)

Shelley's attempt to salvage an integrity for the quotidian from the professed supremacy of the Spirit has resulted, in the final stanza, in an inadvertent *privileging* of the quotidian, or at least, a sense of the value of the spiritual in terms of the temporal. A reconstructed normative predication would read: "the Spirit is (or "is like") the serenity and harmony of the autumn day." But Shelley identifies "day" first: the "day" and its serenity form a vehicle whose tenor is "power," but even after five lines of preparation in figures for the signified, "power" immediately is converted into a vehicle, whose tenor brings us back to the initial vehicle—that is, the tenor is virtually the same as the first vehicle: "which like the truth / Of nature on my passive youth / Descended, to my onward life supply / Its calm." The latter suggests the kind of calm described in the first five lines. This is all the more remarkable when we recall that the poem is intended as a "Hymn *to* Intellectual Beauty." Such an undertone of privilege is a direct reversal of the problem which he is more used to, in which his experience of the world is valued only to the degree that it can be abstracted to stand for something else. Furthermore, since the day's grandeurs are compared to the calm which Shelley hopes to experience in the world of time and space, "day" stands as a synecdoche, an experience to be assimilated, not obliterated by the percipient.[21] Is he resigning himself to the seductive appeal of self-created metaphors? Or is he merely celebrating the work of human imagination in the world of time and space, the world in which it is compelled to operate?

Shelley's vacillation bespeaks a continuing anxiety that his idea of the Absolute relies on an unconscious conflation of metaphor with reality, but one in which metaphor is good enough to lie like truth only because truth is thought to be worthy of its collapse into metaphor. Since, as it would seem, the autumn noon and Intellectual Beauty trope each other, do the forms of Shelley's conceptualization of spirituality owe more than they should to his need to idealize existence? "Essay on Christianity" further complicates the problem, as discussing the Christian concept of a "sleep of life" from which we waken after death, Shelley muses:

> How delightful a picture even if it be not true! How magnificent and illustrious is the conception which this bold theory suggests to the contemplation, even if it be no more than the imagination of some sublimest and most holy poet who, impressed with the loveliness and majesty of his own nature, is impatient and discontented with the narrow limits which this imperfect life and the dark grave have assigned forever as his melancholy portion. ("Essay on Christianity" 205)

This qualification comes in the midst of a vindication of the metaphorical import of Jesus' sayings, and an argument that he did profess a higher truth which nonetheless must not be interpreted literally.[22] Indeed, it is resonant of the uneasy balance the hymn strikes, that between desire for healing and reparation of our felt absences, and belief that one's conception of the metaphysical does not grow exclusively out of such desire. One common denominator, however, in all Shelley's anxieties during this period is his attempt to value the processes of the human mind—if only as a last resort, and in spite of all the ambiguities that attend on such a valorization. When he turns to "Mont Blanc," then, he is conscious first and foremost of his own perceptual faculties as they encounter the world.

"Mont Blanc"

Shelley's reaction to Mont Blanc is at once an encomium of the mind, and a response to his failure to reconcile the various contrary claims of imagination and the world. The mountain itself, as I have already noted, did impress him as an actual object of the empirical world, and it did startle his imagination into a reverie on the sublime. I have also remarked Shelley's implicit struggle with Locke's notion that the insane suffer from an inability to distinguish certain fictions from reality. Now, Mont Blanc strikes him with such force that he virtually allows himself an indulgence in madness, as he writes to Peacock: "The immensity of these aerial summits excited, when they suddenly burst upon the sight, a sentiment of extatic wonder, not unallied to madness" (22 July 1816; *Letters* 1: 358). The madness of reverie is not an uncommon trope in Shelley's day (witness all the mad protagonists in *Lyrical Ballads*), but it is significant that the very object that inspires a meditation on the inescapable significance and gravity of Power, and on its relation to the mind and to the objective world, should also lead to an approbation, however light-hearted, of madness. We may see where his initial response to the mountain is leading: loosely following the common Romantic indulgence in the sublime of nature, he comprehends a sense of power inherent in the grandeur of the mountain, so that he can then virtually forget the mountain. Imagination may score a qualified triumph in such an instance, but still more questions will be begged about the value of the mountain *as* mountain, and—perhaps more important for now—about the independent integrity of his conception of Power.

   In fact, for a poem that, presumably, is so fervently committed to a transphenomenal presence, "Mont Blanc" begins in a manner that is potentially suspect: "The everlasting universe of *things*." "Thing," in any case, has always been an immensely shifty word. In "On Life," Shelley is to explain that by the word *thing* "is to be understood any object of thought, that is, any thought upon which any other thought is employed, with an apprehension of distinction" (478). Kant's "thing in itself," of course, has a particularly long progeny, and Horne Tooke, according to a much quot-

ed passage from his *Diversions of Purley*, sees the Latin *res* (thing) as etymo-
logically related to *reor* (I think). He concludes: "Remember, where we
now say, *I think*, the antient expression was—*Me thinketh*, i.e. *Me thingeth*,
It thingeth me" (2:406). In the Shelleyan world gradually being defined,
there is an inextricable relationship between thinking and the marking of
things.[23]

Indeed, the poem itself had been initially printed at the end of Mary's
*History of a Six Week's Tour through a Part of France, Switzerland, Germany,
and Holland*, in which Shelley's journal-letter to Peacock was also printed.
The context of travel within and witness to the world is thereby firmly suggested, especially since, at the end of the preface to the *History*, Shelley pro-
claims that "Mont Blanc" "rests its claim to approbation on an attempt to
imitate the untameable wildness and inaccessible solemnity from which my
feelings sprang." The problematic of "Mont Blanc," and indeed of this
entire period in Shelley's career, thus reaches something of a climax in the
first stanza of the poem, for, though Mont Blanc serves as a kind of extended metaphor for Shelley's notions of "Power," the first section does not so
much as introduce the actual mountain's presence. This situation suggests
some degree of consonance with Coleridge's "Hymn Before Sun-Rise, In
the Vale of Chamouni," a poem about God (not mountains) professedly
inspired by the awe-inspiring scene; Coleridge, however, had never actually laid eyes on the scene. The latter fact, though certainly unknown to Shelley, is still noteworthy in at least one respect; in *his* poem, Coleridge deems
it a happy occasion that his religious effusion has obliterated his professed
sight of the mountain:

> I gazed upon thee,
> Till thou, still present to the bodily sense,
> Didst vanish from my thought: entranced in prayer
> I worshipped the Invisible alone.
>
> ("Hymn Before Sun-Rise" 13–16)

Coleridge, who in the preface to his poem had asked, "who could be an
atheist in this valley of wonders," never saw this as a problem; Shelley
counts among his many anxieties in "Mont Blanc" a concern for the integrity of actual objects.[24]

Opposing Shelley's to Coleridge's hymn, Angela Leighton offers that
"Shelley still distrusts the habit of substituting a word for a thing and thus
creating a presence from devices of rhetoric" (*Shelley and the Sublime* 61).

In taking a thing for an invisible presence, though, Shelley becomes particularly nervous about the consequent compromising of the inherent value of "things." Furthermore, the first stanza of "Mont Blanc" suggests complexities even greater still. Ronald Tetreault observes that the poem "begins not with the mountain itself but with a metaphorical displacement into a mental context of the river that flows from it" (*The Poetry of Life* 72). But in terms of metaphorical displacement Shelley has gone one step beyond Tetreault's formulation. Shelley gives as his first concern the existence of "things," but his description of how they flow "through the mind" is evocative of a river, and only because we have the title "Mont Blanc" are we able to guess that this is the Arve river: "and rolls its rapid waves, / Now dark—now glittering—now reflecting gloom." The first line and a half of the poem would have it that "things," and their effect on the mind, form the poet's point of departure; however, it quickly becomes obvious that the universe of things is a trope for the Arve River and that the mind is a trope for the Ravine of Arve—a strange situation given that the entire Arve scene is itself a trope for many of the philosophical conceptions of the poem, and indeed its actual presence, as a member of the real "universe of things," is wholly appropriated to stand for that which transcends the universe of things.[25]

But so Shelley begins:

> The everlasting universe of things
> Flows through the mind, and rolls its rapid waves,
> Now dark—now glittering—now reflecting gloom—
> Now lending splendour, where from secret springs
> The source of human thought its tribute brings
> Of waters,—with a sound but half its own.
> Such as a feeble brook will oft assume
> In the wild woods, among the mountains lone,
> Where waterfalls around it leap for ever,
> Where woods and winds contend, and a vast river
> Over its rocks ceaselessly bursts and raves.
>
> ("Mont Blanc" 1–11)

The universe of things flows through the mind and, like a feeble brook's assimilation of the sounds of its surroundings, it brings its waters with their accumulated sounds as a (again figurative) "tribute" to the ravine of Arve. The universe of things (Arve River), however, flows from "secret [hidden, perhaps submerged] springs," and these secret springs are the "source of human thought."[26] The strangeness of this situation cannot be emphasized enough: what has just been described is in fact a tenor, whose vehicle (the Mont Blanc environment) is the organizing trope of the poem. But in the initial presentation this tenor serves as the vehicle to what only later becomes the obvious trope. Unlike a traditional allegory, in which "river," say, would equal flow of consciousness, Shelley makes flow of consciousness suggest—by figurative allusion ("rolls its rapid waves," for example)—river, but only so that river and the scene along with it can be employed as another vehicle. F. R. Leavis's infamous complaint that "The metaphorical and the actual, the real and the imagined, the inner and the outer, could hardly be more unsortable and indistinguishably confused" (*Revaluation* 177), turns out to be not very far off the mark; Shelley *is* confused, but he is conscious of it in ways that would never have occurred to Leavis.

Can a vehicle also be a tenor? The obvious deconstructive reading, of course, is that there is no stable referent to be finally achieved, and that the poem's deferrals and ambiguity in reference form an aporia which deconstructs Shelley's assertions about the transcendental status of "Power." David Simpson, in *Irony and Authority in Romantic Poetry*, holds a view about metaphor in Shelley and the Romantics which is similar to the way in which mainstream deconstruction, especially in its North American manifestations, approaches this problem in Shelley.[27] Simpson remarks of Shelley's general use of metaphor that

> the oversupply of metaphor is as much an onslaught on the received fabric of language as is the Wordsworthian paring down into simplicity. Shelley's hyperarticulacy poses the same threat to the mind's confidence about its position in the world; excess and vacancy can almost be seen as the two interchangeable extremes of a common polemic. The reification through metaphor which Wordsworth fears so much is countered by Shelley with an oversupply of metaphor which prevents us ever coming to a stop in the production of meanings. (*Irony and Authority* 160–61)

This is a valid reading, but one which must be qualified by Shelley's desire to realize an articulation of what is thought to be a transcendental presence, or at least a vague intimation of one. The real struggle pushes against the limits of language, against the limits of imagination in its attempt to apprehend Power; but again, Shelley knew perfectly well that the impediments to human satisfaction do not themselves define the limits of metaphysical possibility. He is consciously exploiting metaphor because he is trying to deal poetically with a kind of faith whose object, he believes, is not merely metaphoric. Since, however, he must have recourse to figurative language, he tries to employ it in ways that will not denigrate the value of the actual by rendering it merely as an abstraction. Hence the investment of multiple figurative images for single speculative conceptions that, precisely because of the confusion that they cause, continually bring us back to the objects which serve as poetic images, for they are our only stable ground.

Shelley by 1816 has already had years of anxiety over the implications of the fictions of figurative language; he knows that there is no ontological sanction for metaphoric predication. When he insists on an easy equation, then, we had best be on the look-out. In the last stanza of "Hymn to Intellectual Beauty" Shelley describes the calm of nature; then, in comparing it to the effect he hopes the Spirit will have on his mature years, he bridges the rhetoric of comparison with a definitive-sounding "thus"—"Thus let thy power, which like the truth . . . ." In "Mont Blanc" something similar is at work, as Shelley introduces the second stanza, finally giving us at least some guidance in untangling his figures: "*Thus* thou, Ravine of Arve— dark, deep Ravine— / Thou many-coloured, many-voiced vale" (12–13). But surely he has not gone to the trouble of imaging the mind only as a convenient way of describing the ravine. Or if so, if Mont Blanc is sufficiently magnificent in itself to warrant description, or to require figurative language to deal with a magnificence beyond discursive expression, then why not just begin with the scene and keep Mont Blanc as the consistent signified?   What is the meaning of the "thus" which introduces the second stanza: "thus" the ravine is as unusual, inscrutable, and multi-faceted as the process of mind encountering objects, or alternatively, "thus" the ravine will now take over as the explicit trope of the main subject of the poem, which is the mind and objects and the secret source of human thought?

Shelley's ostensible purpose is to write a meditation on the philosophical conceptions that are inspired by his look at the great mountain. This would place him squarely within the tradition of philosophical landscape poetry, beginning with Sir John Denham's moralizings over Cooper's Hill, up through the eighteenth-century loco-descriptive poem, and on to Coleridge's Conversation poems, in which description is followed by meditation which in turn is followed by a concluding description.[28] It is true that the lime-tree bower, qua lime-tree bower, is more important to Coleridge than Cooper's Hill is to Denham, but Coleridge's guilt is abetted when he realizes that he can make spiritual metaphors even out of a lime-tree bower. In addition to questioning the efficacy of his metaphors for "Power," Shelley also questions the danger of making tropes out of objects. This is one of the reasons that referents remain so obscure and entangled in the poem; as Stuart Curran observes in *Poetic Form and British Romanticism*, "the impulse to hymn continually runs against the urge to understand the nature of hymning" (61).

But hymn Shelley does nonetheless, and though he also has need to question the nature of hymning, this questioning is an anxiety betrayed, an undertone of self-doubt, not a self-conscious way of writing a self-referential poem.   For by line 14, while apostrophizing the ravine, he finally engages in the main thrust of his argument: "awful scene, / Where Power in likeness of the Arve comes down." But the expected form of metaphoric predication is reversed again.   If Power is like the Arve, what stands for what in the system of metaphoric substitution?   Should it not be that the Arve river flows down with such tremendous force and grandeur that it bears a consonance with our conception of the might of Power?   This would be so if Shelley were privileging the mountain, but since this is not his explicit agenda, he instead draws attention to the impression it actually had made on him by again causing slight confusion in the tenor-vehicle relationship.

Shelley is trying to assert belief in a transcendent "Power" which, in the language of "Essay on Christianity," harmonizes with the human will. The human mind, in its turn, sustains an interdependence between mind and objects, because of the synthesizing power of perception "which passively / Now renders and receives fast influencings, / Holding an unremitting interchange / With the clear universe of things around" (37–40).   But he realizes this only after acknowledging that when he gazes on the ravine what he confronts is not ravine, nor even its immediate displacement into metaphor.   Instead, he confronts the image-maker: "I seem as in a trance sublime and strange / To muse on my own separate phantasy, / My own, my human mind" (35–37). Curran suggests that "The closer he draws to the symbol, the closer he comes not to what it symbolizes—mental formulation in general—but to what in the first place has designated its symbolic quality" (*Poetic Form* 61).   I would add that Shelley, because he is drawn to the designator of symbolic qualities, is also drawn to the object which provided the symbol, in its pre-symbolic being. As Lloyd Abbey remarks, in a provocative comment which he unfortunately does not develop, "To make phenomena into hypothetical symbols of ultimate reality is one thing, but to see phenomena as having value *only* as symbols of the Ultimate is to lose one's humanity in the preoccupation with transcendence" (9). Later in his book Abbey clarifies: " 'Mont Blanc' and the Hymn emphasize the necessity for both imaginative symbol making and imaginative iconoclasm which will prevent symbols of the unknowable Power from being taken as realities" (*Destroyer and Preserver* 19). Thus Shelley's "thought," imaged as "wandering wings," now rests "In the still cave of the witch Poesy, / Seeking among the shadows that pass by / Ghosts of all things that are, some shade of thee" (i.e., Power) ("Mont Blanc" 44–46). In alluding to Plato's myth of the cave, the poet again signals his anxiety over the delusions of figurative language. Yet he is also described as one whose poetry seeks an intimation of Power from the "shadows that pass by," the latter being in apposition to "Ghosts of all things that are." His "Power" is not of the world, but he acknowledges the implications of being consigned to understanding it only in terms of the world. Since, however, such a formulation will have implications for the way we think about the world qua world, it is acknowledged that the "Shadows that pass by" the "cave" of poetry are the "Ghosts of all things that are." Whatever we make of them in our quest for a reality beyond them, the "ghosts"—which I am reading as the images appropriated by the poet—remain the ghosts of "all things" that really are.

This is a complicated business: in the cave of the newly personified "witch Poesy," "that [the speaker's thoughts] or thou [Power] art no unbidden guest," and when Poesy seeks, as in "Hymn to Intellectual Beauty," "some shade of thee, / Some phantom, some faint image" (46–47), the latter "traces" become the figures for intimation of the Power. The impetus that conditioned the writing of "Hymn to Intellectual Beauty" has not changed, for the poet still desires to realize an articulation of an incorporeal Presence which defies discursive reasoning. This time, however, he makes conscious reference to the limitations of his own writing and understanding; bowing again in the direction of the *ut pictura poesis* tradition, Shelley acknowledges that Power can be suggested—to both reader and poet—only by assimilating one's conception of it to sensible objects. As we have seen, Shelley takes exception to the various implications of such a theory, because of his familiar concern over taking a word (or in this case, image) for a real being. Yet one still detects the qualified resonances of, for example, Joseph Warton's prescription that "The use, the force, and the excellence of language, certainly consists in raising, clear, complete, and circumstantial images, and in turning readers into spectators" (Warton, *An Essay On the Genius and Writings of Pope* 2: 160).

Indeed, Shelley is very much aware of the mid-to-late eighteenth-century ode's emphasis on the image; he is trying to revise it, however, to make it more responsible in its comportment both to the abstract and to the integrity of sensible objects. Where Lord Kames, in *Elements of Criticism*, confidently declared that "the eye is the best avenue to the heart" (2: 35), Shelley would join his Romantic contemporaries, most notably Wordsworth and Coleridge, in decrying some of the effects of the "tyrant eye." In *The Prelude* Wordsworth is concerned about "that thraldom of the sense," when the "bodily eye" threatens his creative potential. But Shelley is equally nervous about the opposite side of this coin. He is so used to appropriating "things that are" to give him an apprehension of "Power," so concerned that even if the deep truth is imageless he is still helpless but to present it in images, that in "Mont Blanc" he shows signs of wavering between writing an ode to Power and writing a poem about the mountain. Thus, when he concludes the second section of the poem by insisting "till the breast / From which they fled recalls them, thou art there!" (referring, of course, to the "breast" from which fled the "shadows that pass by"), he is clearly referring to the manner in which he is left to conceive of Power: the "*shadows*" of "things that are" form the subject matter of poetry, are the mere images of poetry. Our conceptions of Power reside there because we are inexorably compelled to the act of appropriating images in our quest to understand our metaphysical beliefs.

Shelley is shortly to quote the skeptical philosopher Sir William Drummond in the preface to *The Revolt of Islam*, and C. E. Pulos has aptly shown the importance, throughout Shelley's career, of Drummond's *Academical Questions*. Drummond's suspicion of philosophical verification would have been very much on Shelley's mind during such times as the writing of "Mont Blanc," especially the following assertion from *Academical Questions*: "The conviction of the philosopher, like that of the lunatic, has no support but from itself" (152). Indeed, Shelley's general debt to the skeptics in matters of belief during this period is enormous, despite his own skepticism over *their* premises. The quotation from Drummond would also have served him as a fine antidote to the one following, from Hume's *An Inquiry Concerning Human Understanding*: "And in philosophy we can go no further than assert that *belief* is something felt by the mind, which distinguishes the ideas of the judgment from the fictions of the imagination. It gives them more weight and influence, makes them appear of greater importance, enforces them in the mind, and renders them the governing principle of our actions" (63). For Shelley, not judgment but imagination is the conveyor of belief, however uncertain and ineffectual its images (and thus our belief) may be; and our need to bridge the gap in our uncertainty leads to an endangering, in perceptual terms, of the integrity of the objects which provided us with our images of, maybe even our belief in, the object of faith.

Shelley's contemporaries responded in various ways to these philosophical cruxes, and Shelley himself further responded to their responses. Wordsworth's *Excursion* provides precisely the kind of example he continued to work against. Book Four in particular is evocative of a number of issues to which he took exception, as in the following effusion of the Wanderer:

> 'Tis, by comparison, an easy task
> Earth to despise; but, to converse with heaven—
> This is not easy:—to relinquish all
> We have, or hope, of happiness and joy,
> And stand in freedom loosened from this world,
> I deem not arduous; but must needs confess
> That 'tis a thing impossible to frame
> Conceptions equal to the soul's desires;
> And the most difficult of tasks to keep
> Heights which the soul is competent to gain.
>
> (*Excursion* 4.130–39)

For Christians, of course, conversation with heaven involves the incarnation, rituals of worship (including prayer and the eucharist), grace, and so on, which serve as intermediaries between the temporal and divine. *The Excursion* has a Christian context, one which is irrelevant to Shelley and his concerns with an absolute, rather than a humanized, deity. Shelley rejects the religious short cuts taken for granted by many of his contemporaries, but the contrast with *The Excursion* is useful in pointing up a correlative issue, one which for Shelley is a great anxiety and for Wordsworth is occasion for joyful devotion. It was not so easy for Wordsworth to shun earth at all; the point is, however, that the Wanderer indulges in the common predilection for valuing "converse with heaven" in inverse proportion to his professed ability to despise earth. In fact, precisely because the Wanderer most emphatically does not despise earth, we learn of his tremendous want of conversation with heaven by indirection. The Wanderer, and

Wordsworth, and Shelley and the rest of humanity are bound to a language of the temporal world, and Shelley is concerned that such wants, and the disappointments over them, foster a too-facile willingness to shun the empirical world, the very world which has given us the objects from which we construct our representations of the "soul's conceptions."

The opening of the third section of "Mont Blanc" simply answers such concerns with more questions:

> Some say that gleams of a remoter world
> Visit the soul in sleep,—that death is slumber,
> And that its shapes the busy thoughts outnumber
> Of those who wake and live.—I look on high;
> Has some unknown omnipotence unfurled
> The veil of life and death? or do I lie
> In dream, and does the mightier world of sleep
> Spread far around and inaccessibly
> Its circles? ("Mont Blanc" 49–57)

Some say that the "remoter world" in whose existence he so desperately wants to believe, is accessible—a comforting thought, even if such accessibility is given in gleams that are shown only in sleep. But Shelley is, after all, looking "on high." His meditation on a remoter world proceeds because the mountain peak of "Mont Blanc" is remote also (but in a very physical sense), and it is one which he is trying to render as a virtually incorporeal dream-vision. Rendered as a symbolic vision, the mountain serves as a convenient pointer to the "remoter world." Is he poised, like the Wanderer, to "despise earth"? Is he allowing, like Hume, his beliefs to govern his actions, in this case literary actions?

Shelley knows, with a nod to Drummond, that he will not be able to separate the educated beliefs of his philosophical nature from the "mad" fictions of his belief in the symbolic value of the mountain, especially given his letter to Peacock in which he claimed to have been thrown into a frenzy akin to madness, upon first sight of Mont Blanc. Thus the mountain, as fictional representation of a belief, cannot discursively be separated from the independent identity of the object of belief. Since he also cannot separate the value of the mountain as naturally sublime object of nature from his transmutation of it into a symbol of Power, he begins to feel guilty, and starts to elucidate the physical attributes of the mountain. Just when his "spirit fails" and he is on the verge of losing his tentacles to the empirical world, he mentions Mont Blanc itself as "still, snowy, and serene." Brought back to the life of the senses, he recalls the "subject mountains," falling again momentarily into the language of displacement of the physical: "Its subject mountains their unearthly forms / Pile around it" (62–63). Shelley is in awe, however, over a mountain that is literally and physically earthly; here he is describing not the Power but the earthly forms themselves, irresistibly robbed of their temporal circumscription by a poet who continues to manifest desire for a perfection which precludes the temporal world.

But he does continue with the landscape description for a few lines, until, overwhelmed now not with the expanse of Power implied in the mountain but with the mountain itself *and* its consequent value as a symbol, he starts to engage in obtrusive mythology: "Is this the scene / Where the old Earthquake-daemon taught her young / Ruin?" (71–73). The mountain had been a symbol for Power, because its greatness suggested Power, and Power must have its metaphors; but he is also overwhelmed enough with the grandeur of the mountain itself, that he feels compelled to mythologize *it*, to fictionalize what is also the vehicle of another conception.

Shelley's honesty here enables him to be more cautious about the mountain for the rest of the poem, even as he holds to the inevitability of image-making: if even the mountain requires a fictional framework, there is little hope that the Absolute will fare much better. Thus, addressing the mountain with this double vision, he solemnizes:

> The wilderness has a mysterious tongue
> Which teaches awful doubt, or faith so mild,
> So solemn, so serene, that man may be
> But for such faith with nature reconciled,
> Thou hast a voice, great Mountain, to repeal
> Large codes of fraud and woe; not understood
> By all, but which the wise, and great, and good
> Interpret, or make felt, or deeply feel. (76–83)

William Cowper, in "Yardley Oak," had also betrayed an anxiety over the merits of his symbol relative to his professed belief in a Christian God:

> Could a mind, imbued
> With truth from heav'n, created thing adore,

I might with rev'rence kneel and worship thee.

("Yardley Oak" 6–8)

Cowper at this point (1791) may not be perfectly satisfied with his feelings about the "truth from heav'n," but he is satisfied to move on, and to use the precise delineations of his oak as a good index of the mutable world in which it has stood its ground. If trees could talk, he says, "By thee I might correct, erroneous oft, / The clock of history, facts and events / Timing more punctual, unrecorded facts / Recov'ring, and misstated setting right" (45–48). Yardley Oak, like Mont Blanc, has stood witness to history, and like Mont Blanc it provides the poet with a concrete locus in the world from which to proceed with meditation. But Shelley's apostrophe to the mountain in its pedagogical manifestations is qualified by the context of the uncertainty of symbols. The language of reconciliation ("the beautiful") is different from the language of awe-inspiring worship ("the sublime"). We are not reconciled to nature itself because we appropriate nature as a convenient analogue of that which transcends it.

Shelley will recall the above effusion ("The wilderness has a mysterious tongue . . .") when he comes to write the final stanza of the ode. For now, his apostrophe seems a staged, entirely inadequate attempt to reconcile himself to nature in the manner of his eighteenth-century precursors, such as Cowper, who acknowledged the value of the object about to be usurped and then quickly made it over into a dress for their thought. Mont Blanc, as a particularly impressive part of nature, can be a vehicle for teaching about the Power that transcends nature; in the awful truth of its resistance to the winds and storms that would wear on lesser examples, it can remind its percipient about the dangers and ultimate weakness of "codes of fraud and woe"; but the "faith" it teaches in the context of this poem reconciles us to nature only in nature's capacity as provider of symbols. We become reconciled to an idea of faith *through* nature, then, which precludes the possibility of reconciliation *with* nature as such. The poem's many warnings about this situation do not obliterate the very real value derived from the mountain-as-symbol, but Shelley again recalls us to the pre-symbolic aspects of the object itself by reminding us of the instability of symbolic representation, and of the inevitability that there are those for whom Mont Blanc will stubbornly remain just a big mountain: the "voice" of the "great Mountain" is "not understood / By all", and those who do insist on investing it with meaning—necessarily the wise and great and good—are involved in an uncertain process of transference of feeling: "Interpret, *or* make felt, *or* deeply feel."

Skeptical philosophers such as Locke and Hume, who otherwise are suspicious of figurative language, make allowances for its use in poetry. Shelley, who claims always to be vigilant for truth, who indeed insists throughout his life that he sacrifices virtually everything in the name of Truth, insists in "Essay on Christianity" that deceit can sometimes be justified. The kind of deceit operating in "Mont Blanc" and in figurative substitutions in general would not have been lost on him, for he defends Jesus' "justifiable" lies even in the same essay that warns about the dangers of taking him "literally": "But this practice of entire sincerity towards other men would avail to no good end, if they were incapable of practicing it towards their own minds" ("Essay on Christianity" 199–200). Thus Shelley claims that Jesus only pretended to accept the Jewish Law, because he needed a way of finding admittance into the opinions of the men to whom he was preaching. This special view of deceit, politically naïve as it may appear, plays a role in Shelley's decision to claim, in the middle of a poem clearly anxious about its appropriation of objects, that the "wilderness has a mysterious tongue." If the end of lying can justify its means in matters of spirituality, then Shelley's "lies" about the mountain, as it were, are well served. And whatever takes precedence in the object-symbol conflict, it is the human being's spiritual quest, he would maintain, which is finally at stake.

Valuing the mind and its capacity for imaginative organization, synthesis, or even creation is not tantamount to rejecting the world of human history, however, and Shelley is soon brought around once again to a realization of the historical world's absolute disjunction between desire and its spiritual objects. Deception must therefore eventually be qualified as such, because the ultimate revelation is never to come. Hence, still working within the context of his fictional framework—"glaciers creep / Like snakes" ("Mont Blanc" 100–101), and "Frost and the Sun in scorn of mortal power" (103) pile precipices—he details the mutability to which the entire world, including the Arve and its tributaries, are subject: "All things that move and breathe with toil and sound / Are born and die; revolve, subside, and swell" (94–95). The mountain is of the mutable world; the first line of the fourth section immediately catalogues "The fields, the lakes, the forest, and the streams, / Ocean, and all the living things that dwell / Within the daedal earth" (84–86) as part of the process of nature. Man too is part of a larger and mutable scheme whose "work and dwelling / Vanish, like smoke before the tempest's stream, / And their place is not known" (118–20). Man's work is still remarked, because imagination performs its calling regardless of external sanction; but even imagination, and its capacity to alter perception, does not objectively alter the rush of history in an anti-intellectual and unspiritual world.

"Power," however, is a different matter, and Shelley approaches the end of the poem by attempting to expose his appropriation of the mountain:

> Power dwells apart in its tranquillity
> Remote, serene, and inaccessible:
> And *this*, the naked countenance of earth,
> On which I gaze, even these primaeval mountains
> Teach the adverting mind. (96–100)

Whatever processes the mountain is subject to, Power is not part of it. Shelley in this section virtually reverts back to a more traditional view of figuration and signification, and to a (temporary) belief that language wholly and accurately transmits thought. For he is trying to make language an inoffensive dress of thought, and so he reveals his codes: power is no part of the symbol he employs to describe it, but the natural scene can "Teach the adverting mind" about human littleness, and human arrogance in so expansive a world.

Shelley's caveat about the insignificance of man comes toward the end of the poem, after he has voiced his preoccupation with what he takes to be the primary signified of the mountain's symbolic potential. He might have felt chastened by Lord Byron, whose Canto Three of *Childe Harold's Pilgrimage* he had been reading in manuscript in the summer of 1816. Seeing the Alps, Byron also thinks of the "vast walls" that have "throned Eternity in icy halls / Of cold sublimity," and he also notes "How Earth may pierce to Heaven, yet leave vain man below" (*Childe Harold's Pilgrimage* 3.62). Unlike Shelley, however, he interrupts himself at this point, and defers first to the evocations of human history: "But ere these matchless heights I dare to scan, / There is a spot should not be pass'd in vain" (3.63). He then goes on to narrate details of history that took place on the sites around him, such as the 1476 Swiss victory over Burgundy which occurred at Morat. In this particular instance, Byron has clearly placed priorities, and he is not agonizing over the inherent value of his metaphors. Since Shelley is questioning whence his priorities derive, and since he is unable to decide between the world of objects and the conceptions of transcendence that require the symbolic manipulations of that world of objects, in the final stanza Shelley ends up impaled on both sides of the fence.

He tries first to solve the problem by putting the Power in the mountain: "Mont Blanc yet gleams on high:—the power is there" (127). The Power is most assuredly not there, except in the most obvious (and facile) possibilities of symbolic representation, and so after a few lines of reminding himself about the real existence of the real mountain ("In the lone glare of day, the snows descend / Upon that Mountain" 131–32), he returns to his consciously constructed confusion:

> The secret strength of things
> Which governs thought, and to the infinite dome
> Of heaven is as a law, inhabits thee!
> And what were thou, and earth, and stars, and sea,
> If to the human mind's imaginings
> Silence and solitude were vacancy? (139–44)

Shelley can claim that the "secret strength of things" inhabits the mountain only because of his notion, forwarded in "Essay on Christianity," that deceit is necessary in certain select matters of communication. The Power which governs thought and which is as a law to the infinite dome of heaven can reside in a mountain only when the mountain ceases to be a mountain and becomes a trope. This process immediately begs the question asked in the final three lines of the poem: not, what is Power, but what are the mountain and earth, and stars and sea. If Mont Blanc becomes an object only to be troped upon, then what is the mountain as mountain? If the silence and solitude of Mont Blanc were only vacancy to its percipient, a mere vehicle looking for a tenor, a gap waiting to be filled by a transcendent presence, would it retain its value as a mountain? Shelley's anxieties suggest that it retains quite a bit of value; indeed he will spend the rest of his career trying to balance the contrary claims imposed by his question.

3. The Language of the Dead

The Revolt of Islam

Shelley concludes "Mont Blanc" with a question, and though it is one he never answers definitively, the fact that he is able to formulate it at all marks an important step in his development. What—as we may recall it—is the mountain as mountain, and what is the "Power" if the formation of a principal symbol for it is not only inadequate, but also morally suspect? *The Revolt of Islam*, composed at Marlow primarily between March and September of 1817, manifests Shelley's continuing compulsion to respond to his own self-exposure, indeed suggests just how profoundly he experienced his philosophic and poetic uncertainties. For *The Revolt of Islam* directly responds to the poet's realization that his fictions are suspect, that they potentially deflect his attention away from the very world he presumably wants to redeem and to spiritualize. It is not, to be sure, a satisfying response or a particularly good poem, but it is the last major effort of his English period, and it marks a transition between the Shelley who tried to battle uncertainties and the Shelley of the Italian period who instead turned his attention to living with them.

    The Revolt of Islam is an epic in twelve cantos that tells a story about Laon and Cythna, a pair of lovers[1] who try to reform the world, and who fail. After being murdered by the masses of an evil empire, they are transported to a wondrous "Temple of the Spirit," another ill-defined, apparently transcendent realm that provides a forum for the perfect bliss of its inhabitants. The tale in fact virtually opens and closes in the realm of the Temple of the Spirit: in the opening canto, the narrator comes upon a woman who goes with him to the temple, and then the tale of Laon and Cythna per se begins in Canto Two. Before the initial journey, though, the woman of Canto One gives a brief synopsis of her own history: after falling in love with a Spirit who instructs her to prove her worth, she achieves great success fighting in the French Revolution, or rather in what appears to be allegorically represented as the French Revolution.[2] Already we are morally beyond the *Alastor* questor, for his vision led him to forsake the world, and this vision leads the woman-questor to embrace it radically. She thus returns to her home and is happy for a time, knowing the bliss of communion in Nature with the "Spirit"; but when she "was awakened by a shriek of woe" (I.xlvi.537)—presumably Shelley's reference to the Reign of Terror—the visionary aspect of life rather conveniently takes over:

> And over me a mystic robe was thrown,
> By viewless hands, and a bright Star did glow
> Before my steps—the Snake then met his mortal foe.
>
> (I.xlvi. 538–40)

Shelley has learned one of the important lessons of "Mont Blanc," for even the synecdoche of "hands" is immediately vulnerable: they are *"viewless hands,"* an imageless trope obtrusively (and hence with full acknowledgment) appropriated from the realm of the visible, and when they have done their work, another symbol—emphatically acknowledged as a symbol—is made possible. For the "bright Star" that glows is not in apposition to the "viewless hands," that is, it is introduced with the important conjunction "and"; the "mystic robe"—itself suggestive of a personalized "dress of thought" that does have transcendental authority—is "thrown" (thrown down from on high, then), *"and"* a bright star glows, because having established the invisibility of the giver of the robe, Shelley takes care not to re-image it. The snake and foe story itself is explained earlier in Canto One: "The earliest dweller of the world," after seeing the "blood-red comet" defeat the morning star in combat, slew his brother. Thus evil triumphed, and the Spirit of evil changed his foe (the morning star) into a snake, while evil itself took on the shape of the eagle. Since then, explains the woman, the two have renewed their battle whenever mankind strives with his oppressors.

The Revolt of Islam begins, then, in its very opening situation, with an implicit meditation on the efficacy of symbols, with an immediate warning about the complacency with which we construe them. Good and evil have reversed their traditional symbols, and even the narrator is initially horrified by the comportment of *his* female narrator toward the snake, until he finds out that it is in fact the maligned spirit of good. Here image-making is a function of fiction-making. Where "Hymn to Intellectual Beauty" began by pondering an implicit rejection of the *ut pictura poesis* tradition, then, *The Revolt* begins by qualifying it: anxiety over interpretation is now joined to recognition of the inevitability of image-making, or more precisely now to the human predilection for interpretation specifically in response to—and often in terms of—images. "Good" and "Evil" are easily confused in their manifestations in the world, and indeed in their manifestations in symbolic orders, but even what Shelley offers as their abstract meaning is conceived exclusively in terms of their symbolic rendering. "Mont Blanc" had disclosed the anxiety over not knowing what comes first: the image or the supposed ground of its interpretation. But since writing the hymns helped Shelley to understand the vulnerability of image-choice and consequent image-interpretation, *The Revolt*, which has more of an explicit political agenda, tries to re-focus attention on the potential triumphs of interpreters, of human beings *as* potentially effective interpreters. He must, of course, suppress certain unresolved issues in order to do so, but he is determined nonetheless to salvage an integrity for the peculiarities of human powers and human propensities.

For Shelley is trying to convince himself and his readers that he has arrived at a more sophisticated understanding of the implications of unconscious interpretive acts: contrary to what we in our complacency might assume, the snake, in the explicit equations of Canto One, does not equal "evil"; however, it does not equal snake either. It is instead to be understood as some sort of short-hand for "good" (snake equals not snake but morning star, which equals "good"). Shelley does not then pause to ponder the value of snake qua snake (as he had pondered the mountain qua mountain), or the implications of assuming an entirely unproblematic substitution of the morning star for his conception of good, but his point about the arbitrariness of symbolic identity does not, after all, provide him with an easy alternative. By putting us on the alert to symbology, he does at least manage to make the not very subtle point that things are not always as they seem.[3]

The poem begins by manifesting its preoccupation with the representation of abstract nouns, then, but this is precisely what prepares for—paradoxically perhaps—its anxieties about the poetic attenuations of the quotidian. But in attempting to answer to the anxieties of "Mont Blanc" without fully subjecting his instincts to the rigors of logical synthesis, Shelley instead makes his anxiety the most remarkable aspect of the poem. Indeed, *The Revolt of Islam* is clearly caught between both sides of the conflict between desire and the actual, with each position bordering on an attenuation of the value and integrity of the other. In a letter to his publisher of 13 October 1817, Shelley explains: "The whole poem, with the exception of the final canto & part of the last is a mere human story without the smallest intermixture of supernatural interference" (*Letters* 1: 563). The previous month he had insisted in a letter to Byron, "It is in the style and for the same object as *Queen Mab*, but interwoven with a story of human passion, and composed with more attention to the refinement and accuracy of language, and the connexion of its parts" (24 September 1817; *Letters* 1: 557). These two assertions virtually cancel each other out. It is a "mere" human interest story if the human drama is of paramount concern, but its "object" is the same as *Queen Mab*'s if the poem promotes a particular political and ideological philosophy and merely utilizes a mass-appeal human interest plot as a subordinate vehicle for propaganda. Spenser, whose *Faerie Queen* is the poem's immediate influence, may well have been concerned with the relevance of the actions performed by the Red Cross Knight, for example, but the principal appeal of *The Faerie Queen* does not reside in stimulating plot and intriguing human passion—a fact Shelley is not yet fully willing to assimilate. Indeed, Shelley's impulse for allegory is underscored by the Greek origin of the names of his heroes: "people" for Laon and "seed" or "germ" for Cythna. He does try to link his two impulses in the Preface, but he still resists the designation of clear priorities: Shelley calls *The Revolt of Islam* his "first serious appeal to the Public" (Preface, *The Revolt of Islam* 36), and insists that in the cause of "a liberal and comprehensive morality" (32) he has chosen "a story of human passion in its most universal character" (32).

But there are further obvious problems even here. First, the very fact that he would maintain the "supernatural interference" specifically to frame a poem which purports to be at least partly about "human passion" and its manifestations immediately suggests the strength of his disinclination to do away with such interests.[4] Indeed, the first canto is almost entirely allegorical, with some form of transcendent hierarchy implicitly being invoked as its moral standard, and most of Canto Twelve takes place after the deaths of the protagonists, who return to the Temple. How are we to understand these references? In fact, whatever warning the snake-eagle combat provides about the ease with which symbols become abused is muted by the canto's allegorical mode and its peculiarities; its full meaning is not transparent, and the dejected narrator's journey to the Temple is vulnerable to the same kind of criticism that I have suggested in Chapter One of Ianthe's ascent to the Fairy Queen's abode. If the supernatural aspects are so dispensable—as indeed they ought to be in an atheistic poem that celebrates human aspiration for liberation from religious, political, and sexual oppression—then is the transcendent once again in Shelley's verse being made into a trope for human perfection, as it had been in *Queen Mab*?

Such a situation would in some respects answer the problems posed at the end of "Mont Blanc," for instead of an empirical object being turned into a symbol of the transcendent (which would implicitly call into question the value of the temporal world), our already metaphoric conception of the transcendent is being made into a trope for a hyperbolic view (itself a trope, then) of human perfectibility. That such an attempt is pondered in direct response to the problematic of "Mont Blanc" is most evident in the concluding stanza of *The Revolt*. Here, the narrator's approach to the "Temple of the Spirit" recalls us to Mont Blanc the mountain:

> Motionless resting on the lake awhile,
> I saw its marge of snow-bright mountains rear
> Their peaks aloft, I saw each radiant isle,
> And in the midst, afar, even like a sphere
> Hung in one hollow sky, did there appear
> The Temple of the Spirit; on the sound
> Which issued thence, drawn nearer and more near,
> Like the swift moon this glorious earth around,
> The charmèd boat approached, and there its haven found.
>
>   (XII.xli.4810–18)

In the 1816 hymn, he had reconciled himself to nature only in its tropological manifestations, only insofar as he could place the "Power" in the mountain: "Mont Blanc yet gleams on high—the Power is there." In *The Revolt*, the mountains also gleam on high ("rear / Their peaks aloft"), but the Spirit has its own temple, "in the midst" of them, certainly, but not identical to them. The impulse for approach is unequivocally related to the Spirit, for unlike the hymn's exclamation that "Thou hast a voice, great mountain," here the boat approaches the Spirit, *past* the mountains, "on the sound / Which issued thence," that is, from the Temple of the Spirit. And, as if to recall his previous ambivalence, he introduces a simile that reminds us of the nearly forgotten earth and of the explicit source of his images for metaphysical otherness: "*Like* the swift moon this glorious earth around." We shall see, though, that Shelley's troping betrays him yet again, for it is still not clear exactly what this post-mortem world is supposed to be or to evoke. Finally, he fails to gain comfortable control of the new twist his fiction-making has introduced.

Indeed, *The Revolt of Islam* tries, as the hymns had tried, to resolve on an affirmation of the mind's prowess in despite of the epistemological doubt and political disillusion we are consigned to live with. But *The Revolt* is more adamant in its direct affirmations, while also being more resigned — or perhaps *because* it is more resigned — to the irresolvable paradoxes and ills of the world. The other-worldly frame gives an authoritative — albeit uneasy and somewhat facile — sanction to the mind's quest to actualize its powers. Thus Shelley moves from hymn to epic, and in so doing attempts to shift emphasis from the appropriation of specific, concentrated representations of particular objects, to the larger conception, to a bold presupposition of some of the premises over which he had agonized in the hymns. Anagogy, he seems to hope, may well proceed finally from allegory, but Shelley's allegory may also be said to presuppose its anagogical reference point in such a way that to dispute the allegorical equations of certain parts does not necessarily threaten the integrity of the whole.[5] In this context we may recall Wordsworth's claim that Spenser is freed from bondage to definite form specifically because of his "allegorical spirit." One of the problems here, though, is that Shelley is too unsure about *what* his anagogical point is supposed to be, for he looks forward in the poem both to a transcendent bliss that precludes temporal contexts and to a rejuvenated temporal world born solely of human agency.[6]

Ideological extremism is usually an index of the times, and 1817 was again a year of tremendous turmoil: insurrections, the executions of the Derbyshire rebels, widespread famine, parliamentary suspension of Habeas Corpus — all these issues were of great moment to Shelley, who responded directly with two public pamphlets, signed in pseudonym by the "Hermit of Marlow."[7] But he also renewed his efforts to make of his poetry an adequate forum for political and social response, as his heroes actually give speeches about the evils of political and sexual oppression, and in their battles they illustrate the values of pacifism and of honest, just rebellion.[8] In all these various and complicated factors, then, we have a hearkening back to the central paradox of *Queen Mab* (which also coincided with the writing of overtly political pamphlets); that is, what Shelley hopes to present as radical truth, finally resolved upon after much soul-searching and worldly wisdom, is in fact embodied in a radical fiction. This pattern is one which he learns to work within again, and which he will continue to employ for some of the more radical experiments in poetic form and conception for the rest of his life.

But *The Revolt of Islam* in some respects represents a regression, for notwithstanding the famous, triumphant lines about language in Canto Seven, on the whole the poem manifests more artistic anxiety and confusion than it does conviction. It is torn between commitment to the political ardour that motivated it, and the irresistible habit of allegory that Shelley has already discovered in himself; between its human domestic and political statements, and the obsession with language and fictions betrayed in it. It is not uncommon for both extremes of these polarities to be manifested in any given artistic work; what is noteworthy about *The Revolt of Islam* in particular, though, is that its irresolutions do not work well with its over-riding attempt to herald an optimistic view of the human being's place in the world. Shelley's effort to balance the issues is simply too precarious at this point, perhaps because he rushed too quickly into an effort to resolve his 1816 perplexities.

I will present some of the more salient examples: The Temple of the Spirit is, as Ronald Tetreault points out, also a Palace of Art (*Poetry of Life* III). Just as Mab's pageant had been beyond human imagination, so the temple is "such as mortal hand / Has never built, nor ecstasy, nor dream / Reared in the cities of enchanted land" (*Revolt* I.xlix.559–61). This is so because it is replete with gorgeous fane, sculpture, paintings, and various other objects of art that provide, presumably, the ideal location for the "Spirit." Shelley is clearly trying, at least, to avoid the problems he had encountered in "Mont Blanc," for the "Spirit" is not analogized along an ineffectual extended metaphor. But what is the Spirit in relation to human desire? What is the Spirit in relation to the heroic feats of the poem's protagonists, or more importantly, to the pacifistic, peaceful world of love to which their revolution looks forward? Shelley provides no sure answers, and we are still left dangling with respect to his metaphysical philosophy. This is a serious problem, for in the rest of the poem a standard of morality and a standard of political reform are being advocated that rely on the sanction of the human heart, indeed rely on our understanding that the human heart offers the only valuable moral sanction. Cythna's address to the sailors in Canto Eight is paradigmatic in this regard, as she lectures them on the evils of enslavement to a God they have constructed in their own image. Indeed, her admonition suggests the kind of warning a guilty Shelley might have offered to himself, as she complains that they "give / a human heart to what ye cannot know" (VIII.v.3235–36).

But then what of the art in the temple of the Spirit? Is Shelley simply acknowledging that he can only portray a spirit-world by adorning it with the work of human hands? Or is it truly constructed by human hands, thereby suggesting that ultimate value does reside in human industry, that the Spirit is really a metaphor for human potential? Given that virtually the entire poem attempts to place definitive value in the possibility of a humanly constructed temporal order, this is a tempting possibility, and indeed may have been Shelley's initial motive for taking care to adorn the Temple. But we will recall that it is finally inaccessible to most of us, that at the end of the poem Laon, Cythna, and the child only gain entrance to it after they die, and that even then it is an arduous journey. The Preface again wavers uneasily in this regard, as Shelley insists that in the poem he has spoken out only against the erroneous idea of the Supreme Being, "not the Supreme Being itself" (37). Although he was clearly trying not to alienate potential readers, and was mindful of the censorship to which the poem was finally subjected, there is still the problem of the first and last cantos, and still the difficulty of the virtually supra-human qualities manifested by the heroes. In responding to his own poetic uncertainties as well as to the encroaching ills of the world, Shelley tries to elevate the human will and human heart above all external impediments to self-fulfilment, but in so doing he also betrays again a disinclination to endure the loneliness of the mind's complete autonomy in the universe. If "Mont Blanc" taught him that his tropes presuppose a virtually Platonic view of the world in conflict with an abiding sensuousness, *The Revolt of Islam* begins to teach him, as *Queen Mab* might have taught him, that his assertions of human potential could as easily serve for tropes of transcendence, but also, that all tropes of transcendence (whether or *not* the transcendent exists) are the topoi of human failure.

Indeed, returning to the primacy of the temporal world is not tantamount to conviction that it is more than a world of becoming. In such contexts it is useful to recall that Shelley's study of Plato resumes at Marlow, during this very period in which he is trying to make the best of his temporal world—even if he draws back in the poetry from making it *the* best world. The absolute disjunction of Plato's realm of Ideal Forms from the world of becoming would have struck resonant and unavoidable chords in Shelley, as would have Plato's condemnation of art on the grounds that the deceptions of mimesis are dangerous for the soul. Book Ten of *The Republic* provides the standard Platonic answer to the allures of mimesis, of which poetry is the prototype:

Then an imitator will no more have true opinion than he will have knowledge about the goodness or badness of his models? . . . the imitator has no knowledge worth mentioning of what he imitates. Imitation is only a kind of play or sport, and the tragic poets, whether they write in iambic or heroic verse, are imitators in the highest degree. (*Republic* X: 477)

But it appears that Shelley would also believe, almost simultaneously, that the Forms reside in the human mind, and that self-actualization is necessarily tantamount to the acquisition of ultimate truth. Witness, as one example among many, Cythna's account of the powers she exercised after her self-education was completed: "For, with strong speech I tore the veil that hid / Nature, and Truth, and Liberty, and Love" (*Revolt* IX.vii. 3523–24). She tears the figurative veil and "sees" abstract nouns, welcoming the Forms, as it were, into the world of becoming.

Still, Shelley's inability in *The Revolt of Islam* to offer an adequate or even a consistent response to his internalization of the Platonic censure of art is most evident in Canto Seven. Here Cythna is telling Laon about the events of her imprisonment in the cave, and how she nursed herself back from madness (a Platonic requisite for poetic inspiration)[9] by making an instructive, self-contained world out of the resources of her own mind:

We live in our own world, and mine was made
From glorious fantasies of hope departed:
Aye we are darkened with their floating shade,
Or cast a lustre on them. (VII.xxx.3091–96)

Only in a world of "hope departed" is the heterocosm one of "glorious fantasies." The British skeptics are echoing in the background of Shelley's thought yet again, for they are *fantasies* that form this world of Cythna's spiritual sustenance, and they are called forth into art because of her impoverishment, indeed because of the failure to produce happiness of the empirical world to which she is bound. Chimeras of hope departed either darken the world by comparison or are susceptible to further embellishment, adulteration, "lustre." For a poem which celebrates concrete political action, and which was partly motivated by the political distress of its author, this is a dangerous proposition.[10]

Nevertheless, this very admission is turned into the precarious raison d'être for art, without sufficient apology for its problematic origins, as Cythna continues:

And on the sand would I make signs to range
These woofs, as they were woven, of my thought;
Clear, elemental shapes, whose smallest change
A subtler language within language wrought:
The key of truths which once were dimly taught
In old Crotona. (VII.xxxii.3109–14)

The subtler language within language is of course metaphor, the language which is wrought from the manipulations ("small changes") of the normative language code ("clear, elemental shapes"), itself a product of evolving, constructed signs (she would "*make* signs to range / These woofs"). This subtler language is not quite truth itself, but rather the "key of truths" which were only "*dimly*" taught in old Crotona. Unlike Plato's crazed poet, Shelley's heroine does learn from her inspiration, but it is an inspiration of the self, a *weaving*, a generative function deduced in the possibilities of the transformations of language. If the key of truths is "know thyself," then it is appropriate that the revolutionary Cythna learns about the world's injustice, and the compulsion for reform, in her cave of the mind. But we are not yet in the realm of Asia's exploration of the mind in *Prometheus Unbound*; rather, the above quotation follows uneasily from the former one ("We live in our own world . . ."), the exclamation of conceded impoverishment and the self-conscious fiction-making of the last resort. Are we now with Shelley in a world of "glorious *fantasies* of hope *departed*," or are we manipulating what began as "clear, elemental" shapes into something more genuinely glorious, that is, the "key of truths"? Or are the changes to the shapes, the subtler language, to be equated with the mind's "lustre" cast on the fantasies of stanza VII.xxx?

We have been identifying more questions than answers in Shelley's poetry, but for every answer that he actually formulates, several more questions must be deduced. The problem of *The Revolt of Islam*, however, is that Shelley is not as prepared to see many of his implicit questions *as* questions, or at least not as problematic ones. They are taken up in far more responsible fashion in *Prometheus Unbound*, the poem which asks the most questions, but which, if it does not propose actual answers, still manages the most courageous responses in the entire Shelley canon. In *The Revolt of Islam* he wants desperately to assert an optimistic vision, and his desperation betrays him.

Prometheus Unbound

When Shelley embarked on *Prometheus Unbound*, he did not pretend to have all the answers, nor even a grasp of all the questions. The poetic issues and difficulties that had been plaguing him since *Queen Mab* are manifold and complicated, and he embarks on his greatest period of productivity, on his *annus mirabilis*, with a sense of productive irresolution—not necessarily with conviction that it is his irresolution which is productive or worthy of being cultivated, but merely that it is time finally to write poetry of mature vision. Indeed, he issues a warning to clarify the point: "But it is a mistake to suppose that I dedicate my poetical compositions solely to the direct enforcement of reform, or that I consider them in any degree as containing a reasoned system on the theory of human life" (Preface, *Prometheus Unbound* 135). Having written *The Revolt of Islam*, he could already claim a substantial bulk of lines written for the benefit of a public he gravely distrusted anyway, and written with an aim to raising politically efficacious consciousness. *Prometheus Unbound* is offered, as he remarks in the Preface, for "the highly refined imagination of the more select classes of poetical readers" (Preface, *Prometheus Unbound* 135), which means not that he is uninterested in reader response, but that he is less concerned with how the lower classes might translate his lines into discursive prescriptions for survival.

In *Prometheus Unbound* Shelley achieves full understanding of the resistance of certain poetic thoughts to discursive language; indeed, the poem betrays a new desire to celebrate the possibility that certain thoughts exist as thoughts at all only by virtue of their rendering in poetry.[11] He might also have been thinking of Coleridge, whose *Biographia Literaria*, according to Mary's Journal, he had finished reading by 8 December 1817. In Chapter One of the *Biographia*, for example, Coleridge complains of poetry in the tradition of Pope that "the matter and diction seemed to me characterized not so much by poetic thoughts, as by thoughts *translated* into the language of poetry" (1: 19). Such reading may have helped Shelley to assimilate more fully the concept—gaining currency in his own poetry and in the thought of the period—of the irreducibility of higher forms of poetry to "literal" discourse. The *Statesman's Manual* of Coleridge exerted a similar influence; also read by Shelley in 1817, this "Lay Sermon" contains the now famous lines about allegory, the literal, and the metaphorical. For our immediate purposes, I am most interested in its invective against allegory, for the most striking difference between *Prometheus Unbound* and *The Revolt of Islam* is that the former yields meaning in less discursively translatable, less allegorically obvious ways: "Now an Allegory is but a translation of abstract notions into a picture-language which is itself nothing but an abstraction from objects of the senses; the principal being more worthless even than its phantom proxy, both alike unsubstantial, and the former shapeless to boot" (*Statesman's Manual* 30). But precisely because of his sharpened understanding of the potential inherent in poetic language, Shelley is also cautious of its various dangers—many of which he first took notice of in the 1816 hymns—and so he tries also to construe a truth which, though resistant to normative discursive explanation, is still a truth which possesses an integrity distinct from its necessary metaphors.

In the spring of 1818 Shelley sailed for the continent, never to return to England. The composition of *Prometheus Unbound* was undertaken sporadically between September 1818 and late 1819. Yet again, the list of the poet's personal tragedies during this period is long and familiar: he had been denied custody of his children by Harriet in a chancery suit the previous Spring; the Shelleys' baby, Clara, died on 24 September 1818; and their beloved William died on 7 June 1819, at the age of three. Problems in the domestic arrangement of Mary and Percy were already setting in, and Shelley's health continued in a precarious state. But personal and political problems had already just occasioned a radical, panicked attempt (*The Revolt of Islam*) to affirm the value of the mind and of the imagination in despite of the doubts and horrors we are consigned to live with. The most obvious practical difficulty that he always encountered in the process had been with the failure of language to embody his conceptions, with consequent epistemological anxiety quickly following. The Shelley of the Italian period is equally plagued by uncertainties, but he has learned to take certain things for granted: the value of the human mind, the presence of evil in the world, and the probability of the existence of some metaphysical ultimate which defies discursive representation. The host problem now is not so much how to make language work for him, but how to reconcile himself to living with the given limitations of language. Furthermore, the "givenness" of the limitations of language comes with its own set of philosophical problems, and Shelley is no less attuned to them.

Indeed, a change had been brewing even before the final departure from England. On 11 December 1817, in a letter to William Godwin, Shelley insists on the strength of his talents in ways that clearly indicate a shifting of poetic allegiances: "I am formed,—if for any thing not in common with the herd of mankind—to apprehend minute & remote distinctions of feeling whether relative to external nature, or the living beings which surround us, & to communicate the conceptions which result from considering either the moral or the material universe as a whole" (*Letters* 1: 577). He seems, then, to be suggesting that his real talent—and perhaps his real virtue—lies in his ability to express subtle thoughts, indeed the kind of thoughts that prose analysis cannot delineate. I do not intend to suggest that *Prometheus Unbound* has not been productively read, in the capacious history of scholarship on the poem, in terms of its revolutionary zeal and the political acumen of its author.[12] I do, however, want to assume that Shelley has by now internalized the political implications of all aspects of human endeavour. By the end of 1817, he perceives expressibility itself to be so large an issue that he claims it as the chief preoccupation of his life. It is not as simple, clearly, as Shelley would have liked Godwin to believe, but his handling of poetic language and poetic form had become so manifestly angst-ridden that it is entirely appropriate he should turn to them for proof that his endeavors possess some justification.

Prometheus Unbound: A Lyrical Drama in Four Acts is an extended meditation on voice, language, and the peculiarities of communication: on what we hear and assimilate, and on how we respond to it.[13] By fusing lyric, the genre of the internalized meditation, with drama, the form of public performance and presupposed auditors, Shelley exposes public gesture and quotidian context as constituting the ground for private deliberation and understanding; language as we normatively experience it (though not necessarily as we theorize about its origins) exists only insofar as it is actualized (in reading as well as speaking and writing), and that actualization is only possible because communities publicly subscribe to certain shared assumptions about sounds and signs.[14] Even thought is understood to take place under the rubric of a *conversation* with the self, and leaving aside for the moment the problem of determining priority (thought or the language of its articulation), it is clear that Shelley is immediately indicating the possibilities, for better or for worse, that are inherent in shared, virtually unconscious assumptions about the transparency of language. He is alerting us also to the precarious status of the individual who engages in private meditation in a forum—poetry—which is offered for the public benefit, but which yet does not have the kind of public pretences that political pamphlets or obtrusively political poems possess. Shelley is keenly aware of the political implications and indeed the political presuppositions of *Prometheus Unbound*, but he is now more reconciled to the notion that the key of truths, the human being's only vehicle for belief in truths—even political truths—is wrought on the small changes made to the seemingly clear, elemental shapes of language.

Cythna learned about this process while exploring the cave of her mind; in *Prometheus Unbound* Shelley ponders further the implications of language-as-instrument-of-socialization feeding into privately held convictions. Indeed, Shelley's consideration of this problem is particularly susceptible to irresolvable paradoxes; in Act IV, the Earth sings out about the regenerated individual:

> Through the cold mass
> Of marble and of colour his dreams pass;
> Bright threads, whence mothers weave the robes their
>   children wear. (IV.412–14)

Here, all language is the language of desire. If the robes woven by the mothers are the children's artistic heritage, as the Norton editors suggest (*Shelley's Poetry and Prose* 205n.3), then individual desire ("his dreams") determines language-as-vestment (the "dreams" are the foundation of the "robes"); but that same language is still priorized by given conventions: "mothers" weave the robes and then give them to their children as prescribed heritage, received orthodoxy.

The lyric traditionally manifests the private meditations of the poet, and the closet drama calls attention to its refusal of a public presentation of perceptible images, in favor of private response. The poet is immediately preparing us, then, for Demogorgon's pronouncement in Act Three that "the deep truth is imageless," but in a highly qualified fashion; the audience here is a reading audience, and so we do not actually see a coalescence of physical objects. All vision is confined to interpretation of signs of images, many of which recall us to the absence of a physical (that is, dramatically performed) image. Even the masque which is Act IV—the very act that affirms and prolongs the triumphs in the poem—tantalizes with its chorus of happy dancers and united singers, but the form makes of it virtually a private joke of Shelley's. For a closet masque is more frustrating, more indicative of what is absented from the reader's direct view than is a conventional closet drama. In Act Two, to cite an earlier example, Asia tells Panthea that the spoken narration of her dream-vision of the absent Prometheus is virtually unheard. This problem is similar to the reader's dilemma, but Asia's solution recalls us to another absence, one which is the reader's own:

Asia: Thou speakest, but thy words
          Are as the air. I feel them not . . . oh, lift
          Thine eyes that I may read his written soul!

Panthea: I lift them, though they droop beneath the load
          Of that they would express—what canst thou see
          But thine own fairest shadow imaged there?

                                                        (II.i.109–13)

One hears in "fairest shadow" more than just a periphrastic naming of Asia: seeing herself physically reflected in the mirror of Panthea's eyes, she sees but a shadow; accommodating her sense of self-definition in response to someone else's erotic dream of *her* object of desire—that is, mimicking the reader's experience of lyric—she may see, Panthea hints, an imaging of her "fairest shadow," or *fairest* materialization of what has been felt as a discernable absence, "shadow" serving as the indicator of presence displaced. Like Asia, the reader knows that the poet "speakest," but his voice is absent, as are the dramatic images with which closet drama teases and withholds visual, and even aural, satisfaction. When we turn then to reading, as Asia tries to do, we are perhaps only more anxious to find our absences answered by the gratification of fictions that resolve tension, and reinforce the contexts by which we would define self-worth ("thine own *fairest* shadow"). But Shelley withholds even this satisfaction. Asia serves as displaced mouthpiece of the reader's frustrations by reading Panthea's (poetic) dream, in which she sees an image of the absent Prometheus; but then a second, related dream is evoked, which supplies not a forum for reunion, but invitations for further reading: "Follow, follow!" (II.i.131)[15]

Indeed, what is inscribed in the language of *Prometheus Unbound*, in the subtler language within language, is the absence of the object that language tries to evoke; however, being tantalized by an absence which cannot be recovered by analysis of a poem's parts is precisely what suggests, in minutely subtle ways, those non-discursive poetic thoughts which are the special province of *Prometheus Unbound*. Even in the essay "On Love," written probably in July of 1818,[16] Shelley is aware of the inefficacy of language, and of the embellishments to which it is prone, precisely because he feels so overwhelmingly the plenitude and importance of his ideas about love; he complains in a footnote: "These words are inefficient and metaphorical—Most words so—No help—" ("On Love" 474). There may well be no help, but there is also no alternative, and Shelley becomes triumphantly aware of it.

The drama that cannot be publicly performed also calls emphatic attention to the absence of *heard* voices. Since *Prometheus Unbound* exploits the idea of speech more than any other form of communication, and since audible speech is necessarily excluded from lyrical, closet drama, the poem exposes the virtual impossibility of its own mode of articulation. As we shall see, Shelley encodes his own necessary failure as poet in the service of affirming the value of, and "protecting" the extra-textual integrity of, his vision. The poem opens with Prometheus's anguished vocalization of his despair, addressing first an absent Jupiter and then a Nature which he believes to be inattentive to his cries. Neither does the reading audience, however, *hear* what Prometheus angrily complains is unheard by those characters who ought to hear, and who then ought to act in some measure on that hearing. In the opening situation, while Prometheus is still agonizing over his pain, he queries the unresponsiveness of nature. But not only have natural forces not *seen* him writhe, he asks of the sea, "Have its deaf waves not *heard* my agony?" (*Prometheus Unbound* 1.30; italics mine). When he finally repents for having cursed Jupiter, he finds that he cannot remember the words of the curse, and so turns to nature and demands: "If then my words had power / . . . / let them not lose it now! / What was that curse? *for ye all heard me speak*" (68–72; italics mine). A chorus of "voices" then appear (in poetry, of course, speaking voices *appear* inaudibly), from the mountains, springs, air, and whirlwinds, but he complains still, "I hear a sound of voices—not the voice / Which I gave forth" (112–13). The crisis of the first act thus revolves around Prometheus's frantic quest first to be heard, and then to "hear that curse again" (131). In attempting to communicate with Earth, the Titan's mother, she tells him, "How canst thou hear / Who knowest not the language of the dead?" (137–38). Clarifying the issue, she then explains, "No, thou canst not hear: / Thou art immortal, and this tongue is known / Only to those who die" (149–51), the latter group shortly after being referred to as "the inarticulate people of the dead" (183). When the phantasm of Jupiter is summoned to utter the curse, Prometheus commands it, "Speak the words which I would hear, / Although no thought inform thine empty voice" (248–49). And after the furies have worked their evil, Prometheus refuses to tell Panthea what he had seen: "There are two woes: / To speak and to behold; thou spare me one" (646–47).

Wry as it is, the above quotation perhaps holds the key to the first act. The implied ellipsis (there are two woes *related to the communication of my recent experience of horror*) suggests that to speak and to behold horror of the manner he has just experienced are the two kinds of woes. The syntactical ambiguity allows for a reading which would suspend the ellipsis, though, and assert the woe—the inadequacy, the suspect nature, the self-defeating uncertainties—of speaking and of beholding, exclusive of context. Prometheus wishes to be spared the one of speaking since he has already had no choice but to behold. The reader, however, neither hears nor sees the spectacle per se, and so in this respect the reader stands to Prometheus as Panthea, in her interest in a narration of the events, stands to Prometheus. But the reader is "witness" only to the written language, which enacts an imagined scene whose central character does not even want to talk about it. Shelley finally realizes that if poetry, and indeed all language, involves necessary embellishments and metaphoric displacements, then all communication can only rely on the nuances of its mode of articulation and on the interpretive skills of its audience. Even more important now, communication must rely on the revelation of its inexorable ellipses, which nonetheless expose the *something* that is missing. If *Prometheus Unbound* is preoccupied primarily with voice, language, and their manipulation, that is because Shelley is reconciling himself to the necessary simultaneity of prophetic vision with such preoccupations; if there is an extra-textual meaning in the universe which we nevertheless come to understand only in terms of our mode of articulation, then we must also come to understand the suspect aspects and limitations of articulation.

Indeed, we belong to the "inarticulate people of the dead" because language does not recuperate our losses; Prometheus is denied his "own words" at first because words, as he finally realizes, "are quick and vain" (I.303), not the unmediated or uncomplicated actualizations of "thought" which, in isolation from his interpretive abilities, can enact his need to repent for his cursing. The furies torture him with this very knowledge and its implicit extension to the unfulfilled desires embodied in poetry:

Dost thou boast the clear knowledge thou waken'dst for man?
Then was kindled within him a thirst which outran

Those perishing waters; a thirst of fierce fever,
Hope, love, doubt, desire—which consume him forever. (I.542–45)

The "clear knowledge," as Asia is to tell Demogorgon in Act Two, is "speech," and "speech created thought, / Which is the measure of the Universe" (II.iv.72–73). Unquenchable thirst (recall the limitless desire of the *Alastor* questor) is kindled by the "clear knowledge" which is the self-consciousness of thought, and language is thought's only forum.[17] But the measure of the universe is a synecdoche of, not identical to, the universe; and though the knowledge which language yields is not entirely "clear" (these are, after all, the furies speaking), it is still the condition of consciousness. Infinite desire is unleashed when it is discovered within the infinite manipulations of the language within language—and such manipulation, of course, is the condition of all language, even what we sometimes naively call literal language. The pain of infinite desire, the pain of the *Alastor* questor, is now understood to be the legacy of language and its tropes, which are the ground of human consciousness.

The source texts here come from Rousseau; first *A Discourse on the Arts and Sciences*, which claims that "the arts and sciences owe their birth to our vices" (*Discourse on the Arts and Sciences* 15). More important, we hear clear echoes of the *Second Discourse*, in which Rousseau claims that "The imagination, which causes such ravages among us, never speaks to the heart of savages, who quietly await the impulses of nature, yield to them involuntarily, with more pleasure than ardour, and, their wants once satisfied, lose the desire" (*Second Discourse* 78). It is the "civilizing" force of language which has obliterated the possibility of human contentment:

> Let us conclude then that man in a state of nature, wandering up and down the forests, without industry, *without speech*, and without home, an equal stranger to war and to all ties, neither standing in need of his fellow-creatures nor having any desire to hurt them, and perhaps even not distinguishing them one from another; let us conclude that, being self-sufficient and subject to so few passions, he could have no feelings or knowledge but such as befitted his situation; that he felt only his actual necessities, and disregarded everything he did not think himself immediately concerned to notice, and that his understanding made no greater progress than his vanity. (*Second Discourse* 79; italics mine)

We create, as the old cliché goes, from the fragments of impoverished desire, but it is no less true to Shelley for being a cliché; we can conceptualize only in terms of our manipulations of our received language code, but language, and specifically poetic language, withholds satisfaction even as it holds out the promise of its potential.[18] Northrop Frye has taught us to understand that poetry originates in desire, itself an immediate sign of absence.[19] If this is the special condition of poetry, for Shelley it is also the more general condition of our experience of life, in which desire implies absence, which we often take to imply an untapped plenitude.[20] For Shelley, the furies and Rousseau are right, though within certain qualifications: self-consciousness, even in all its agonies, is still the condition of human spirituality, and infinite desire is the spur to whatever spiritual fulfillment and self-actualization we do experience. Negation is the introductory mode of *Prometheus Unbound* not only, as Earl Wasserman suggests, because Jupiter is the "privative mode" of Prometheus (*Critical Reading* 260), but because author and reader share in a collusion of withheld desires in an effort to come to terms with the ground of their desires. What Shelley has been learning is that his mode of articulation and even his deficiencies in articulation are what often precipitate his conceptualizations, themselves inextricably linked to their articulation, and hence doomed finally to obscurity.

Yet another important "source text," which Shelley probably has in mind while writing the "speech created thought" section, is also from the *Second Discourse*, in which Rousseau advances a theory of linguistic origins which implies a theory of metaphor, and of language *as* metaphor:

> Purely abstract beings are . . . only conceivable by the help of language. The definition of a triangle alone gives you a true idea of it: the moment you imagine a triangle in your mind, it is some particular triangle and not another, and you cannot avoid giving it sensible lines on a coloured area. We must then make use of propositions and of language in order to form general ideas. For no sooner does the imagination cease to operate than the understanding proceeds only by the help of words. If then the first inventors of speech could give names only to ideas they already had, it follows that the first substantives could be nothing more than proper names. (68–69)

We expand vocabulary, then, in response to a need to move from the particular to the general, in short, to conceptualize and to experience thought.

For Prometheus to recall his curse on Jupiter, is not so much for him to realize that Jupiter is but an absence, or a privative mode, but rather to reconcile himself to the inextricability of articulation and conceptualization. I thus see the curse-voice (Prometheus) and the "cursee"-image (Jupiter) as two aspects of the same issue. Both the utterance and recalling of the curse, and the defining features of the image-object of the curse, are equally emblematic of Shelley's linguistic concerns. Language, and the language of myth and of metaphor and of common fiction, are part of a received orthodoxy which Shelley wants to question, but can only work within. For Prometheus—himself a myth—to curse Jupiter is to curse the only system of meaning available to him. He must try to work within it, then, or to create a new one from the fragments of the old.

Thus the poem also serves, as some commentators have helpfully suggested, as anti-myth. Prometheus himself begins to learn such a lesson when he beholds the "phantasm" of Jupiter, brought from the world of "shades" to re-present the curse. Prometheus recalls us again to our own dilemma as readers confronting a poetic concretization of an abstraction, as he exclaims:

> Tremendous Image! as thou art must be
> He whom thou shadowest forth. I am his foe
> The Titan. Speak the words which I would hear,
> Although no thought inform thine empty voice.
> (*Prometheus Unbound* I.i.246–49)

The "tremendous image" of Jupiter is tautological because it shadows forth the idea of Jupiter's mythic image: there *is* no Jupiter qua Jupiter to begin with.[21] The Jupiter of a poem and of a representation is but an image—albeit a tremendous one—yet we cannot help but understand in terms of the image: "as thou art must be / He whom thou shadowest forth." The problem is that the discursive representations of Prometheus's mythology have hardened into the received ideology, and Shelley sets out to correct the error.

This does not necessarily mean that Shelley is discarding belief in a metaphysical dualism; he is, however, exposing the more facile responses to and dangerous consequences of belief. In *Shelley's Process*, Jerrold Hogle points to the multitude of mythic structures embodied in the poem, and the incongruence of Greek and Persian mythology, for example, and concludes that

> they are mythographs, the written remains of what occurs when poetic interrelations become symbolic systems of control in which each symbol denotes a

standard to be obeyed or avoided. When Shelley takes on these forms by radically rearranging them, their uprooted status allows them to be recombined with ones from different times and ideologies. (*Shelley's Process* 171)

Such a pattern, Hogle continues, allows myth "to negate its claims to exclusive power" (172).

Another consideration must be added to this difficult problem: Shelley is wary of myth also because he is wary of the attenuations of the value of the quotidian to which metaphor and myth are prone. Thus Paul Cantor asserts that *Prometheus Unbound* is "an anti-mythic myth," but that the poet employs myth "to suggest how myths distort man's view of the world, and to show the need to break through their rigidity of meaning" (*Creature and Creator* 94). He goes on to point out the central paradox of the personae:

> As a dramatist Shelley must make his mythic figures behave like characters in a play, with a life of their own. But he also feels it necessary to undermine the literal reality of his creations, suggesting that Prometheus, Asia, Jupiter, and Demogorgon are only imperfect embodiments of a deeper spiritual truth which will always elude concrete expression. (94)

We may see why the poem must doom itself to failure, but also why that failure must be seen as Shelley's ultimate triumph: Prometheus will be able to treat Jupiter as the mythic creation and abstraction that he is, indeed one which he can obliterate from his own perception, only when he learns deeper self-knowledge. But it is our very experience as readers witnessing Prometheus's success that cautions against taking even Shelley's anti-myth as any kind of definitive expression. To understand Prometheus's success is also to acknowledge Prometheus's failure to be fully answerable to the spiritual needs we turn to in poetry. As the conclusion to Act Four suggests, in which Demogorgon offers advice on how to deal with the next tyranny, the poetic version of apocalypse does not entirely work; we feel better, but only for a limited time. To us, the mortal, inarticulate people of a received, imperfect language which yet is our only vehicle for spiritual growth, the best we can do is to learn some form of intuitive knowledge of the absences—and possibly the untapped plenitude—which poetry in particularly implicitly encodes.[22]

It is for this reason that Act Two shows Asia's descent to the realm of Demogorgon. In Act One, Prometheus confronts images and learns of their inherent absences. In Act Two, Asia confronts, in a sense, the

absences themselves, the "anti" part of the "anti-myth," and she learns of
our need, in the world of temporality, to encode them. The unification of
Asia and Prometheus will be the realization of poetic vision which under-
stands its own limitations.

I have already discussed the scene in which Panthea and Asia "read" a
dream which sets them on their journey to the realm of Demogorgon.
They are drawn, according to some "spirits" who see them, "By Demogorgon's mighty law" (*Prometheus Unbound* II.ii.43), which I take to mean
simply the urge for understanding. Demogorgon himself is an enigmatic
character, a "mighty Darkness" (II.iv.2) who lives in an enigmatic, obscure
underworld—"the world unknown" (II.i.190), according to the Echoes"—
and virtually no two Shelleyan critics are alike in defining his role.[23] I take
this to be Shelley's intention, for Demogorgon is but the vehicle for revelation of what we lack, of what cannot be represented in tactile images.
According to Tilottama Rajan, the Cave of Demogorgon is "where the
philosophical foundations of traditional hermeneutics are eroded" (*Supplement of Reading* 310).   He is "a voice unspoken" (II.i.191), and the
Oceanides descend to his dark realm, out of the way of sound and sense, so
that they will learn of desire and of understanding de-contextualized; or
rather, that they must re-ascend to their world of actual contexts because
the abysm does not vomit forth its secrets. In "Potentiality in *Prometheus
Unbound*,"[24] D. J. Hughes sees the poem as "restoring our sense of the
potential, turning, through a series of verbal strategies, the actual back
upon itself" (605). He therefore suggests that Demogorgon's law is "the
restoration of the potential to itself" (613). I would qualify this helpful
reading by adding that we understand the potential only in terms of our
sense of the given world of the actual, and further, that we respond to the
empirical world often in terms of our preconceived notions of its potential
for fulfillment.

We are, then, perpetually being cued to the interpretive skills necessarily endemic to life. Arriving at the entrance to the realm of Demogorgon, Panthea explains:

> Hither the sound has borne us—to the realm
> Of Demogorgon, and the mighty portal,
> Like a volcano's meteor-breathing chasm,
> Whence the oracular vapour is hurled up
> Which lonely men drink wandering in their youth
> And call truth, virtue, love, genius or joy—

> That maddening wine of life, whose dregs they drain
> To deep intoxication, and uplift
> Like Maenads who cry loud, Evoe! Evoe!
> The voice which is contagion to the world.
>
> (*Prometheus Unbound* II.iii.1–10)

Shelley refines and qualifies, again and again, the view that we create from our impoverishment. The above image is an ambiguous one: Maenads are dangerous, and the *lonely* men who become intoxicated with the "wine of *life*" are doing so, it seems, as compensation for spiritual incompletion (why else would lonely men be wandering?). Does the quest for spiritual fulfilment, that is, does the hint of spiritual aridity, originate the quest for "oracular vapour"? The "oracular vapour" is in apposition to "That maddening wine of life," because such "lonely men" are prototypes of poets as myth-makers, their frenzied desires becoming equated, in their minds, with "truth, virtue, love, genius or joy." For Shelley, such postures are "contagious," for they lead potentially to the mistaking of reverie for ideological truth: they "*call*" their frenzies "truth, virtue, love, genius or joy," and we have learned already the ominous implications of *naming* visions and desires. Shelley would see his poem as the oracular vapor of a lonely man who knows that all he knows for sure is the "maddening wine of life." *Caveat emptor, caveat lector.*

It is therefore entirely appropriate that, just before the final descent, Asia utters an apotheosis of the natural world: "Fit throne for such a Power! Magnificent! / How glorious art thou, Earth! and if thou be / The shadow of some Spirit lovelier still . . ." (II.iii.11–13).[25] Shelley has epistemological problems that are similar to Milton's. He is recalling Raphael's explanation in *Paradise Lost* that Earth is possibly "but the shadow of Heav'n, and things therein / Each to other like, more than on earth is thought" (*Prometheus Unbound* V.574–76). What Asia learns, though, is that her images of the empirical world have virtually nothing at all to do with such a "Heaven," nor with what *Prometheus Unbound* labels the "deep truth." She is about to encounter a "shadow" because, for her at this point, the empirical world defines the limits of absolute epistemological certitude, even as it betrays its susceptibility to being rendered in terms of what it is not.[26] To be an anti-myth, the poem has also to be, in part, an anti-image. Shelley's inheritance is one in which metaphor is generally held to involve images; the tyranny of the image is not his only concern, but it looms large enough to be a worthy opponent.

Thus Asia asks Demogorgon a series of questions, to which she receives only the answers she already knows. To "who made the living world?" (*Prometheus Unbound* II.iv.9), she is told "God." To "Who made all / That it contains . . . ?" and who made yearning and "Terror, madness, crime, remorse" (19), she receives the same answer, modified to "Merciful God," and then to "He reigns" (28). But Asia is still behaving like an irresponsible poet, believing that the convenient metaphoric predications of God will yield satisfactory responses. She demands again, "Utter his name—a world pining in pain / Asks but his name; curses shall drag him down" (29–30), to which she is told again, "He reigns." Cursing a "name," however, will emphatically not drag down the embodiment of evil. Shelley is again signaling the error of predicating attributes of that which by its very nature is abstract, as Asia goes on: "I feel, I know it—who," to which she finally offers a mythological history of the origin of the universe, culminating in Prometheus's torment, and the repeated query about the origin of pain:

> but who rains down
> Evil, the immedicable plague, which while
> Man looks on his creation like a God
> And sees that it is glorious, drives him on,
> The wreck of his own will, the scorn of Earth,
> The outcast, the abandoned, the alone?—
> Not Jove: while yet his frown shook Heaven, aye when
> His adversary from adamantine chains
> Cursed him, he trembled like a slave. Declare
> Who is his master? Is he too a slave? (II.iv.100–109)

William Drummond's *Academical Questions* asserts the danger of assigning causes, in prose that should help us to detect the hint of Asia's false assumptions: "To assign causes for everything has been the vain attempt of ignorance in every age. It has been by encouraging this error, that superstition has enslaved the world" (*Academical Questions* 39). It is clear why Demogorgon has been casually answering "God" to Asia's questions. It is the answer she expects, but beyond that, "God" is as good as any name of ineffable—and therefore imageless—truths. We do not have a language that can indicate the limitations of discursive representation, and the language within language which is metaphor is so self-referential that we are always in danger of substituting a solipsistic vision for our sense of incompletion. What is important is not God's name, which in Shelley's vision is entirely arbitrary, but His attributes, which by their very nature cannot be univocally predicated. We do not need to know who "God" is; we need to know only that the naming of Him belongs not to the real meaning of a metaphysical absolute, but to the language within language which poetry in particular manifests. Asia inches closer to this realization when she finally asks, "Whom *calledst* thou God" (II.iv.112; italics mine), for she is beginning to understand the disjunction between "calling" and inherent attributes.

We thus arrive at the central issue of the poem, as Demogorgon asserts:

> —If the Abysm
> Could vomit forth its secrets:—But a voice
> Is wanting, the deep truth is imageless. . . .   (II.iv.115–16)

to which Asia responds:

> So much I asked before, and my heart gave
> The response thou hast given; and of such truths
> Each to itself must be the oracle. (121–23)

For Shelley, language does not fully incarnate thought. The poet has finally declared, then, that his linguistic difficulties are rooted in the basic epistemological problems inherent in any metaphysics. He may convey, in tropes already doomed to failure, his own intimations of transcendence, but they are intimations offered by a self-consciously subjective poet. We must each to ourselves be oracles where such matters are concerned because the deep truth that is imageless is also silent; we learn of the inherent inefficacy of our metaphors and myths, and so, like Asia, we also learn both the danger of and the inescapable need and compulsion for interpretation, in the terms of what we do claim as knowable.[27] Paul Cantor offers a compelling interpretation of the dilemma: "In a sense, the central aim of *Prometheus Unbound* is to suggest the limitations of literal meaning, to show that however much we try to embody our visions in the concrete form of myth, something is always left over which transcends the images we create" (*Creature and Creator* 95). This is a bold gesture for Shelley,

being heir, as he was, to the eighteenth-century revival of syncretic mythology,[28] for the only immutable truth forwarded by *his* own answer to the
Prometheus myth is the vulnerability of all tropes, all fictions, all myths,
indeed all language.[29]

What remains for the rest of the poem, then, is virtual commentary.
Asia, having learned her lesson, need only ask to understand that "the destined hour" of Prometheus's release is immediate, is instantaneous with the
liberation of perception from its subjugation to fictions. Two cars thus
arrive, one to take Asia and the sister Oceanides to Prometheus, the other
to bring Demogorgon to Jupiter, where the imageless voice, in his aspect
of "Eternity," will de-throne the embodied voice of projection. Act Two
closes out with an extended apotheosis of Asia, because once the poet frees
himself from the burden of an audience's instinctive belief that his language
is the incarnation of his thought, and frees himself from trying to image
his thought as the legitimate license for metaphysical vision, he is free to
sing out. We move, then, into the realm of self-conscious poetic celebration, into Shelley's embracing of the redemptive moments of poetic vision;
but one which is also a kind of *Liebestod*. For we move now into the
qualifications of poetically fulfilled desire, our absences all the more keenly
felt for their only partial completions in a poem that has already drawn
emphatic attention to its artifice, and to its necessary failures. We have
learned that we cannot easily reify what can be conceived of only in
metaphor. But in *Prometheus Unbound* Shelley acknowledges that only
metaphors can serve to reproduce, however vaguely, our already ill-
defined, metaphoric conceptions of the ineffable. Thus, unlike the case in
The Revolt of Islam, the obtrusive mythic structure of the poem is never broken, never taken down to the level of human beings who just might, if they
try hard, approximate the heroic feats of the protagonists. We have not
Laon and Cythna, but two myths who, as myths, are manipulated by us,
not ideal models of how we ought to live. We have celebration by fictional failures who sing out in the triumph of their release from prescribed duty.

This is not to suggest that Shelley holds out merely linguistic self-revelation as the triumphant end of poetic vision. Indeed, for him the discovery of the epistemological limitations of language in general and of his
poetry in particular also frees him to take chances. He holds out a vision of
a society that regenerates itself because of its cleansed vision, but just as he
had warned against taking parables and poetic fictions as literal truths in
"Essay on Christianity," the vision here need not be cheapened by having
anyone believe that it is "literally" true. The maturity of the Prome-

thean/Shelleyan vision relies partly on its acknowledgment of the limitations of vision.

Shelley's answer to political meliorism and to visionary idealism is a qualified faith in the potential latent in perception. *Prometheus Unbound* teaches that the mind's apperception is tantamount to the healing which takes place when images and fictions are acknowledged as such. Shelley and Byron seem to be again feeding off one another. Canto Four of *Childe Harold's Pilgrimage*, which was published in 1818 and which Shelley read in manuscript, also refers to an abyss, but this one has Byron for a voice, and it does vomit forth its political secrets:

> Hark! forth from the abyss a voice proceeds,
> A long low distant murmur of dread sound,
> Such as arises when a nation bleeds
> With some deep and immedicable wound;
> Through storm and darkness yawns the rending ground,
> The gulf is thick with phantoms, but the chief
> Seems royal still, though with her head discrown'd,
> And pale, but lovely, with maternal grief
> She clasps a babe, to whom her breast yields no relief.
>
> (*Childe Harold's Pilgrimage* 4.167)

The consonance of images—the voice from the abyss, the gulf "thick with phantoms"—is clear enough. The differences, however, are most telling. Byron is referring to the death of Princess Charlotte, which had occasioned a political pamphlet from Shelley while he was still at Marlow. Byron is equally concerned with the efficacy of fictions; he reminds himself throughout the *Pilgrimage* that he has held to airy dreams.[30] But Byron's consolation in these contexts is historical, or rather, by taking a historical perspective he holds that all things are equidistant, and therefore of equal traumatic effect. This does not make Shelley less earth-bound in his politics; it does underline his fear of rendering the actual as an abstraction, and the abstract ineffable as a member of the temporally confined, empirical world. The rest of *Prometheus Unbound* therefore proceeds on the level of mythic abstraction which obtrusively resists the drawing of analogies to specific, contemporary political issues. The heightened consciousness which his vision inspires is applicable, he hopes, in all areas of human conduct, including the political.

In the final analysis, however, it is difficult to know what constitutes responsible imaginative vision, or politically appropriate fiction-making. Shelley tells us in his Preface that he presents "beautiful idealisms of moral excellence" in the service of enlarging our capacity to love; moral regeneration is possible only once our sympathetic capacities have been expanded, and it is in this sense that the poem avoids the simple didacticism Shelley so reviles. But to arrive at such a position is not easy. In a letter to Peacock of 6 November 1818, he seems almost ready to slip back into the naive poetic posturing which he had scolded himself for in "Mont Blanc": "You know I always seek in what I see the manifestation of something beyond the present & tangible object" (*Letters* 2: 47). Just a few months later, though, he writes to Peacock again:

> At present I write little else but poetry, & little of that. My 1st Act of Prometheus is complete, & I think you wd. like it.—I consider Poetry very subordinate to moral & political science, & if I were well, certainly I should aspire to the latter; for I can conceive a great work, embodying the discoveries of all ages, & harmonizing the contending creeds by which mankind have been ruled. (23–24 January 1819; *Letters* 2: 490–92)

This statement is sometimes taken as Shelley's implicit approbation of mythological syncretism; I read it as a guilty gesture toward the potential inefficacy of art which is aware of its own failures. Poems and political treatises, he has learned, accomplish different ends, and his poetry manifests interests which cannot be satisfied in the writing of political prose. His claim that he would write a socio-political account of the world is a disclaimer, but one that clearly shows his conscious separation of visionary poetry from political efficacy, or even from political savvy.[31] Shelley is also aware of the suspect aspects of poetry that offers poetic vision as an answer to societal ills; he knows that it cannot compensate for the pain of experience, for political upheaval, or social injustice. Apprehensive of consigning human suffering, or indeed any human activity, to the domain of abstract thought, he has also learned the need to qualify his propensity to see beyond the immediate, tangible object. And precisely because of his intensified awareness, the visionary poetry of *Prometheus Unbound* exempts itself from certain charges of naïve presumption, even as it indulges its impulses for metaphysical speculation and abstract thought.

Act Three thus shows the place of retirement for the mythic heroes, a pastoral retreat reminiscent of those treated in Cowper's *The Task* and Wordsworth's *The Excursion*, but with a difference: rather than serving as a concrete locus for the mind, this is a haven for the mind's fictions, a place of anagogic fantasy which serves as Prometheus's watching place for the commerce of human beings. Prometheus delineates the pastoral attributes of the cave, and then explains:

> A simple dwelling, which shall be our own,
> Where we will sit and talk of time and change
> As the world ebbs and flows, ourselves unchanged—
> What can hide man from Mutability? . . .
>
> *   *   *   *   *   *   *   *   *   *
>
> And lovely apparitions dim at first
> Then radiant—as the mind, arising bright
> From the embrace of beauty (whence the forms
> Of which these are the phantoms) casts on them
> The gathered rays which are reality—
> Shall visit us, the progeny immortal
> Of Painting, Sculpture and rapt Poesy
> And arts, though unimagined, yet to be.
> The wandering voices and the shadows these
> Of all that man becomes, the mediators
> Of that best worship, love, by him and us
> Given and returned, swift shapes and sounds which grow
> More fair and soft as man grows wise and kind,
> And veil by veil evil and error fall . . .
> Such virtue has the cave and place around.
>   (*Prometheus Unbound* III.iii.22–25; 49–63)

Pastoral, as Stuart Curran reminds us, is a state of mind (*Poetic Form* 98). Shelley is also recalling King Lear's hopes that in prison, he and Cordelia will enjoy a haven where they will "pray, and sing, and tell old tales, and laugh / At gilded butterflies, and hear poor rogues / Talk of court news" (*King Lear* V.ii.12–14). Lear had progressed from claiming the entire kingdom as his rightful domain, even his domain of retirement, to contentedness with a small square space of confinement. Prometheus's cave is much grander, certainly, but this is no ornate kingdom. It is an enclosed space where they can watch: instead of human beings observing Prometheus and company, that is, instead of individuals reading poems, observing their fictions, this retreat in effect describes the fictions observing the human beings. We will recall "Mont Blanc": "Seeking among the shadows that pass by / Ghosts of all things that are, some shade of thee, / Some phantom, some faint image; till the breast / From which they fled recalls them, thou art there!" ("Mont Blanc" 45–48). Here is our haven where we can go to claim *our* fictions, our records of spiritual striving. Like the cave of the mind in *The Revolt of Islam*, it yields the subtler language within language, for it is the closest Shelley will ever come to literalizing, as it were, the forms of desire. Indeed, the cave is a place of seclusion from the world because, in the final analysis, we must be reminded that in their aspects of fictions Prometheus and Asia are not properly of the world. They are "unchanged," not because our fictions do not alter, but because as myths of projected fulfillment they are closer to the visionary ideals of perfectibility than they are to the world of temporality. Furthermore, as we learn shortly after, the cave is beside a temple "Distinct with column, arch and architrave / And palm-like capital, and overwrought, / And populous most with living imagery" (*Prometheus Unbound* III.iii.162–64). The scene resembles the Temple of the Spirit in *The Revolt of Islam,* except that here Shelley is not burdened by the incongruity of placing supposedly real human beings in its inexplicable midst. *Prometheus Unbound* rests assured in its absence of human personae.

Poetic fictions, we have learned, cannot be fully answerable to experience. But since, in any case, they provide us with our only approximations of our inarticulate notions—ones which can be expressed only within the nuances and intimations of poetry—we must develop new art forms. Or rather, as language yields subtler language, art encompasses the seeds of new art forms: the progress of cleansed perception dictates that to "Painting, Sculpture and rapt Poesy" will be added other arts, "though unimagined" for now.[32] The fragmentary essay "On Life," written sometime in 1819, speaks to this issue:

> What is life? Thoughts and feelings arise, with or without our will, and we employ words to express them. We are born, and our birth is unremembered, and our infancy remembered but in fragments; we live on, and in living we lose the apprehension of life. How vain is it to think that words can penetrate the mystery of our being! Rightly used they may make evident our ignorance to ourselves, and this is much. (475–76)

And so who knows what a new art form will make of our ignorance? The prose quotation is of a piece with Prometheus's explanation that art forms, which have their origin in the mind ("whence the forms / Of which these are the phantoms"), become actualized ("dim at first / Then radiant") "as the mind. . . . / casts on them / The gathered rays which are reality." These "lovely apparitions," it must be remembered, visit Prometheus—they emanate from the world outside, because art is the province of human beings. Art is actualized within human contexts, and this is so because we intimate, sometimes vaguely, some spiritual truth ("arising bright / From the embrace of beauty") which, we believe, cries out for form.

As if to remind us of the disjunction between Prometheus and family and our status as still temporally confined human beings, Earth repeats, to Asia, her explanation that the immortals cannot understand problems pertaining to mortality: "Thou art immortal and this tongue is known / But to the uncommunicating dead.— / Death is the veil which those who live call life: / They sleep—and it is lifted" (*Prometheus Unbound* III.iii.111–14). We are, in the final analysis—and even as spectators watching the reveries of Prometheus and Asia—but the "uncommunicating dead." Our spirituality is still, in the end, ineffable, and what we wake to after our sleep of life—which I take to be the sleep of, in the language of "On Life," "the mist of familiarity" which "obscures from us the wonder of our being" (172)— is left unspoken even by the Earth. Indeed, her celebration of renewed faith in the oracular can be construed as a warning by indirection about our own presumptions with fiction-making. The Earth explains that Prometheus's cave is in fact the cavern which, in Act Two, had been the place where men go mad with oracles on the "maddening wine of life." Now it is redeemed:

> There is a Cavern where my spirit
> Was panted forth in anguish whilst thy pain
> Made my heart mad, and those who did inhale it
> Became mad too, and built a Temple there
> And spoke and were oracular, and lured
> The erring nations round to mutual war
> And faithless faith, such as Jove kept with thee;
> Which breath now rises as among tall weeds
> A violet's exhalation. . . . (III.iii.124–32)

Again we are recalled to the temple of *The Revolt of Islam*, but here, we have just been reminded by the Earth that we are still the "uncommunicating dead." So too is Shelley. Given that we still have faith in the value of our own created images, indeed given that Jupiter, or even our own effusively pronounced convictions of self-reliance, or even whomever we think of when we say "God," is still the issue of our unactualized desires, we had best beware of our oracular urges. Fictions may be our only hope for spiritual sustenance, but they are also to be approached with caution.

Indeed, if, while the mythic figures unite with one another and anticipate a future full of harmonizing bliss, we are still left reading in the language of the dead, what has the point been? If the mist of familiarity obscures from us the wonder of our being, then an unveiling of it discovers to us its wonder, and hence also, its mystery, its impenetrability. We uncover grounds for further epistemological uncertainty, which, however refreshing the process, still does not yield discursive information. What we are left with finally is an implicit injunction to experience some form of *gnosis*—at least as close to it as we can reach—even while we acknowledge the unstable possibilities inherent in a world where the ineffable holds out infinite potential for infinite constructions of meaning, itself precarious and hence never static. It is this issue that the Spirit of the Hour and the Spirit of the Earth address when describing the changes effected by Jupiter's fall. The Spirit of the Earth exclaims first:

> and soon
> Those ugly human shapes and visages
> Of which I spoke as having wrought me pain,
> Past floating through the air, and fading still
> Into the winds that scattered them; and those
> From whom they past seemed mild and lovely forms
> After some foul disguise had fallen—and all
> Were somewhat changed, and after brief surprise
> And greetings of delighted wonder, all
> Went to their sleep again: and when the dawn
> Came—wouldst thou think that toads and snakes and efts
> Could e'er be beautiful? (III.iv.64–75)

The sleepers remark only "brief surprise" and "delighted wonder" after waking and finding themselves changed. The most remarkable aspect of the human transformation is that they take it almost entirely for granted; the loveliness is their true nature, and therefore presents so little shock that they have no difficulty at all falling back to sleep again. They accept their new life with ease. This scenario strikes in several directions. The most obvious reading is that the Shelleyan rejuvenation is just that—a rejuvenation, not an utter transformation. According to this reading, earth is the reality of heaven when earth is allowed to manifest its genuine reality.

Still, there is something disturbing about the human response described by the Spirit: can rejuvenated humanity do no better than briefly remark the change and go back to sleep? If humanity has finally achieved its highest level of self-actualization, if it has become the spiritually awakened apotheosis of everything we aspire toward, why does the poet not have them stay up and do something useful? Shelley's back-handed compliment is hardly subtle: we are still, after all, those ugly human shapes and visages that would cause any rejuvenated being pain, and even were we to change, we would still be of the uncommunicating dead who must go back to some form of "sleep again."

The Spirit of the Hour is less hard-hitting:

Soon as the sound had ceased whose thunder filled
The abysses of the sky, and the wide earth,
There was a change . . . the impalpable thin air
And the all-circling sunlight were transformed
As if the sense of love dissolved in them
Had folded itself round the sphered world.

* * * * * * * * * * *

      I wandering went
Among the haunts and dwellings of mankind
And first was disappointed not to see
Such mighty change as I had felt within
Expressed in outward things; but soon I looked,
And behold! thrones were kingless, and men walked
One with the other even as spirits do,
None fawned, none trampled; hate, disdain or fear,
Self-love or self-contempt on human brows
No more inscribed. . . .

* * * * * * * * * * *

     even so the tools
And emblems of its last captivity
Amid the dwellings of the peopled Earth,
Stand, not o'erthrown, but unregarded now.

         (III.iv.98–103; 126–35; 176–79)

The "negatives" in *Prometheus Unbound* have been remarked many times, but it is usually assumed that Shelley is simply playing on the assumption that evil is the privation of good. To this I would add that, if we create the forces of evil by projecting, and then regarding, our own insecurities, then we also construct a mythology of goodness by inversion and indirection. For the mythology we have to work with relies on our myths of evil: in a fallen world, virtue is achieved by demythologizing evil. We do not arrive at an absolute and positive definition of goodness, and as such, the mythology of evil sets the standard. If *Prometheus Unbound* is an anti-mythic myth, that is because Shelley's expression of goodness is a negation more than it is a positive formulation. The familiar Christian understanding has been inverted, then: good in *Prometheus Unbound* is the privation of evil. This partly resembles the manner in which we understand the metaphysical in terms of our virtually a priori assimilation of it to the phenomenal, and then to our insistence that it is qualitatively different from the phenomenal.

Such understanding prepares, then, for the assertion of humanity's time-bound orientation, as the Spirit of the Hour goes on:

> The painted veil, by those who were, called life,
> Which mimicked, as with colours idly spread,
> All men believed and hoped, is torn aside—
> The loathsome mask has fallen, the man remains
> Sceptreless, free, uncircumscribed—but man:
> Equal, unclassed, tribeless and nationless,
> Exempt from awe, worship, degree,—the King
> Over himself; just, gentle, wise—but man:
> Passionless? no—yet free from guilt or pain
> Which were, for his will made, or suffered them,
> Nor yet exempt, though ruling them like slaves,
> From Chance and death and mutability,
> The clogs of that which else might oversoar
> The loftiest star of unascended Heaven
> Pinnacled dim in the intense inane.   (III.iv.190–204)

When the fictionality to which we enslave ourselves is acknowledged, it is torn aside, and the "loathsome mask" falls. What, however, takes its place? Prometheus and Asia will retire to a cave, and remain unchanged. We will be released from self-imposed forms of bondage. But the problematic of identity, of separating our familiar fictions from the reality of human existence, is never entirely resolved. The question of the millennium scene, then, is not simply how to differentiate millennial fictions from "inane" ones, but how to join them with a new, mutable, everyday, but transformed reality. In moving from an old, negated, quotidian reality to a new quotidian reality, we find again a resistance to clear articulation, indeed, we find an ineffable of the quotidian. Some of the negations in particular (notably "Sceptreless," "unclassed," "tribeless," "nationless") illustrate the inefficacy of presenting the new reality in terms simply of the absence of the old: the mask has fallen, but "man" is . . . what? In the post-lapsarian world in which poems are written and read, we predicate negative adjectives, not nouns, because a demythologized humanity is—for those of us still speaking the "language of the dead"—a humanity without identifiable attributes. The impulse for metaphoric equations may well have been vanquished (in the millennial world), or at least checked (in the world in which we read the poem), but the point of stasis has no language we yet know of. For the abstract concept of "man," then, a voice is still very much wanting. We are not enslaved by "chance and death and mutability," but that too is a negation, and even then, no-one knows what it could possibly mean to be not exempt from, but yet to rule, mutability.[33]

Prometheus Unbound falls clearly on the other side of the dilemma of the *Alastor* questor, who had overleaped the bounds of temporality in his fruitless quest for meaning.[34] The negatives cited above, then, move toward the nothingness of the inane, until the final qualifications pull the reader (and the inhabitants of this millennial society) back down to earth. The heaven on earth to which Shelley now yearns is one in which humanity is actualized in time, not obliterated in an all-consuming unity. To give up temporal confinement, that is, to ascend heaven and enter an "intense inane," would be to relinquish finite consciousness, which is the ground of individuality.[35] By making the heaven unascended, by refusing to enter that inane, and yet by making his fictionalized millennium itself a triumph of negations, a failure of fictions, Shelley discovers the freedom within necessary confinement, the grand celebrations implicit in restraint.

Shelley's initial intention had been to suspend his readers in the negations and the demythologizing that conclude Act Three, and to end his poem there. Having finished the act in the spring of 1819, he went on to write *The Cenci*, based on details of a tragic case history, as he explains in the Preface, "which has already received, from its capacity of awakening and sustaining the sympathy of men, approbation and success" (Preface, *The Cenci* 239). Having already insisted that the millennium still precludes our ascension of "heaven," Shelley turns his attention to a very real world of Italian domestic history. He did add a fourth act to *Prometheus*

Unbound—the masque David Perkins has famously referred to as "an extended exclamation point" (*The Quest for Permanence* 113)—probably because he gained a more emphatic sense of the essential differences between the redemption looked forward to in poetry and the real world from which it is abstracted. The play differs also from *The Revolt of Islam* in that the latter's obtrusive allegorizing had attempted a commerce with quotidian existence that the poem could not finally sustain. In *Queen Mab* and *The Revolt*, Shelley had appropriated a radical fiction to work out a point—*Mab* a more philosophically literal point, and *The Revolt* a politically motivated one. *The Cenci* employs a true story—a *literally* true story—to suggest that our deepest thoughts and subtlest passions are not only imageless, but also unspoken.

The play follows the story of the Cenci family in the late sixteenth century, Count Cenci's rape of his daughter Beatrice, his family's successful scheme to have him murdered, and their execution. Shelley is still articulating the subtle thoughts that now determine his professed expertise (recall the letter to Godwin), but they relate in a more obvious manner to the agonies of the inarticulate. Indeed, he clarifies in the Preface: "Imagination is as the immortal God which should assume flesh for the redemption of mortal passion" (Preface, *The Cenci* 241). The drama, however, suggests that he is uncertain of his own success.

The Cenci's plot is so replete with horrors that what is articulated most clearly is the ineffable horror of the world—not the metaphysical ineffable, but the ineffable of emotional outrage, the primal scream that can find no proper language. Again the Preface is instructive in this regard, as Shelley clarifies that self-revelation is the highest end of drama: "The highest moral purpose aimed at in the highest species of the drama, is the teaching the human heart, through its sympathies and antipathies, the knowledge of itself" (Preface, *The Cenci* 240). But this is the highest end of *drama,* which is still a form of artistic representation. When Asia experienced her revelation that her "own heart" was the best "oracle," she too was in the center of an artistic exhortation to an audience of readers learning the virtues of self-knowledge. In the world from which poetic vision is projected, the formula is not so easy. Shelley tries to remind us of this, even while we recognize that as a play, however faithfully told, it still represents an *aesthetic* response to experience. Orsino, for example, contemplating ill will against Beatrice, exclaims aloud that he fears "Her subtle mind, her awe-inspiring gaze, / Whose beams anatomize me nerve by nerve / And lay me bare, and make me blush to see / My hidden thoughts" (*The Cenci* I.i.84–87). Giacomo, about to wish for his father's murder, is also troubled by self-revelation:

> Ask me not what I think; the unwilling brain
> Feigns often what it would not; and we trust
> Imagination with such phantasies
> As the tongue dares not fashion into words,
> Which have no words, their horror makes them dim
> To the mind's eye. (II.ii.82–87)

The most striking example of this turn on the Shelleyan injunction for self-revelation is Orsino's reconciliation to his own evil attributes:

> even I,
> Since Beatrice unveiled me to myself,
> And made me shrink from what I cannot shun,
> Shew a poor figure to my own esteem,
> To which I grow half reconciled. I'll do
> As little mischief as I can; that thought
> Shall fee the accuser conscience. (II.ii.114–20)

The last two lines echo those negations in *Prometheus Unbound* which point by indirection to the visionary rejuvenation of the world. In the empirical world of experience, doing as little evil as we can is a dangerous qualification. Doing as little mischief as we can when we reveal to ourselves an inherently evil nature is tantamount to a quietism of the imagination.

Shelley is thus exploring, as he had begun to explore in 1816, the implications of artifice, and of aesthetic renderings of human experience in the world. But he is now joining to it the considerations he learned in the later poetry, particularly in the *Prometheus*; if we can formulate no positive definition of the goodness in the world, if the world indeed is such that the only mythology of goodness relies on its conscious opposition to the reigning mythology of evil, can there be any sanction—other than artistic, aesthetic sanction—for believing that human beings are inherently good? If self-revelation shows evil to the self, what is one to do then?

In the world of *The Cenci*, self-revelation results in oracles of, and then actualization of, further evil. It is true that, like the furies of *Prometheus Unbound*, these characters grow evil by looking on it, by contemplating and thus internalizing evil; but Shelley seems to be suggesting that there may be more to it than that. Count Cenci is, after all, a human man, not a negative projection of Beatrice's, not a fury, and not a mythic abstraction. To claim a world view on the understanding that the deep truth is imageless is a precarious business, because it verges on sanction for a kind of moral anarchy.

Beatrice's frenzy after being raped by Cenci is perhaps the most powerful anti-statement to *Prometheus Unbound,* and it is the last one that I shall deal with before returning to the lyrical drama:

> What are the words which you would have me speak?
> I, who can feign no image in my mind
> Of that which has transformed me. I, whose thought
> Is like a ghost shrouded and folded up
> In its own formless horror. Of all words,
> That minister to mortal intercourse,
> Which wouldst thou hear? For there is none to tell
> My misery. (*The Cenci* III.i.107–14)[36]

In *Prometheus Unbound* we learned to celebrate the knowledge that the deep truth is imageless, and that its imagelessness is a condition for mature vision. But Beatrice's pain provides an almost perverse parody of virtually all the central Shelleyan issues: the inadequacy of *ut pictura poesis,* the imagelessness of truth, and the inability of art, or indeed of any form of expression, to recuperate our losses. Since "there is none to tell / [her] misery," and no image for her deep horror, she becomes, not one prepared for the happy obscurities of art, but a tortured woman without any sure form with which to locate her pain. It may be indeed that the subtlest thought is *about* the elusiveness of language. The triumphs of artistic vision, then, are at best precarious.

When Shelley returns to *Prometheus Unbound* it is with a more emphatic need to acknowledge the role of fiction in his particular form of visionary idealism. He concludes with energetic affirmation of everything he had learned in the course of writing the poem, but he is more self-conscious of its artifice, of the still merely latent character of the triumphs it manifests. The fourth act is still bereft of any human dramatis personae, but a chorus of spirits who "come from the mind / Of human kind" (IV.93–94) does join in the song and dance with the rejuvenated "hours," only some of whom have departed in the wake of earthly regeneration. Furthermore, our heroes, Prometheus and Asia, have disappeared, presumably because their celebrations are of a more private nature and already under way. We have grand masque, then, and grand vision, which is more bold even as it is more tentative in its assertions. When the Earth praises rejuvenated humankind, for example, her remark about language stands as the projected potential corrective to Beatrice's troubles:

> Language is a perpetual Orphic song,
> Which rules with Daedal harmony a throng
> Of thoughts and forms, which else senseless and shapeless were.
>> (*Prometheus Unbound* IV.415–17)

In Act Two, Asia recalled that after Prometheus gave man speech, "speech created thought, which is the measure of the universe." Here, in the midst of a celebration of the millennium, a more modest qualification is offered. After the spiritual apocalypse, language only creates thought in so far as it gives it definite form, an image which is in "Orphic" harmony with thought; in a rejuvenated world, sign and signified are united.

The chorus of spirits from the mind come from "that deep Abyss / Of wonder and bliss" (IV.99–100), and they rejoice that "our singing shall build, / In the Void's loose field, / A world for the Spirit of Wisdom to wield" (IV.153–55). The abysm has not exactly vomited forth its secrets to give image to the deep truth, but what can be thought can be articulated. *We* know for certain only a "void's loose field"—the void left in the wake of a demythologized existence—but in a world wielded by the "Spirit of Wisdom" Beatrice would no longer have trouble with expression. Still, those of us who want to know what the deep truth is will have to wait. What the new world does do, at least in the context of Shelley's poem, is give us a vision of hope for real potential to penetrate such knowledge.

But again and then again, the reader is teased and denied. By the fourth act, though the deep truth is not given image, we are instead told of a music. First Panthea remarks "the deep music of the rolling world / Kindling within the strings of the waved air / Aeolian modulations" (186–88). The reader, of course, hears only the silent voice of poetic lyric, not the music of the masque, not the music within the masque that Panthea and Ione hear. Ione's response to Panthea is thus an indication of the boldness of Shelley's vision, but also of our utter separation from it: "Listen too, / How every pause is filled with under-notes, / Clear, silver, icy, keen, awakening tones / Which pierce the sense and live within the soul" (IV.189–91). The poet is doing his best: he gives us visual, synaesthetic images of this sound within sound—"clear, silver, icy, keen"—by way of qualifying his conception. But to describe a musical sound (already unheard) in terms of synaesthesia is to remind one's readers that they are readers, not auditors, not real witnesses to the scene being described. Since sound represents in nondiscursive ways, it may be closer than images are to the deep truth, for it does not indulge in image-fixation. What one hears in a poetry descriptive of an unheard music is a cadence, one which resonates within the mind's structures, but which emanates from an external source of stable (verbal) organization. Of such sounds, indeed, each to itself must be the oracle. But these musical oracles certainly resist explicit construal, and since the reader still shares only the language of the dead, we can neither hear nor fully understand the Oceanides' music.

Their music finally ushers in precisely what we are more accustomed to understanding: images whose interpretation tempts us to believe that we are approaching the deep truth. Ione sees a chariot wherein "sits a winged Infant, white / Its countenance" (219–20), and white its body, hair, and clothing. Holding "a quivering moonbeam" in its hand whose "point" directs the chariot, the infant signifies, as D. J. Hughes suggests, "the perfection of the potential, a potential which, in its stasis, need not seek completed form" ("Potentiality" 607). Panthea's vision is slightly more complicated, as she sees "A sphere, which is as many thousand spheres, / Solid as chrystal, yet through all its mass / Flow, as through empty space, music and light" (238–40). This is a vision of the earth, with the Spirit of the Earth asleep in it, shooting light "from a star upon its forehead" (270). The poet glosses this for us: "Embleming Heaven and Earth united now" (273). With this kind of embleming, the image can function as a language within the language within language: the music is impenetrable to this kind of easy gloss until it is given a symbolic shape (the child asleep in its midst), and delineated (the star upon its forehead) according to the artistic needs of the author. Whatever reading is finally applied to these two visions, it is the very process of—and impulse for—literary interpretation which is most exploited. For the complexity of the scene immediately suggests a hermeneutic puzzle, one that invites and encourages interpretive unraveling. Indeed, when we have something so obviously crying out for exegetical explication, we derive a strong sense of the ultimate meaning latent in the poetic image: by being teased into interpretation in this manner, especially such image-based interpretations, we are at once teased into believing that there is a correct—in the sense of authoritatively accurate—interpretation of the image, and that that interpretation will have some ultimate sanction of truth. Given that we have just been warned of the image-lessness of the deep truth, this is a remarkable situation.

But Shelley knows, of course, that we have no choice. The fourth act turns us back into self-conscious readers interpreting a text full of poetic images, all of which together form a vision of the millennium of the imagination. We have, to be sure, been frustrated throughout the poem by Shelley's consistent reminders that we are merely readers who cannot partake of the action and who cannot hear the voices. But since we have already learned such lessons, Act Four finally celebrates—in the only way we know how—the little, limited knowledge of hope and potential that we do possess. So we are, even in the end—and armed with our new skepticism—readers confronting poetically constructed images once again.

It is for this reason that Demogorgon must warn, at the end of the poem, that lest Eternity "should free / The serpent that would clasp her with his length" (567), the *Prometheus Unbound* story shows the way to overcome tyranny. Shelley draws back, even within the safe confines of an acknowledged fiction, from granting himself ultimate victory. He has thrown down the mantle, and reform, he would claim, is now up to his readers; but even the fictionalized, poeticized victory still leaves the serpent lurking. We are all, finally, unsure of the efficacy of our stories and of our response to stories.

Indeed, the great imageless voice summons all the characters to hear his final exhortation. When he comes to address "the dead," the poem's central paradox is most obtrusively underlined:

Ye happy dead, whom beams of brightest verse
   Are clouds to hide, not colours to portray,
Whether your nature is that Universe
   Which once ye saw and suffered— (IV.534–37)

"A Voice," with the stage direction "from beneath," responds: "Or as they / Whom we have left, we change and pass away" (IV.538). Such assertions occur even in Act Four, the very one which is superficially offered as the apotheosis of Shelley's vision of the potential inherent in language. Even the supposed light, illumination, of poetry ("beams of brightest verse") obscures not only the answers, but also the question ("*Whether* your nature is that Universe") of the meaning of mystery. Here, in the very midst of Shelley's closest and most urgent grasp after anagogic vision, we have an assertion of poetry's propensity for deflection, for abstraction of the kind that is morally precarious. Shelley urges such doubt upon us precisely because in so doing, he urges a double-visioned, qualified celebratory mode, one that finds room for song and hope in the very midst of our frailty.

4. Sweetest Songs That Tell of Saddest Thought

Epipsychidion

Shelley's decision to find room for the qualified celebrations of *Prometheus Unbound* still leaves him, of course, in a precarious position. He remains conscious of the potential for a poetry of professed limitations to slip into a naïve aestheticism or a gratuitous art for art's sake. Finally he must deal with the quotidian world to which his flights of fancy—paradoxically perhaps—now recall him; but he must also return to the possibilities of art within a world increasingly, sometimes unconsciously, negotiated in the very terms of art and of artistic manipulations of language. "To a Skylark," written in June 1820 and published with the *Prometheus Unbound* volume, provides one of the most familiar assertions of the later Shelley's angst:

> We look before and after,
>   And pine for what is not—
> Our sincerest laughter
>   With some pain is fraught—
> Our sweetest songs are those that tell of saddest thought.
> ("To a Skylark" 86–90).

The bird is addressed as an absence; its song, and Shelley's poem, are sweet, but with "saddest thought" of our necessary incompletion. Nevertheless, just as the deep truth, though imageless, is still a deep truth, the laughter and song of the poetry of an unfulfilled world may still be "sincerest" and "sweetest." What is sweet, though, is experienced within the world, even if the song yearns towards transcendence of that world.

Indeed, even in *Letter to Maria Gisborne*, also written in June 1820, and conceived in a light-hearted tone of quiet jubilation, Shelley reminds his addressee of their shared indulgence in the slighting of the mutable world:

> and how we spun
> A shroud of talk to hide us from the Sun
> Of this familiar life, which seems to be
> But is not—or is but quaint mockery
> Of all we would believe, and sadly blame
> The jarring and inexplicable frame
> Of this wrong world:—and then anatomize
> The purposes and thoughts of men whose eyes
> Were closed in distant years—or widely guess
> The issue of the earth's great business,
> When we shall be as we no longer are—
> Like babbling gossips safe, who hear the war
> Of winds, and sigh, but tremble not . . .
>
> (*Letter to Maria Gisborne* 154–66)

Despite the gentleness of the self-mockery, Shelley has not forgotten that poems of absence may still be sweetest songs; but neither has he forgotten that appropriating the world to stand as the sign of absence smacks of an immature, adolescent form of discontentment. To guess comfortably, like "babbling gossips safe," at the issue of the "earth's great business" precisely when that issue is held to be the ultimate corrective to "this wrong world" is to deflect the light of common day—"the Sun"—from "this familiar life." Shelley may be jubilant, but he never forgets: the web of talk of such doing is a "shroud."

Epipsychidion takes its place within an oddly shaped repertoire, then, for it is the acknowledgment of art's inefficacy, and even the poet's concern over the potential for solipsism inherent in a poetry of acknowledged inefficacy, which in *Epipsychidion* leads, paradoxically, to a frenzied fictional rendering of actual human beings. The poem is so obtrusively aware of its failures, so emphatically insistent on its inability to sustain its own fictions, that it virtually escapes the charge of real solipsism on the grounds of egregious transparency. It is as if Shelley's understanding of the implications of his fiction-making has effected not a paralysis but a kind of throwing up of the hands, as it were, and a desperate attempt to embrace an elaborate fiction of solace, if only tentatively.

Indeed, the quotation from the real Teresa Viviani that prefaces the poem's "Advertisement" initially emphasizes the objective reality from which her fictional rendering is drawn (it is signed, "HER OWN WORDS"), but it immediately inverts one of the central lessons of

Prometheus Unbound: "The loving soul launches beyond creation, and creates for itself in the infinite a world all its own, far different from this dark and terrifying gulf" (*Shelley's Poetry and Prose* 373). If in *Epipsychidion* Shelley does transcend the loftiest star of heaven to pinnacle himself and his beloved in an intense inane, it is yet because he knows that the descent back to earth will be all the more severe and unyielding; what he would like for a little while, at least, is a space in which to rest his weariness—not merely a mythic projection acknowledged as such, but himself and his environs rendered as myth like projections. It will be difficult for him to draw the subtle line between naïve or irresponsible fiction, and self-conscious indulgence which is attuned to the world it employs as tensile springboard; but his despair of the world, even his further dissatisfactions with the world which his own poetry has revealed to him, is such that his need for this indulgence is very great. In this sense, *Epipsychidion* is sweetest precisely where it is most indicative of an impoverishment.

The poem was written in the early winter of 1821, during the association of the nineteen-year-old Teresa Viviani, the Emily of the poem, with the Shelleys and Claire Clairmont, who sympathized with her unhappy confinement in a convent. Shelley was in very poor health during the more important days of his relationship with her, and Richard Holmes, noting the rapidity with which the flirtation became one of Shelley's obsessions, comments that "The whole thing had in his mind a strangely unreal quality, almost as if she was part of his illness, as a vivid hallucination is part of a fever" (*The Pursuit* 629). There was no consummation of Shelley's great passion for the young woman, who flattered him with adolescent exclamations of appreciation, ones only too tempting for a poet with so fecund a fantasy life.[1] But his fantasy life also provides the forum, in this poem, for the one visionary composition whose poetic images can be directly translated into the details of his domestic situation: most notably, Mary as (cold, sterile) Moon, Claire Clairmont as (dazzling) Comet, and Emily as (warm, ardent) Sun.[2] It is so derivative of his life experiences, so evocative of his own literal, quotidian circumstances, that he distanced himself from their poetic rendering by writing an "Advertisement," one which claims that the real author of the poem has died. As "an idealized history of [his] life," as he describes the poem to John Gisborne (18 June 1822; *Letters* 2: 434), it also provides an implicit description of his life as self-conscious idealization, as thing of art. The tension of the poem, however, derives from the fact that this self-conscious idealization is enacted from within descriptions that virtually cry out for literal reduction.

This discussion is not to suggest that Shelley abandons his under-standing that metaphors are rarely reducible to literal paraphrase; but in the "Advertisement," he inverts the tone of the quotation from Teresa Viviani by quoting, from Dante's *Vita Nuova*, an assertion that claims a priority for so-called literal meaning: "Great would be his shame who should rhyme anything under the garb of metaphor or rhetorical figure; and, being requested, could not strip his words of this dress so that they might have a true meaning" (*Shelley's Poetry and Prose* 373). He is, admittedly, telling his audience that incomprehensibility is their difficulty, not his failing, but he is also expressing anxiety over the nature of his composition. For the later Shelley, stripping his words of their over-laden dress might render mean-ing, but not of the variety that finds definitive discursive expression: in *Epipsychidion* Shelley is seeking a happiness for himself—not just for a Promethean hero, not for a neutral substitute—that exists exclusively in his garb of metaphor and rhetorical figure.[3] And this is so not only because the great ecstasy he longs for can only yield metaphoric thought, but also because physical consummation with the real Emily is but a fantasy. If, as he has learned, only mythic abstractions like Prometheus and Asia can be real heirs to ecstatic completion, then in his need he will make himself and his literal environment into myth. It is for this reason that there exists in the poem an uneven balance between "reducible" fiction and visionary flight. But precisely because Shelley has by now progressed far beyond the naïve postures of *Queen Mab* as well as *Alastor*, his ascent is consciously marked by its inverse correlation with his clasping of earth. Always there lurks the question, "how / Shall I descend, and perish not?" (*Epipsychidion* 124–25), precisely because when he does descend he would prefer not to perish. Emily is neither an object of true physical consummation nor an Ideal Form, and at the last, Shelley will be returned to himself.

The poem proceeds, then, on loosely flowing, but still obtrusive, rhyming couplets, somewhat like that other Romantic yearning toward ful-filment in love—Keats's *Endymion*, for which Shelley had very qualified praise, but which would have reminded him yet again of the difficulty in mediating the disjunction between the quotidian and the yearning for tran-scendent love.[4] Emily's heart is arrayed in "thought":

High, spirit-winged Heart! who dost for ever
Beat thine unfeeling bars with vain endeavour,
'Till those bright plumes of thought, in which arrayed

It oversoared this low and worldly shade,
Lie shattered. (*Epipsychidion* 13–17)

We already know that language does not incarnate thought, but can thought incarnate feeling? And can Shelley's poetic lines, as he refers to them immediately prior to the "invitation" section, truly function as "flowers of thought" (384), as his passion incarnated in pure thought? Shelley is playing subtle tricks with a conception he has already articulated elsewhere: although language does not incarnate thought, thought is generated within and because of the manipulations of language and of art. The necessary and only forum for thought in a temporal world is at once thought's propellant and its sign of incompletion. In the fantasy of this poem, though, Emily's heart is arrayed in "thought," not words—thought is the dress of the heart, instead of language being the dress of thought—because she has ascended the loftiest star of unascended heaven, and so has no need for the temporal circumscription of voice. Furthermore, for Emily "thought" itself functions as forum; if this means very little to us, that is because human thought is circumscribed, and the poet is on his way to annihilating aesthetically Emily's humanity.

But Shelley is not engaged merely in idealizing his desire. In *Alastor* his persona's love had been directed at an always other-worldly source, one who had been revealed to him only in a dream. In *Epipsychidion* we begin with an actual woman for whom he has tremendous lust—recall the *forsaken* Arab maiden in *Alastor*—who then comes dangerously close to imaging, even becoming, an absolute, metaphysical truth. It is important that this process be understood as distinct from the Platonic phenomenon of love for the form of the Beautiful, as precipitated by sensual beauty.[5] It quickly becomes evident that Shelley's most deeply felt desires here are sexual, whatever his claims about chaste love may be, and his lines about free love—which would authorize his passion for the real Emily/Teresa—undermine any lofty claims for her status as catalyst simply for love of Ideal Beauty. To be sure, he sublimates this lust into an idealized, transcendent passion of the souls ("To whatso'er of dull mortality / Is mine, remain a vestal sister still" 389–90), but she also stands as the image of Beauty ("Veiled Glory of this lampless Universe!" 26) who is obscured only because his words fail:

And odours warm and fresh fell from her hair
Dissolving the dull cold in the froze air:

Soft as an Incarnation of the Sun,
When light is changed to love, this glorious One
Floated into the cavern where I lay,
And called my Spirit, and the dreaming clay
Was lifted by the thing that dreamed below
As smoke by fire, and in her beauty's glow
I stood, and felt the dawn of my long night
Was penetrating me with living light. (333–44)

Those images which obviously invoke or recall Platonic desire,become subliminally symbolic of the narrator's sexual passion (note the images of penetration, of "warm" odors dissolving the hardened cold) even while the sexual passion fails to find an adequate image which would fix it, and so becomes elevated to the level of ideal yearning. Finally, as far as the transcendent form of the Beautiful is concerned, Emily is neither imitation nor catalyst, but is virtually, and rather extravagantly, "this glorious One," the radiant form itself. Again, such a status precludes the possibility of a Platonic or Neoplatonic ascension from the many to the One: if she *is* the One, then the poet does not proceed *from* her to perception of the Ideal. This situation would be less interesting or unusual if it were simply a case of imaging the Ideal in terms of a sensual image, but since Emily began life as a human being there is a three-step circular pattern through which she is processed. First she is a lovely human being, too lovely even to describe, and therefore evocative of the Ideal; then she is supra-person enough to be the Ideal; finally the Ideal/Emily, since it is beyond human conception, is described in terms of Shelley's erotica, which he nonetheless tries to suppress. She takes a circular route back to sensuousness, but the sensuality is uncertain and muted because it is offered poetically in the service of the transphenomenal.

Furthermore, though it is often assumed that the poem derives much of its imagery from the Song of Solomon,[6] and though Shelley does, like the biblical author, refer to his beloved as both spouse and sister, in fact the biblical text is at all times consistently and explicitly responsive to the earthiness of the lovers in ways that are utterly foreign to Shelley's poem. The fact that much biblical exegesis had been devoted to spiritualizing the thematic intent of the Song is of only minimal importance to its points of important difference from Shelley's poem. Where the Song of Solomon has the lover exclaim that her "bowels were moved for him" (Song of Solomon [AV] 5: 4), *Epipsychidion* concerns itself only with *her* transformational effect on *him*: "this glorious One / Floated into the cavern where I lay, / And called my Spirit, and the dreaming clay / Was lifted by the thing that dreamed below." More important, Shelley's poem engages again in a self-conscious, obtrusive, and consistent use of metaphor in its quest to find an analogue for Emily, but Emily is all but lost in the process:

> Seraph of Heaven! too gentle to be human,
> Veiling beneath that radiant form of Woman
> All that is insupportable in thee
> Of light, and love and immortality!
> Sweet Benediction in the eternal curse!
> Veiled Glory of this lampless Universe!
> Thou Moon beyond the clouds! Thou living Form
> Among the Dead! Thou Star above the storm!
> Thou Wonder, and thou Beauty, and thou Terror!
> Thou Harmony of Nature's art! Thou Mirror
> In whom, as in the splendour of the Sun,
> All shapes look glorious which thou gazest on!
> Aye, even the dim words which obscure thee now
> Flash, lightning-like, with unaccustomed glow;
> I pray thee that thou blot from this sad song
> All of its much mortality and wrong. (21–36)

There is much here that reminds us immediately of "Hymn to Intellectual Beauty," but the 1816 hymn encodes Shelley's inability to articulate an imageless truth of presumed real transcendental status. Here we have a human woman who, not unlike the Renaissance Petrarchan sonnet ladies, is becoming elevated to the level of feminized deity. Shelley's program, however, is emphatically different from that of the Elizabethan sonneteers; impelled superficially by love of a particular woman, and more specifically by a professed lack in his being, he seeks to actualize his need for spiritual completion. The spiritual completion inevitably becomes confused with sexual longing, which is a problem that the poem never manages to resolve. In this world, and for Shelley the poet, the quest for fulfillment takes the form of a need for the solace of fiction, one in which he can try to experience spiritual—because limited to the linguistic—completion in her love. It is for this reason that, however "dim" are his words that "obscure [her] now" in the dross of temporal matter, the words of the poem are the only visible signs available to us (and to Shelley); and therefore the words—not

Emily, who after all is "too gentle to be human"—alone "Flash, lightning-like, with unaccustomed glow." The language of the poetry obscures Emily, and is itself implicitly prioritized *as* language; Emily cannot give him the satisfaction that the poetry tries to inscribe.[7]

After all, it is not Emily who is illumined; just as the imageless truth, indeed just as the skylark-as-ideal-poet, could not be predicated in terms of concrete attributes, so she is described in terms of a series of ineffectual, "dim" metaphors which Shelley knows can only "obscure" her and recall us to the process of his writing. Again, the Song of Solomon provides an important point of departure in this analysis, for the many attempts of the biblical author to predicate attributes of his beloved in fact rely almost exclusively on similes. In the Song of Solomon, there is no textual rendering of the beloved as a divine abstraction:

> Behold, thou art fair, my love; behold, thou art fair; thou hast doves' eyes within thy locks: thy hair is as a flock of goats, that appear from mount Gilead. Thy teeth are like a flock of sheep that are even shorn, which came up from the washing; whereof every one bear twins, and none is barren among them. Thy lips are like a thread of scarlet, and thy speech is comely: thy temples are like a piece of a pomegranate within thy locks. Thy neck is like the tower of David builded for an armoury, whereon there hang a thousand bucklers, all shields of mighty men. Thy two breasts are like two young roes that are twins, which feed among the lilies. (Song of Solomon 4:1–5)

Here the voice sings of a woman. We are not quite sure what Shelley is singing of because, as he tells us, he cannot find any means of describing her. And it is precisely this inability to describe the flesh and blood, especially when he is attempting to do so partly in terms of abstract metaphors (Wonder, Beauty, Terror, and so on), that ironically recalls us to the Intellectual Beauty, or Power, or Spirit of the Universe that Shelley elsewhere has been at pains to describe in similar fashion.[8]

In *Endymion* Keats also has his hero describe the Moon in terms of a series of possible analogues, but the effect is different. Endymion is still learning the lesson of mortal love, and the Moon-goddess is soon to be revealed as his lover:

> thou wast the deep glen—
> Thou wast the mountain-top—the sage's pen—
> The poet's harp—the voice of friends—the sun.
> Thou wast the river—thou wast glory won.

Thou wast my clarion's blast—thou wast my steed—
My goblet full of wine—my topmost deed.
Thou wast the charm of women, lovely Moon!

(Endymion 3.163–69)

What distinguishes Shelley's catalogue of analogues for Emily is the virtual absence, in the opening descriptions, of a controlling possessive, which
would release his metaphors from the burden of masquerading as absolute
equations; the Moon for Keats is *my* steed, *my* topmost deed, and so even
when the possessive is not employed, there is no difficulty in determining
the significance of the metaphor's source. But Shelley's persona forsakes
the sensuousness of the Song of Solomon and the uncomplicated effusive
postures of the young Keats, and even the more conventional efforts to
image a metaphysical truth, in favor of conflating into one precarious idea
his wish for fulfillment in all these areas.[9]

Indeed, after another catalogue of ineffectual metaphors, he finally
moves closer to recognition: "I measure / The world of fancies, seeking one
like thee, / And find—alas! mine own infirmity" (*Epipsychidion* 69–71).
Shelley is acknowledging the solipsism of the particular apostrophe and of
the poems's larger conception; but unlike the *Alastor* situation, it is a solipsism that finally calls into question not the integrity of the vision as vision,
but rather (like "Mont Blanc"), the real value of the human being qua
human being. We are more accustomed to poets returning to themselves,
to their own symbolic capacities, when they are describing metaphysical
conceptions. Here we have a poet loving a flesh-and-blood woman, which
in fact *still* returns him to himself, to the very same sense of spiritual incompletion and theistic angst which had previously caused him to see a mountain and make it into a symbol for his a priori assumptions about the
transcendent. *Endymion*, itself something of a response to *Alastor*, is again
resonating in the background; resolving to forsake his unearthly love,
Endymion exclaims:

<blockquote>
I have clung
To nothing, loved a nothing, nothing seen
Or felt but a great dream! O I have been
Presumptuous against love, against the sky,
Against all elements, against the tie
Of mortals each to each. . . . (Endymion 4.636–41)
</blockquote>

Shelley takes his something, and makes her first into nothing that can be described, and then into nothing that can be properly conceived, even intellectually. By the end of the poem, she has no distinct identity left at all. But Shelley does try to make her into something that can stay his longing. Even Endymion, after all, is satisfied finally because the human woman he turns to eventually proves to be his unearthly beloved. And Shelley is in control, at least partly, of his staged manipulations of Emily's identity. Keats wins no moral victories over Shelley on these grounds.

It is therefore with a certain amount of frantic grasping after straws, a kind of reaction-formation, that Shelley asserts his right, again and again in this poem, to speak from within a life-as-myth. To do so may be presumption, but it also appears superficially to be more satisfying. In *Peter Bell the Third*, the parody of Wordsworth written in October 1819, Shelley had already aligned himself with those poets—"the damned"—who are committed to salvaging a faith in the value of the world:

> And some few, like we know who,
>   Damned—but God alone knows why—
> To believe their minds are given
> To make this ugly Hell a Heaven;
>   In which faith they live and die. (*Peter Bell* 242–46)

The narrator of *Peter Bell* moves on to describe the condition of all of humanity:

> All are damned—they breathe an air,
>   Thick, infected, joy-dispelling:
> Each pursues what seems most fair,
> Mining like moles, through mind, and there
> Scoop palace-caverns vast, where Care
>   In throned state is ever dwelling. (257–62)

When the value of the world becomes hard to salvage, though, one builds palace-caverns in the mind, where Care nonetheless reigns. In *Epipsychidion* the palace-caverns of the mind are predicated on the beauties—and, perhaps, the spiritual qualities—of a woman of flesh and blood, while the woman of flesh and blood herself becomes in the poem an unearthly, quasi-transcendent being. The solipsism of the visionary yearning and the conscious symbolic structuring may be acknowledged, but such self-exposure

still will not ease the discomfort of all readers who themselves recoil from
the poet's metaphorizing of the woman out of existence:

See where she stands! a mortal shape indued
With love and life and light and deity,
And motion which may change but cannot die;
An image of some bright Eternity;
A shadow of some golden dream; a Splendour
Leaving the third sphere pilotless; a tender
Reflection of the eternal Moon of Love
Under whose motions life's dull billows move;
A Metaphor of Spring and Youth and Morning;
A Vision like incarnate April . . .   (*Epipsychidion* 112–22)

To exclaim "See where she stands" does not finally give him much
help: it is impossible to imagine Emily in terms of the images and abstract
nouns that the poet has been presenting. In her own essential reality, she
may well be "a mortal shape," but "love and life and light and deity" are not
indices of a bodily configuration. What, indeed, can be *seen*? As readers,
what we see is—literally—all we get; that is, the verbal structure before us
is our only forum for imagistic detail, and Shelley is at pains, in this poem,
to emphasize the artistry not only of his descriptions but also of his human
relations. In *Epipsychidion*, perhaps more than in any other of Shelley's
poems, what we *see* is a verbal virtuosity, one that has been consciously
adopted to "stand" in for various existential needs. "See where she stands"
is an exclamation of the deepest complexity, then. For in a linguistic space
so constructed, where could a woman stand? His catalogue of ineffectual
metaphors has reached, depending on one's critical perspective, either the
apex or the nadir of his efforts: unable to fix her within one of his images
of "bright Eternity," he finally says that she is "A *Metaphor* of Spring and
Youth and Morning." Neither tenor nor vehicle, she becomes the metaphor itself. What does it mean to *be* a metaphor? Shelley has attempted
several metaphors in his efforts to describe her and her place in his poetic
world; now she has degenerated to an "equals" sign in a poem. The word
"incarnate" in line 121 works in a similar fashion: she is not like April, she
is like the incarnation (the figure) of April. Shelley has metaphorized Teresa Viviani out of existence.

Indeed, we know that Emily cannot be the deep truth, because we
have learned from *Prometheus Unbound* that the deep truth is imageless.

Emily may be without equations in this poem, but she is still a corporeal figure (or at the very least we are sure that she began life that way), still an image who is rendered in terms of some metaphoric function. In a letter to John Gisborne of 22 October 1821, he refers to the poem in a disclaimer that reveals more anxiety than it conceals: "The Epipsychidion is a mystery—As to real flesh & blood, you know that I do not deal in those articles,—you might as well go to a ginshop for a leg of mutton, as expect any thing human or earthly from me" (*Letters* 2: 363). And later, on 18 June 1822, he writes of *Epipsychidion*: "I think one is always in love with something or other; the error, and I confess it is not easy for spirits cased in flesh and blood to avoid it, consists in seeking in a mortal image the likeness of what is perhaps eternal" (*Letters* 2: 434). Shelley acknowledges this to be an error, even while he knows it to be standard fare. I cite the first lecture of William Hazlitt's *Lectures on the English Poets* by way of indicating the orthodoxy Shelley was conditioned by and straining against:

> Poetry then is an imitation of nature, but the imagination and the passions are a part of man's nature. We shape things according to our wishes and fancies, without poetry; but poetry is the most emphatical language that can be found for those creations of the mind "which ecstacy is very cunning in." Neither a mere description of natural objects, nor a mere delineation of natural feelings, however distinct or forcible, constitutes the ultimate end and aim of poetry, without the heightenings of the imagination. The light of poetry is not only a direct but also a reflected light, that while it shews us the object, throws a sparkling radiance on all around it: the flame of the passions, communicated to the imagination, reveals to us, as with a flash of lightning, the inmost recesses of thought, and penetrates our whole being. (*Lectures* 5: 3)

It is the fantasy of the poet that such a pleasing sense of aesthetic value should apply to the radiant objects of his own romantic poetry. In fact, Shelley extrapolates from the transformations inherent in the metaphors of poetry, to a valorization of the multiple images of free love, and then concludes by paralleling the functions of free love, understanding, and imagination:

> Love is like understanding, that grows bright,
> Gazing on many truths; 'tis like thy light,
> Imagination! which from earth and sky,
> And from the depths of human phantasy,
> As from a thousand prisms and mirrors, fills
> The Universe with glorious beams, and kills

Error, the worm, with many a sun-like arrow
Of its reverberated lightning.   (*Epipsychidion* 62–69)

Claiming both aesthetic and moral sanction for the infidelity which he is about to render metaphorically in the autobiographical history of his life, is too transparently facile: Shelley's sense of guilt sounds consistently in this poem; his appeal to the "glorious beams" that issue from unharnessed desires—both sexual and poetical—reads as an intentionally feeble excuse, especially given his concern that poetical "beams" are susceptible to becoming dangerous embellishments.

It is, however, with such attempts in mind that Timothy Webb, in *Shelley: A Voice Not Understood*, claims that Shelley's poetic progression is one from simple didacticism to highly imaginative flights: "Finally, there was a growing delight in the 'brilliance and magnificence of sound,' in the harmony of language itself and in the vitally metaphoric mode of poetry, all of which melted away the puritanical reserve of the younger Shelley" (85).[10] One must always bear in mind, however, that, for Shelley, conscious delight in such effects as the "harmony of language itself" is concomitant with a guilty consciousness over the empirical world from which he derives his metaphors and symbols, and a persistent need to justify aesthetic pleasures on moral grounds.

Still, his construction of a world for himself within poetry does bespeak a resigned effort to live within the mundane world: escapism is virtually acknowledged as escapism, and desire is virtually understood as the ground of aesthetic/poetical power, often linked to a sense of unfulfilled sexual power. Narrating the history of his love life, he refers to "a Being whom my spirit oft / Met on its visioned wanderings" (*Epipsychidion* 190–91). Not surprisingly, the scene is reminiscent of the *Alastor* questor's error: "She met me, robed in such exceeding glory, / That I beheld her not" (*Epipsychidion* 199–200). The latter phrase is particularly telling, for indeed the entire embellishment process which is poetry is the primary anxiety of Shelley's later career. Here, when he cannot behold his vision, it is not because she is a deep truth who is imageless, but rather because his ornamentation obscures normative vision. He continues, still seeking the Being of his desire:

And in that silence, and in my despair,
I questioned every tongueless wind that flew
Over my tower of mourning, if it knew

Whither 'twas fled, this soul out of my soul;
And murmured names and spells which have controul
Over the sightless tyrants of our fate;
But neither prayer nor verse could dissipate
The night which closed on her; nor uncreate
That world within this Chaos, mine and me,
Of which she was the veiled Divinity,
The world I say of thoughts that worshipped her . . .

(*Epipsychidion* 235–45)

Shelley is refining the sentiments he had pondered in the 1818 work, "On Love." There he claims, without evidence of anxiety over the assumption, that love "is that powerful attraction towards all that we conceive or fear or hope beyond ourselves when we find within our own thoughts the chasm of an insufficient void and seek to awaken in all things that are, a community with what we experience within ourselves" ("On Love" 473). One cannot have a relationship, though, with a chasm of an insufficient void; neither can one reasonably be expected to worship one in prayer. In "On Love," to be fair, he does go on to explain that, for desire to emerge from the void, the void must first be peopled with an ideal prototype seeking its antitype; but the primacy of that needy void is potentially problematic, certainly disturbing. Shelley's later poetry is more self-consciously indulgent of his needs, and so his writing becomes exposed as the rite of need.

What is more, Shelley's easy equations of his various beloveds with the astronomical elements strike us, perhaps, as unfair. Why should they, after all, become entities who are physically transcendent to the earth (the poet gets to be the earth itself, who keeps his fictions/planets determining the course of his life), even if he is acknowledging the fictionality of such rendering? In addition to the Sun-Moon-Comet triad, he refers, for example, to Harriet's suicide by remembering a quenched "Planet of that hour" (*Epipsychidion* 313), of which James Rieger angrily observes:

Metaphor has again failed Shelley, but in a way more frightening than before, because poetic integrity has collapsed with it. Shelley is now more concerned to excuse his actions than to do them actual or "poetic" justice. The symbolist deprecates the world of experience he has undertaken to illuminate and lapses into that fake eloquence, known as phrasemaking, which always attends the divorce of words from things. (Rieger, *The Mutiny Within* 204)

Whether we see the entire *Epipsychidion* problematic as staged or inadvertent (and in this case, it is difficult to tell the difference with assurance), there is something unsettling here about the permutations of Shelley's human metaphors. Can he implicitly apologize for, and still sustain, his lofty flight of fantasy?

Indeed, if he fictionalizes human beings, including himself, into non-existence, then his return to himself, his coming to terms, if only implicitly, with solipsistic thought, is startling: "Twin Spheres of light who rule this passive Earth, / This world of love, this *me*" (*Epipsychidion* 345–46). Returning from the planets who have become his lovers, he is brought to himself emphatically because he is returning from the self-annihilation that results from constructing himself poetically, in the exclusive terms of metaphor. This notion is introduced again, prefatory to the grand annihilation at the end of the poem, when he tries to describe love once more, in yet another series of ineffectual analogues: "like Heaven's free breath, / Which he who grasps can hold not; *liker Death*, / Who rides upon a thought, and makes his way / Through temple, tower, and palace" (400–403; italics mine). Love, we will recall, is also like imagination. To equate love with death in a poem where individuals disappear into poetic embellishment is to call attention to the one great danger of metaphor in the poem: in a world where all things are equal (because all are failures) as equations of an ideal, the identity yielded by metaphor is always potentially an annihilation. "I know / That love makes all things equal" (125–26), he exclaims early on; in the love-equality of this poem, individual human identities are tropes.

The poet then departs from his Shelley-centric world of revolving planets, and rather abruptly envisions for himself and Emily an escape by boat to a secluded island that keeps a "Soul," one who is "An atom of th'Eternal" that "may be felt not seen" (477–80). In this world inhabited by an imageless deep truth, they will reside in "a pleasure-house" (491), but unlike the poetic pleasure-dome which, in "Kubla Khan," Coleridge would build in air (if the music of the Abyssinian maid could be revived), our poet has already conveniently sent "books and music there, and all / Those instruments with which high spirits call / The future from its cradle" (519–21). He is trying to guard against the uncertainty of vision of Coleridge's persona in "Kubla Khan," for if he has sent books and music and objects of art there, then he has sent what is needed to sustain his world and house of artifice. The house itself no longer shows signs of *humanly* constructed artifice: "For all the antique and learned imagery / Has been erased, and in the place of it / The ivy and the wild-vine interknit / The volumes of their many twining stems" (498–501). As William Keach notes, "increasingly remote natural phenomena function as artifice" (*Shelley's Style* 153). But where Keach sees this tendency as "virtuosic," I view it as an example of Shelley virtually losing control of his fictions; the human art has given way not to nature simply, but to a kind of nature-as-miracle—ill-defined, inexplicable, and desperately trying to claim a retreat where nature *is* art.[11]

The retreat represents, then, a coalescence of the Spirit of the Temple in *The Revolt of Islam*, the cave retreat of *Prometheus Unbound*, and—most important perhaps, and in ways that only become apparent at the end of the poem—the drift toward death of *Alastor*. Shelley is escaping, but he is escaping with a pseudo-Platonic beloved-turned-idealization, and by this point in the poem we are not quite sure whether his priorities are to remind us of his objective point of departure or to indulge us in his fantasy life. For in describing the island, which is "Beautiful as a wreck of Paradise" but still secluded, he explains: "And, for the harbours are not safe and good, / This land would have remained a solitude / But for some pastoral people native there" (424–26). This is a rather humorous gesture towards realism, as Shelley seems to believe that he must explain why such a beautiful place has not become a tourist trap. Is he worried that we will wonder why we have not heard of it before? Beyond the inadvertent humor of the attempt, it also recalls us to the central paradox of the poem: how can Shelley justify so obtrusive a fantasy myth, indeed the rendering of his own domestic affairs *as* a fantasy myth, after all the lessons he learned in *Prometheus Unbound*?

The answer lies, perhaps, in his knowledge that this self-imposed, conscious solipsism is only for a limited, qualified time—qualified because, as he tells us early in the poem, they are only his *words* that flash "with unaccustomed glow." His song is sweetest where it most despairs, and even in the island retreat he reminds us of the mutable world where life is bitter:

> It is a favoured place. Famine or Blight,
> Pestilence, War and Earthquake, never light
> Upon its mountain-peaks; blind vultures, they
> Sail onward far upon their fatal way:
> The winged storms, chaunting their thunder-psalm
> To other lands, leave azure chasms of calm
> Over this isle. (*Epipsychidion* 461–67)

This act of description is self-imposed cruelty. For in escaping he recalls all that we—and he and Emily—must actually endure, because in fact he has *not* escaped from the world of storms and of uncertain weather. Compare a fragment by Leigh Hunt, "Fancy's Party," first published in 1818. This poem opens by noting the books and flowers and busts "In this poetic corner," and insists, "Why think of these fatalities, / And all their dull realities?" ("Fancy's Party" 6–7). The poet then goes on, like Shelley, to imagine an escape voyage:

> Far, far away we're going
> From care and common-places,
> To spots of bliss
> As fine to this,
> As yours to common faces;
> To spots—but rapture dissipates
> The pictures it anticipates.—
>
> And hey, what's this? the walls, look,
> Are wrinkling as a skin does;
> And now they are bent
> To a silken tent,
> And there are chrystal windows;
> And look! there's a balloon above,
> Round and bright as the moon above. (22–35)

Leigh Hunt's poetical skills could never have rivaled Shelley's, and his poetic imagination is not so intense. But we do see in the first quoted stanza a familiar disinclination to image a picture of "rapture," and in the second a conscious rendering of the given world within an escape fantasy, as the walls of his room wrinkle into the skin of a hot air balloon. The important difference lies in the extent to which Hunt's fantasy escape still cleaves in obvious ways to the given world (his walls become the walls of the balloon), and is therefore a felicitous fantasy, not an endangering of the integrity or value of his world. Where his fantasy is sweetest may still lurk the traumas of an objective reality, but Hunt's is still without the intense agony of imminent fictional collapse.

I began this chapter by suggesting that Shelley's choices in *Epipsychidion* suggest a willingness to engage in obtrusive fiction precisely because he acknowledges now the dangers inherent in certain forms of fiction-making. But I also noted that it would be difficult for him to sustain such a program, and indeed, it is difficult not to conclude ultimately that his success is highly qualified. Finally in this poem it would appear that Shelley simply does not know whether he wants language to veil or to unveil his imaginative desires; whether he wants thought to feed off desire; whether he can cope with a fiction which presages his return to a quotidian world that offers only the comforts of potential for further fictions.

Thus, addressing Emily, Shelley tells of possible *veils* of caverns for their seclusion (*Epipsychidion* 553–56), and of exhalations from the sea, "Veil after veil, each hiding some delight, / Which Sun or Moon or zephyr draw aside" (472–73),[12] finally culminating in full awareness, not necessarily of the ineffable but of the condition of ineffability:

> And we will talk, until thought's melody
> Become too sweet for utterance, and it die
> In words, to live again in looks, which dart
> With thrilling tone into the voiceless heart,
> Harmonizing silence without a sound.
> Our breath shall intermix, our bosoms bound,
> And our veins beat together; and our lips
> With other eloquence than words, eclipse
> The soul that burns between them. (560–68)

Even the language within language, then, is not answerable to certain forms of "thought's melody." Indeed, thought *dies* in words, and is re-born in a very physiological impulse: the body *eclipses* the soul, and not by words either. In "Shelley's Veils: A Thousand Images of Loveliness," (an early) Jerome McGann offers an optimistic view of this poem and of this particular difficulty: "Love dalliance here is a succession of talk and silence, with a 'death' the point of mediation" ("Shelley's Veils" 215). He holds to this reading as part of a general understanding of the issue in Shelley, in which he claims that the poet exercises full control of his fictional collapses: "Language is a veiled vision, and the poet's veil of imagery must be destroyed if the power of vision is to be sustained, if fresh creations are to be brought forth and new figured curtains to be woven" (214). This is so in a world of art, and it is true of the imagination when it is not actively engaged in fending off the encroaching horrors of the external reality. But Shelley's melody that becomes too sweet for utterance is here tantamount to the intense inane in which, far beyond that reality, he had wanted to pinnacle himself and Emily; having lost the temporal circumscription of the quotidian, they lose the temporal embodiments (that is, language) even of poetic thought. They fall silent, then, not because they are themselves deep truths beyond image and sign, but because they have fictionalized themselves out of existence, into silence.

The final apotheosis of their love follows logically, for it is a frightening, deathly embrace, a *Liebestod* which yet has been declared inaudible:

> We shall become the same, we shall be one
> Spirit within two frames, oh! wherefore two?
> One passion in twin-hearts, which grows and grew,
> 'Till like two meteors of expanding flame,
> Those spheres instinct with it become the same,
> Touch, mingle, are transfigured; ever still
> Burning, yet ever inconsumable:
> In one another's substance finding food,
> Like flames too pure and light and unimbued
> To nourish their bright lives with baser prey,
> Which point to Heaven and cannot pass away:
> One hope within two wills, one will beneath
> Two overshadowing minds, one life, one death,
> One Heaven, one Hell, one immortality,
> And one annihilation. Woe is me!
> The winged words on which my soul would pierce
> Into the heights of love's rare Universe,
> Are chains of lead around its flight of fire. —
> I pant, I sink, I tremble, I expire!   (*Epipsychidion* 573–91)

In *Alastor* the questor was led to death because of his over-intense yearning to satiate his longing for a fictional construct. Here Shelley annihilates, for the purposes of his poetry, not only himself but also another human being, the Other who had stimulated him into this particular vision in the first place. He does so, however, by first abstracting away a woman he has great sexual passion for, and then finally turning to a fantasy of sexual consummation that also tries to masquerade as a fantasy of soul-union, beyond the dross of carnality. But bodies that are seen as embodiments of fictional idealizations are necessarily obliterated from perception, and Shelley goes with her to annihilation because he too has been consumed in his fiction of union. Their "one Heaven" gives way also to "one Hell," and they can possess "one immortality" only in "one annihilation." In his earlier days, death had held out the promise of fulfillment, because it is the most obvious archetype of the unknown. In *Epipsychidion*, to lose individual identity in the fiction of unity is to attempt the spirituality of the intense inane, and we already know that to be pinnacled dim there would be to resign our humanity.

Thus his "winged words" are "chains of lead," not only because they cannot praise her as he would, or describe the full bliss he would experience in her love, but also because the explicit sexual imagery of the passage precludes the possibility of a Platonic interpretation of his desire.[13] The best he can do in such an embarrassing situation is to try to make the sexual language strangely metaphoric of their Platonic consummation of soul-love. He cannot do so, of course, and besides he has already seduced himself into a temporary self-obliteration of identity. Questing for a life in art that would enable him to live more contentedly in the world of experience, he has instead drawn near to a life-denying aesthetic.

When he rallies back to bid his verses live, however, he signals at least partial awareness of the dilemma: he tells them to go to her by whom they are inspired, or to whom they are slaves ("kneel at your Sovereign's feet" 591), and that they are "the masters" of the poet (592). Emily is master of the verses, which in turn are masters of the poet. Shelley has enslaved himself, indeed has temporarily reduced himself to a self-imposed fiction; this act surely recalls his own crusade against worshiping a God in our own self-image. Therefore he and the world that has been his tensile springboard will try to effect a sort of peace, because he finally does know that he has no choice, that there really is an absolute disjunction between spiritual desire and poetic fulfillment:

> Then haste
> Over the hearts of men, until ye meet
> Marina, Vanna, Primus, and the rest,
> And bid them love each other and be blest:
> And leave the troop which errs, and which reproves,
> And come and be my guest,—for I am Love's.   (599–604)

The fictional world he has constructed stops just short of utterly abandoning him on the heights of the inane; our descent to the world is all the more keenly felt.

A Defence of Poetry

There is scarcely a poem in the Shelley canon that does not betray an anxiety over its own efficacy and place in the world. Before turning briefly, then, to *Adonais*—the great monument of anguish over the quotidian—I should like to scrutinize the salient points of *A Defence of Poetry*. For it is entirely appropriate that to an attack on poetry, even a light-hearted and transparently comical attack concerned primarily with its inefficacy and obsolescence in the contemporary world, Shelley should react with so urgent and defensive a response. Written almost immediately after *Epipsychidion*, the essay takes Thomas Love Peacock's *The Four Ages of Poetry* as its superficial point of departure, but only because his close friend's complaint seems to speak to everything he was already vexed about. Peacock's essay was merely the catalyst to prompt Shelley into writing an explicit justification of poetry, of his indulgence in what had become for him a compelling need. It is not without inconsistencies or difficulties, but *A Defence* does take its place with the later Shelley who tries to affirm some value for his craft, to live with his choices in some manner that can be justified, even lauded.

There is much in Peacock's short essay, written for *Ollier's Literary Miscellany* of 1820, which is provocative; but I will cite only the two passages most relevant to my purposes, the first being a complaint against the Lake poets.

> They wrote verses on a new principle; saw rocks and rivers in a new light; and remaining studiously ignorant of history, society, and human nature, cultivated the phantasy only at the expense of the memory and the reason; and contrived, though they had retreated from the world for the express purpose of seeing nature as she was, to see her only as she was not, converting the land they lived in into a sort of fairy-land, which they peopled with mysticism and chimaeras. This gave what is called a new tone to poetry, and conjured up a herd of desperate imitators, who have brought the age of brass prematurely to its dotage. (*Four Ages* 15)

> But in whatever degree poetry is cultivated, it must necessarily be to the neglect of some branch of useful study: and it is a lamentable spectacle to see minds, capable of better things, running to seed in the specious indolence of these empty aimless mockeries of intellectual exertion. Poetry was the mental rattle that awakened the attention of intellect in the infancy of civil society: but for the maturity of mind to make a serious business of the playthings of its childhood, is as absurd as for a full-grown man to rub his gums with coral, and cry to be charmed to sleep by the jingle of silver bells. (*Four Ages* 22)

The exceptionally well-read and learned Peacock would have been emphatically aware of Sir Philip Sidney's summary, in his *An Apology for Poetry*, of the time-worn complaints against poetry, as well as Sidney's defense that poetry moves to virtue by teaching and delighting. Peacock slyly reiterates the very indictments Sidney answers, and in so doing emphasizes the full weight of blame and disaffection that had so roused Sidney: "First, that there being many other more fruitful knowledges, a man might better spend his time in them than in this. Secondly, that it is the mother of lies. Thirdly, that it is the nurse of abuse, infecting us with many pestilent desires, with a siren's sweetness drawing the mind to the serpent's tail of sinful fancy" (*An Apology for Poetry* 55). The challenge would have been irresistible, all the more so since Shelley had been reading Plato's *Ion* — the dialogue in which the rhapsodist is shown to be dysfunctional in every department of life save for the ability to recite Homer movingly[14] — when Peacock's essay first reached him. Shelley already worries about his poetic abuse of the actual, his inefficacy in philosophical and practical terms, and his craft as an active displacement of, or delay to, active involvement in the affairs of humankind. *A Defence of Poetry* defends the place of the poetic imagination within the world by making a subtle claim for its inevitability, its irresistibility as a function of humanity, no less so than — in the language of Peacock's polemic — any branch of useful study. In this respect the treatise has much in common with the preoccupations of all the major poetry.

The poet may be the needy singer of *Epipsychidion*, one who is akin therefore to "a nightingale, who sits in darkness and sings to cheer its own solitude with sweet sound" (*Defence* 486), but that sound is a function of, and a constitutive force in, a very elemental humanity. Shelley's contemporaries were no less obsessed with self-vindication; in the Preface to his *Poems, 1815*, Wordsworth had already defended the particular claims of imagination suggested in his "To the Cuckoo," which, like Shelley's "To a Skylark," "dispossesses the creature almost of a corporeal existence" (Wordsworth, *Prose* 3: 32). Of such powers of poetry, Wordsworth triumphantly notes: "These processes of imagination are carried on either by conferring additional properties upon an object, or abstracting from it some of those which it actually possesses, and thus enabling it to re-act upon the mind which hath performed the process, like a new existence" (*Prose* 3: 32). Shelley has been coming to realize that he really does indulge in such modifications, but now he is nervous enough about their implications to attempt an almost guilty answer to them. For Shelley, if we speak a language, indeed if we engage in expression at all, then we all sit and sing to cheer our own solitude; but we are cheered partly because the singing in our solitude effects change in the way we perceive the world and our own songs about it. Furthermore, our singing at once causes us to realize our alienation from the object of song and conditions our desire; it therefore perceptually composes the very object of desire. Poetry thus gives necessary form to, even while it constitutes, ineffable desire.

But for Shelley the poet himself is one of peculiarly refined imagination, or perhaps it is simply that he is self-conscious about the implications of language; either way, it is the ineffable—of metaphysics, of feeling, and of self-definition—that compels him, and the ineffable that he feels an instinctive need to confine in the definite, albeit limited, form of language:

> We are aware of evanescent visitations of thought and feeling sometimes associated with place or person, sometimes regarding our own mind alone, and always arising unforeseen and departing unbidden, but elevating and delightful beyond all expression: so that even in the desire and the regret they leave, there cannot but be pleasure, participating as it does in the nature of its object. It is as it were the interpenetration of a diviner nature through our own; but its footsteps are like those of a wind over a sea, which the coming calm erases, and whose traces remain only as on the wrinkled sand which paves it. (*Defence* 504)

The constitutive function of poetry does not undermine Shelley's belief in a dualism, of metaphysics and, as we shall see, of word and thing. But the poetic impulse is still the ground of the articulation of dualism, and hence its only chance for consciousness within human minds.[15] Poetic language thus yields intuitive approximations of abstract conceptions and thoughts, and of desires that can never find literal paraphrase: "Hence the vanity of translation; it were as wise to cast a violet into a crucible that you might discover the formal principle of its colour and odour, as seek to transfuse from one language into another the creations of a poet" (*Defence* 484). "Poetry redeems from decay the visitations of the divinity in man" (505), because poets "can colour all that they combine with the evanescent hues of this etherial world; a word, a trait in the representation of a scene or a passion, will touch the enchanted chord, and reanimate, in those who have ever experienced these emotions, the sleeping, the cold, the buried image of the past" (505). Because deep truths are imageless, the representation of scenes or passions *reanimates* images of the past: they do not equate themselves with definitive presentations of things or ideas-in-themselves. We derive from poetry an intuitive grasp of certain concepts and ideas which, though they cannot find extra-poetic articulation, are resistant to discursive representation precisely because they do refer to an extra-poetic existence. Like Wordsworth's, then, Shelley's imaginative reconstitution is tantamount to a heightening of the *effect* of the object, but devoid of the dangers of willful distortion. Poetry is still the pursuit of the ineffable, though acknowledged now *as* the ineffable—even his escape with Emily, which gives linguistic form to his feverish passion for her—and it is this very disjunction of feeling and intuition from their objects which defines the worth of poetry. It is vestment, but a vestment which makes us aware that there is something to cover:

> It arrests the vanishing apparitions which haunt the interlunations of life, and veiling them or in language or in form sends them forth among mankind, bearing sweet news of kindred joy to those with whom their sisters abide—abide, because there is no portal of expression from the cavern of the spirit which they inhabit into the universe of things. (505)

The above quotations are themselves clarifications that follow from the famous description of the creative process itself: "for the mind in creation is as a fading coal which some invisible influence, like an inconstant wind, awakens to transitory brightness: this power arises from within, like the colour of a flower which fades and changes as it is developed, and the conscious portions of our natures are unprophetic either of its approach or its departure" (503–4). Shelley's poetry, written in the self-consciousness of the necessary qualifications of imaginative vision—and hence written in the self-consciousness that accompanies those of us who do not ascend into the intense inane—is a poetry of the *hyper-quotidian*, as it were, a poetry of the desire for and failure of transcendent vision, a poetry that betrays that vision is finally a seeing in terms of the signs of its absence, but where absence is recognized in the terms of a presented quotidian world. Indeed, seen finally and always is the quotidian, temporal world—appropriated again and again as the sign of absence—but that world is still what gives us, if we are astute enough to recognize it, our forum for the most spiritual actualization of vision of which we are capable:

> All things exist as they are perceived: at least in relation to the percipient. "The mind is its own place, and of itself can make a heaven of hell, a hell of heaven." But poetry defeats the curse which binds us to be subjected to the accident of surrounding impressions. And whether it spreads its own figured curtain or

withdraws life's dark veil from before the scene of things, it equally creates for us a being within our being. It makes us the inhabitants of a world to which the familiar world is a chaos. It reproduces the common universe of which we are portions and percipients, and it purges from our inward sight the film of familiarity which obscures from us the wonder of our being. It compels us to feel that which we perceive, and to imagine that which we know. It creates anew the universe after it has been annihilated in our minds by the recurrence of impressions blunted by reiteration. It justifies that bold and true word of Tasso—*Non merita nome di creatore, se non Iddio ed il Poeta.* (505–6)

Here, finally, is the defense of the heterocosm which Shelley has taken all these years to actualize.[16] The poet may create a world, not simply to escape the old bad one, but to release the quotidian from the recurrence of impressions blunted by reiteration.[17] In this sense, the poetry of imagination is akin to the process of love itself, as it had been in *Epipsychidion*, and as Shelley clarifies earlier in his essay: "The great secret of morals is Love; or a going out of our own nature, and an identification of ourselves with the beautiful which exists in thought, action, or person, not our own" (487). We will recall that even at the conclusion of *Epipsychidion*, which is more of an indulgence in a fantasy escape than it is an acknowledgment of the poet's objective external reality, the poet bids his verses live, and tells them to bid his domestic circle to love one another. If he had created a habitation to which his own world was only chaos, it was nonetheless constructed, he hopes, in the subtle service of that world.

If we are consigned to the quotidian, temporal world, then our poetry is a poetry of and for the quotidian; the being created by poetry is one within the normative quotidian being, and the poetic world as conceived in the *Defence* is what I have referred to above as the hyper-quotidian, especially when it strives toward some modulation of the ineffable, and even when it is in the service of intimating (or, for that matter, deconstructing) some transcendent order. There is no real ontological status for poetry or for its tropes: poetry both spreads and uncovers a curtain because, in a dualistic universe, both processes of embellishment amount to the same thing. When we become attuned to the wonder of the attributes of the quotidian and the marvels of the external, empirical world—when we realize that Mont Blanc is actually a tremendous mountain—then we are also made aware that we have been conceiving of metaphysical otherness, for example, in terms of unconscious interpretations of an external world that we no longer even notice. If mountain does not equal Power, then we understand something important about both the mountain and Power. But we also begin to understand the manifold implications this represents, for meta-physics and for the poetry of desire—or for poetry *as* desire. That is, since things exist as they are perceived, at least in relation to the percipient, our truths are truths *to us* when we in our temporal circumscription actualize them.

Indeed, Shelley is now coming to terms with his latent awareness that his metaphysics, and his conception indeed of any ineffable construct, are unconsciously predicated on his inheritance of language and of metaphor. Again, Sidney's *Apology* provides a point of departure, but one which Shelley finally sees as self-destructing,

> for any understanding knoweth the skill of the artificer standeth in that *Idea* or fore-conceit of the work, and not in the work itself. And that the poet hath that *Idea* is manifest by delivering them forth in such excellency as he hath imagined them. Which delivering forth also is not wholly imaginative, as we are wont to say by them that build castles in the air, but so far substantially it worketh, not only to make a Cyrus, which had been but a particular excellen-cy, as nature might have done, but to bestow a Cyrus upon the world to make many Cyruses, if they will learn aright why and how that maker made him. (*Apology* 16)

Sidney is dealing with the imaginative rendering, the poetic translation, of discursive thoughts into moral exempla. His "Idea" is understood as a fore-thought which itself is independent of the writing process. In *A Defence of Poetry* Shelley makes an aesthetic out of clarifying that we arrive at ineffa-ble thoughts by becoming aware of the conventions of language:

> Their language is vitally metaphorical; that is, it marks the before unappre-hended relations of things, and perpetuates their apprehension, until the words which represent them, become through time signs for portions or class-es of thoughts instead of pictures of integral thoughts; and then if no new poets should arise to create afresh the associations which have been thus dis-organized, language will be dead to all the nobler purposes of human inter-course. (*Defence* 482)

The being within our being which is poetry is therefore a relational appre-hension of the quotidian, even a relational synthesis of desire with the empirical world.[18] Most important, Shelley is attempting to exonerate himself from any potential charges of naïve aestheticism or of image-fixa-tion, particularly where ineffable concepts are concerned; apprehension is itself only "represented" by tentatively placed words which are immediately vulnerable, and they are intended as pictures of integral thoughts, not the dead metaphors which would make them signs for whole portions or classes of thought. Poetry creates afresh the associations—it lifts the veil of familiarity which obscures from us the wonder of our being—and by disorganizing our dead metaphors, it breaks the complacency by which thought and thing, desire and its actualization, are feebly conflated by lazy interpreters. John W. Wright helpfully clarifies: "The sign, which once signified, becomes in time the thing signified. . . . 'Before unapprehended relations,' once nothing for the mind, emerge in metaphor as novel, immediate, and integral apprehensions and then slide into dotage as entities in a world system" (*Shelley's Myth of Metaphor* 30).

Under such assumptions, all language is metaphorical, and all poetry is a function of the linguistic manipulation without which we cannot experience thought. Poets thus command a wide province, because the poetic impulse is the same as the human impulse for actualization of our humanity:

> they are the institutors of laws, and the founders of civil society and the inventors of the arts of life and the teachers, who draw into a certain propinquity with the beautiful and the true that partial apprehension of the agencies of the invisible world which is called religion. Hence all original religions are allegorical, or susceptible of allegory, and like Janus have a double face of false and true. (*Defence* 482)

Because we have only a partial apprehension of the agencies of the invisible world, all religious expression can only be allegorical, and hence Janus-faced. So in such terms must our existing systems of thought be understood: Shelley claims that evil in the Christian religion "sprung from the extinction of the poetical principle, connected with the progress of despotism and superstition" (496). The poetical principle here means relational apprehension, so that exoteric expressions are understood in their proper contexts: "It is unfortunate for those who cannot distinguish words from thoughts, that many of these anomalies have been incorporated into our popular religion" (496). We need the metaphorical principle, then, first to arrive at a partial apprehension of the invisible world, and then to understand that the form that apprehension takes is allegorical, is composed of words which are not to be confused, in any simplified equation, with thought.

Such attempts to exonerate poetic fictions from their ominous implications, however, do not guide readers to a clear understanding of what we are to take as essentially "true," and what as more self-consciously poetic.[19] Shelley himself is qualifying again Sidney's defense of fiction-making:

> Now for the poet, he nothing affirms, and therefore never lieth. . . . The poet never maketh any circles about your imagination to conjure you to believe for true what he writes. He citeth not authorities of other histories, but even for his entry calleth the sweet Muses to inspire into him a good invention; in troth, not laboring to tell you what is or is not, but what should or should not be. And therefore, though he recount things not true, yet because he telleth them not for true, he lieth not. (*Apology* 57)

For Shelley it is not so easy, because his poetry finds justification, not only as a forum for instruction and incitation to virtue, but also as a medium for, and in qualified ways, a constituent part of, knowledge. Shelley needs the release for fiction which Sidney offers, and which many of his contemporaries were also offering as standard fare; but he also often needs its virtual rival—the truth claims of the fictions themselves—because the metaphors of relational apprehension yield pictures of integral thought which *do* serve an epistemological as well as a didactic function, and which *do* encompass a cognitive content. *Prometheus Unbound* is self-conscious fiction partly in the manner Sidney is referring to, and it was with such self-vindicating considerations in mind that Shelley engaged in obtrusive myth for the poem. It is also one more Janus-faced allegory, one that very much encircles the imagination with the intent, not of offering Prometheus and company as literally true, but of providing readers with intimations of the poetic thoughts—the ineffable thoughts—that are the issue of the poem as whole. In poems such as *Epipsychidion*, which take literally true events as their starting points, and in "Mont Blanc" and "Hymn to Intellectual Beauty," which present respectively an empirical object and a transcendent order, the license for fiction, even of the variety that Coleridge had in mind in his famous "willing suspension of disbelief that constitutes poetic faith," does not function as smoothly.

Shelley has been attempting to salvage an integrity for his craft, however, not to undermine it, and so he makes of poetic failure finally a triumph:

> His very words are instinct with spirit; each is as a spark, a burning atom of inextinguishable thought; and many yet lie covered in the ashes of their birth, and pregnant with a lightning which has yet found no conductor. All high

poetry is infinite; it is as the first acorn, which contained all oaks potentially. Veil after veil may be undrawn, and the inmost naked beauty of the meaning never exposed. (*Defence* 500)

William Keach has provided the most useful gloss to this passage:

> The infinite potential meaning of poetry is seen to depend upon the inability of words ever completely to conduct and therefore to discharge the mental energy they signify. So when Shelley goes on to transfigure words-as-ashes into words-as-veil, he does so not to lament the discrepancy between thoughts and words, but to expand his claim that "All high poetry is infinite." (*Shelley's Style* 28)

Shelley's poet puts veils on, but not because there is a reducible meaning to be found when the veils are withdrawn. Indeed, it is this very irreducibility that saves him in the end, for, if there were literal paraphrase behind the veils of poetry, then he could well be accused of the indulgence of lies and of merely self-gratifying fantasies. But his embellishments and ornamentation and elaborate structures—he hopes—in his mature years are the signs of ineffable meaning, which must always take on perpetually changing forms. They are also the very ground of the unveiling process that lifts the film of familiarity which obscures from us the wonder of our being. Shelley knows, clearly, that he does not always succeed; but in the *Defence* he asserts a successful aesthetic from the ruins of failed vision.

Adonais

By the time we arrive at *Adonais*, Shelley has already reconciled himself, at least partially, to the inefficacy of language. He has already assimilated his consideration that language cannot provide a satisfying alternative to, or a satisfying metaphoric equivalent of, an absence. The physical absence—the death—of a real human friend, however, one such as Keats had been to Shelley, would have shocked him even out of the complacency of acknowledged inefficacy.[20] It is one thing to reconcile oneself to losses of objects we never had in the first place; it is another to write about the loss of a human being who had held an important place in our lives.[21] If Emily had been metaphorized out of existence, then *Adonais* reminds him that he cannot metaphorize anyone back *into* existence. It seems a cruel irony after the poetic difficulties he had encountered in *Epipsychidion*, but Keats's death, or rather, Shelley's attempt to write a pastoral elegy on Keats's death, confirmed him in his final orientation—one of obsessive attention to the quotidian in the very midst of failed vision.[22]

I should like to offer a very brief account of *Adonais*, then, one that concentrates on its concluding movement. For those issues in the poem which bear upon my particular argument are relatively tractable, and they reach their fullest and most fascinating actualization in "The Triumph of Life," which is the focal concern of my next chapter. It is clear that the poem is modeled on the familiar conventions of the pastoral elegy,[23] that it rejects the consolation of "Lycidas" and of other well-known pastoral elegies, both Christian and pagan, and that various Platonic and British empiricist elements are manifested throughout the poem.[24] I do not believe that it gives evidence of any significant solace, and I do not believe that Shelley intended that it be read, or even written, as practical consolation. The elegy that offers "Peace" to its mourners in the "consolation" section and in the same stanza reminds us that " 'Tis we, who lost in stormy visions, keep / With phantoms an unprofitable strife" (*Adonais* 345–46), and that "*We* decay / Like corpses in a charnel" (348–49), is as inimical to assuagement as a poem could be. The suicidal note on which the poem ends—which would have been interpreted as suicidal even without the benefit of our foresight about Shelley's death by drowning—is neither shocking nor indicative of assurance of transcendence. Even as an example of Platonic pathos, the poem's strongest emphasis is not its yearning for the Ideal from which we in our temporality are irrevocably separated, but the temporality to which we are consigned, and how we are able to manage within it.

Following Shelley's own lead, virtually every critic has noticed that it is one of the most finely wrought of his poems, one of the most obtrusive and artful deployments of poetic skill.[25] Shelley had obvious precedent for this in Milton's "Lycidas" and in the entire long line of pastoral elegies, and he had precedent also for his concern about his fiction's inefficacy.[26] In rejecting Milton's Christian consolation, however, he also resists the temptation to privilege instead his own poetic fictions; neither does he dwell on his fictions' obvious susceptibility to deconstruction. Indeed, it is the immediate assumption of the poem that his fictions will not suffice: "O, weep for Adonais! though our tears / Thaw not the frost which binds so dear a head!" (2–3). *Adonais* is not a fantasy escape from the ills of the world, as *Epipsychidion* had partly been, and it does not look forward to a rejuvenated temporal world, made more beautiful through love, as *Prometheus Unbound* had done. He assumes an anagogical reference point for his claims about the transcendence of Keats/Adonais (couched in the familiar rhetorical fictions and tropes), but he enters into it with very little attention to philosophical rigor or even polemical intention.[27] Shelley has abandoned belief in fictions as possible bringers of real recuperation or even solace, but he still holds to their value for other, more limited ends. I will therefore turn to the problematic of consolation in the poem's later stages; for it is in *Adonais*'s final moments of poetic reckoning that the great theme of the later Shelley is most profoundly revealed.

Indeed, not even and especially not poetic language can compensate for the finality of death; when one confronts a real death which results in a real anguish, it is time to consider whether metaphorical equivalents do not trivialize the affliction inherent in real, lived experience. The experience of loss is the exclusive experience of the temporally confined, indeed marks the condition of temporal confinement. Shelley's gestures toward the convention of elegiac consolation only further mark its inaccessibility, as in the following three quotations:

> he, as I guess,
> Had gazed on Nature's naked loveliness,
> Actaeon-like, and now he fled astray
> With feeble steps o'er the world's wilderness,
> And his own thoughts, along that rugged way,
> Pursued, like raging hounds, their father and their prey. (274–79)

> Who mourns for Adonais? oh come forth
> Fond wretch! and know thyself and him aright.
> Clasp with thy panting soul the pendulous Earth;
> As from a centre, dart thy spirit's light
> Beyond all worlds, until its spacious might
> Satiate the void circumference: then shrink
> Even to a point within our day and night;
> And keep thy heart light lest it make thee sink
> When hope has kindled hope, and lured thee to the brink. (415–23)

> The One remains, the many change and pass;
> Heaven's light forever shines, Earth's shadows fly;
> Life, like a dome of many-coloured glass,

Stains the white radiance of Eternity,
Until Death tramples it to fragments.—Die,
If thou wouldst be with that which thou dost seek!
Follow where all is fled!—Rome's azure sky,
Flowers, ruins, statues, music, words, are weak
The glory they transfuse with fitting truth to speak. (460–68)

In the first quoted stanza, Shelley describes his own place at the funeral of Adonais, and suggests what it might amount to, finally, to create a being within the being which is the quotidian world. The unveiling in which poetry participates, partly through a process of veiling, yields thoughts that, in an unresponsive world, can only lead to anguish. "Where there is leisure for fiction there is little grief" (*Lives of the English Poets* 1: 163), is Samuel Johnson's famous indictment of "Lycidas"; but for Shelley the leisure for grief *is* and must be fiction, because grief itself is an abstract concept that, in a temporal world, relies on fiction for purposes of epistemological clarification. And that is not real definitive clarification at all, of course, but merely articulation of intuitive approximation. The poetry provides a definite form in which to confine his anguish, but beyond that, the poetry *forms* the apprehension of grief over a death and its philosophical and aesthetic implications.

If we can come to terms, only within the confines of fiction, with something as brutally unadulterated as the death of a friend—if we can come to terms indeed with anything at all only in terms of necessary fictions—then we are inevitably compelled to an aesthetic rendering of all experience, and hence a perpetual process of deferral of all experience. Shelley had attempted to defend a similar position in the *Defence* under the rubric of infinite creativity, and its ominous implications do not render such conclusions null and void; but the discovery of new ominous implications does emphasize the grave limitations inherent in the very condition of human understanding. If the speaker presumes to believe that he has confronted nature unadulterated, "naked," without the aid of fictions, then he is on his way not necessarily to spiritual strength, but to a death to the world, to the shock of the incompatibility of desire for knowledge with its objects. His thoughts pursue him when he gazes on nature naked, because they are wild and ruinous, unformed phantoms shorn of necessary, inevitable vestment. It is for this reason too that the second quoted stanza situates the potentially consoled in the intense inane, "beyond all worlds," at "the void circumference." Shelley is recalling, as the Norton editors remind us (*Shelley's Poetry and Prose* 404n2), the *Defence's* claim that poetry "is at once the centre and circumference of knowledge" (*Defence* 503). But if the spirit attempts to go beyond "all worlds"—as the *Alastor* questor had overleaped "the bounds of temporality"—only to hit a "void circumference" from which we must "shrink / Even to a point," then we shrink back to ourselves, back to our fictions of the very "void" from which we have returned, and finally back to the world in which we must try to find a place—and a fiction—for living.

But we arrive instead, again and again, at a fiction of the One which has been troped from the earth through relational apprehension, of the fictions by which we sustain a Platonic pathos. Such self-consciousness over fiction-making is the obvious consequence of anagogic vision; but here, in the shock of the finality of death, it finally demands our acknowledgment that, after returning from Mont Blanc-as-trope to the grand mountain itself, we do not finally want to cope with the mountain.

If Shelley here appears to be forsaking the earth, then it is a forsaking based on a loving despair over it: "Here pause: these graves are all too young as yet / To have outgrown the sorrow which consigned / Its charge to each" (*Adonais* 451–53), he laments, even though—or rather, precisely because—the poem propels him inevitably toward the most despairing statement of the entire Shelley canon: "Die, / If thou wouldst be with that which thou dost seek!" Shelley's intuitive belief in Keats's transcendence still denies him the motivation to return to fresh woods and pastures new. We do seek for ultimate meaning, he knows, and there lies the difficulty in believing in anything which has been constructed—inevitably and irrevocably—in the terms of fictions, themselves constructed from our temporal confinement: "Flowers, ruins, statues, music, words, are weak / The glory they transfuse with fitting truth to speak" (467–68). Thus the One remains, and we are left with "shadows," with what he had called in the *Defence* the ability to "colour all that they [poets] combine with the evanescent hues of this etherial world," which in *Adonais* has become the "dome of many-coloured glass" that stains the white radiance of Eternity.

What consolation can there possibly be, then? The process of Shelley's anguish over fictions confirms his implicit acceptance of their necessity. Thus, commenting on the elegy's images of veiling and of covering, Peter Sacks suggests:

> The presence of these gathering fabrics of shadow, veil, and curtain testifies to an elegist's acceptance not only of Death's castrative power, but also of the

elegist's recapitulated entry into, and submission to, those very mediations of language that interpose between him and his object of loss or desire. The elegist's riposte to Death, his consoling counterassertion, however displaced, of desire and of the trope for a surviving power, must, therefore, come to terms with the enforced fabric of substitutions. This is where one of Shelley's most vexing problems comes to the fore. For while trying to rebut Death's power, Shelley also struggles to purge his counterassertive language of its inherent association, as language, with all the interposing fabrics — of Death's curtain, or of life's erotic but mortal physicality, or of the traces of this latter physicality in the material flowers, however spiritualized, of rhetoric. (*English Elegy* 150)

Shelley is not trying to rebut Death's power, as Sacks would have it, but his assertion does point up the important consideration in the elegy: poetic fictions do not do anything. They do not accomplish anything beyond the subjective potential for limited understanding, and they do not obviate epistemological angst. *Adonais* does not pretend to approximate recuperation of loss. The fiction of this poem has offered death as the only real practical consolation, but Shelley's poetry also knows now that death is the great unknown, that whatever we predicate about it relies on our linguistic and poetic manipulations of our received language code.

Such clarification itself implies the great need for the fictions of poetry; but in *Adonais* Shelley virtually abandons the struggle for sustaining the fictions of the value of the quotidian. In anguish over the torment of living, he privileges his pain over a potential aesthetic redemption for it. Even an unadulterated reality, however, can only be conceived of negatively, or indirectly, and therefore the drift towards death is impelled partly by an abandonment of faith in the value of fictions of the earth. But in *Adonais* the anxiety over perception of a quotidian, virtually unadulterated reality — whatever we finally make of it in the end — is the profound and important legacy of fiction.

5. With More Than Truth Exprest

The last year of Shelley's life, even more than any other, is marked by conflicting tendencies. On the one hand, he never abandons his quest to justify even radical forms of fiction-making, and he engages in subtle analysis, of the kind exemplified in *A Defence of Poetry*, to relate the necessary embellishments of poetry to the quotidian world. He has learned that poetic ornament is not *merely* ornamentation of discursive thought, and that articulation and conceptualization are therefore inextricably linked. But he has also been coming to grips with the notion that, given the inextricability of thought and form, given the necessary embellishments of fiction, given even the imagelessness of the deep truth, he owes special consideration to the empirical world that has been conveniently providing him with metaphors. For, though Shelley is fully sensitive to the necessary problematizations through which an external reality can only be grasped, he also knows, as he explains in "On Life," that mere words cannot finally "penetrate the mystery of our being" ("On Life" 475). And the mystery of our being, though ultimately inscrutable, is the mystery of a life lived in continual misapprehension, in the familiarizations that blunt perception of a world of objects and relations, however constructed. We find him, and we leave him ultimately, suspended between a desire to ascend to some unknowable, other-worldly, ubiquitous One, and a conflicting desire to answer the question he poses at the end of "Mont Blanc"—again, if value inheres in the mountain only as it becomes an object to be troped upon, then what is the mountain as mountain? In *Adonais* he had come dangerously close to abandoning the question altogether, but in the end Shelley knows that it is the impulse to formulate definitive answers which makes the questions so anxiety-provoking in the first place.

In the so-called "Jane poems," and in "The Triumph of Life," Shelley offers neither new aesthetic principles nor a significantly altered conception of metaphysics; or rather, the recognition that he has nothing of truly new significance to offer is the most striking and most important feature of the final poems. Judith Chernaik remarks that "we notice as in all the late lyrics the quiet disappearance of apocalyptic hope, the ambition to change the world" (*The Lyrics of Shelley* 169). Shelley has not abandoned philosophical angst or epistemological uncertainty, but he does extend the hint of "Mont Blanc" and of the 1821 work; that is, his *poetic* attention shifts to his anxiety over the empirically knowable. We find in the final poems, then, an intense feeling of imminence which, manifested variously in different works, becomes a sense of imminent understanding of the value or the meaning in the quotidian world. In "With a Guitar. To Jane," for example, the poet describes the guitar in ways that correspond generally to the tone of his later poetry: "The artist wrought this loved guitar, / And taught it justly to reply / To all who question skilfully" (58–60). But of course such replies are withheld in the poem and denied discursive formulation by their very (musical) nature. The guitar knows all, he insists, but "All this it knows, but will not tell / To those who cannot question well / The spirit that inhabits it" (79–81). The implicit questions, then, not the answers, become most important for the poetry. Assertion of potential—the *Defence*'s assertion of poetic/linguistic potential, *Prometheus Unbound*'s illustration of the potential of human love or human understanding—has been translated into the excitement and anxiety of a qualified expectation.

The Jane Poems

"To Jane. The Invitation" and its companion piece, "To Jane. The Recollection" immediately recall us to the ominous aesthetic and philosophic rendering of Teresa Viviani in *Epipsychidion*, but Shelley's last efforts are more sensitive to the dangers of metaphoric displacement and deflection. Although he cannot entirely obviate such dangers while he continues to write poems, indeed while he continues to exist, the last poems attempt to privilege the empirically actual in ways that suggest some degree of resignation to aesthetic insufficiency, and thereby resignation to the inadequacies of the empirical world itself. It is in such resignation that the promise of imminent satisfaction is held out—even when the sense of imminence has but an ill-defined object—because Shelley plays on the natural predilection to assume modest rewards for the relinquishing of grander visions. This is the obverse of *Adonais*'s "Die! if thou wouldst be with that which thou dost seek," for Shelley now defers to his understanding that he *cannot* be with that which he seeks; that is, he comes to expect some quiet, if brief, contentment in quotidian life. He makes such an effort not as a substitute for complete spiritual fulfillment, but in deference to the unavailability of spiritual completion. Yet the aesthetic rendering of such consciously remarked absences also signals a heightened awareness of, and response to, aesthetic need, and therefore an even stronger sense of the inextricability of quotidian life and aesthetic need.

Thus, in the opening situation of "To Jane. The Invitation," we have an immediate gesture towards an implicit revision of *Epipsychidion*: "Best and brightest, come away— / Fairer far than this fair day" (1–2). In the invitation section of *Epipsychidion*, Shelley had envisioned a full fantasy escape to a world secluded, isolated, and finally unearthly even in its "natural" imitations of artifice. By 1822, Jane Williams had replaced Emily as the focus of Shelley's frantic desires, again in response to his unsatisfactory sexual life with the exhausted, ill, and oft-pregnant Mary. Shelley revises his 1821 stance through the mediation of a modified echo of "Come live with me and be my love," but the differences are telling. Shelley is situated not in a pastoral ideal but in his particularized world, and where he in fact had taken a real walk (with Mary too, but he prefers to recall Jane only). He does not want her to come and live with him, only to come and walk with him, somewhat like Wordsworth's exhortation to Dorothy, in the lyrical ballad "To My Sister," to put on her woodland dress and leave books and cares behind. And he does not want Time to stop for them, only for them to enter into the creative possibilities of their particular moment: she is fairer far than this "fair *day*," and later, he hopes to "take what this sweet *hour* yields" ("To Jane. The Invitation" 32), for she is "Radiant Sister of the *day*" (47; italics mine), not eternity, not all time, just the moment—Shelley's answer to the *carpe diem*.[1]

Here also is no languidly buoyant meter; the poem is written in rapidly moving tetrameter couplets, with a quick progression to an easy, superficially unproblematic fiction of pathetic fallacy, where the retreat world is seen to be the winter world of imminent release into Spring:

The brightest hour of unborn spring
Through the winter wandering
Found, it seems, this halcyon morn
To hoar February born;
Bending from Heaven in azure mirth
It kissed the forehead of the earth
And smiled upon the silent sea,
And bade the frozen streams be free
And waked to music all their fountains,

> And breathed upon the frozen mountains,
> And like a prophetess of May
> Strewed flowers upon the barren way,
> Making the wintry world appear
> Like one on whom thou smilest, dear. (7–20)

We require, in this initial situation of the poem, neither a process of tortuous exegetical work, nor an overly philosophical paradigm in which to read the lines, to construe their sexual connotations, and to mark the obtrusively self-conscious fictionalizing of the scene: in line nine, "it *seems*" that the unborn spring can be anthropomorphized into a Being who "finds" the day of their sojourn, and who then acts out a muted love duet with "the forehead of the earth." Such images anticipate, for the poet, the proto-sexual release heralded by the advent of Spring, and remind us that, as "invitation," the promise of fulfillment could extend to more than just a harmonious walk. We will see, however, that such uncertainty contributes to some extent to the ironizing of the poem's seeming simplicity. For now, the effect of the lovely day is not to imply that there is an even better, transcendent one which this scene mirrors (as Asia had done in *Prometheus Unbound*), and certainly not to suggest that one ought finally to die if he would be with that which he seeks (as *Adonais*, in its despair of the world, had done). Rather, Shelley initially offers that the natural environment, like the Nature which Wordsworth is "fitted" to in the "Prospectus to *The Recluse*," and his affective experiences within it, may be harmoniously joined within a poem which simply celebrates a joyful sense of imminent fulfillment.

But we already know from *Adonais*, indeed from the entire Shelley canon, that, even if we do reconcile ourselves to the inaccessibility of our transcendental yearnings, it does not necessarily mean that humanity and Nature will in turn be united, at least not in any manner that can be sustained on a level of poetic simplicity. In fact, "To Jane. The Invitation," is not in the least an easy "fit" between the poet and Nature, between the poetic personages and Nature, because the Nature to which he is fitted in his scene is a poeticized forum for fulfillment which never comes. We will see also that even in "The Recollection" the most striking feature of the recollection is that the experience is over and the speaker therefore impoverished. Witness the beginning of the second stanza of "The Invitation":

Away, away from men and towns
To the wild wood and the downs,
To the silent wilderness
Where the soul need not repress
Its music lest it should not find
And echo in another's mind,
While the touch of Nature's art
Harmonizes heart to heart.— (21–28)[2]

We are still observing an important instance of progression from some of
the more troubling postures of *Epipsychidion*, for the "heart *to* heart" of this
poem is juxtaposed with the annihilation born of unity in the former poem.
But Shelley has not forgotten his lessons about the inextricability of articulation with communication, of articulation with conceptualization, and
about the problem of voice in a temporal world. We are not seeking here
for a deep truth, only for a moment of supposedly realistic relaxation; but
since we respond to deep truths in terms of the sensory impressions we construct in our (sometimes unconscious) fiction-making, and indeed since, as
it seems, we cannot help but construct some idea of the deep truth in
response to our perception of concrete objects, we remain susceptible to
the unconscious evocation of images of ultimate meaning, no matter what
we are engaged in describing superficially. The wilderness here is "silent,"
but the soul may intimate its ineffable language precisely because the natural world is insentient, inarticulate, and hence open for projected interpretation. The expectation of sympathetic unity, the "*echo* in another's mind,"
is almost a folie-à-deux with Jane in their natural world of muted artistic,
fictional possibilities. He does not try to give the wilderness itself a "mysterious tongue" (as he had done in "Mont Blanc") to be interpreted in
terms of some larger conception of life and the cosmos; instead, he sees it
as at once real forum *and* poetic vehicle. It is Nature as the poet renders
"Nature's art" which "harmonizes heart to heart." We have invitation to
quotidian scene, certainly, but we do not stop there, and possibly Shelley
is suggesting that we *cannot* stop there.

Such lines indicate a sensibility that is not entirely reconciled to our
inability to predicate univocally ultimate meaning in the world. The "silent
wilderness" may not be the one that implicitly speaks of "Power," but it is
one that hints at a meaning that the poem and the natural scene are not
entirely able to provide. The negations of the second stanza remind us of

what the poem is not, but only because there are still things Shelley emphatically wishes it to be. The final couplet of "The Invitation" remarks a philosophical summation which the poem does not fully support: "And all things seem only one / In the universal Sun" (68–69). In *Letter to Maria Gisborne* Shelley had chided himself for hiding in a "shroud of talk" from the sun of common day, and in *Epipsychidion* the sun which was Emily became assimilated to his own being, so that he and his world were one in the sun of his metaphoric making. Here he hints again at the collapse of identity into obliteration; but there the poem ends, anticipating the friendly union and still consciously attempting to remain faithful to its quotidian grounding. The poem, it must be remembered, is an *inviting*, an expecting, at least, of a tangible day of happiness, even if that day is to become also the forum for mild philosophic rendering.[3]

But Shelley is aware also that this rendering is potentially problematic and, for the purposes at least of this poem, he strains against the human predilection to impose meaning which may not necessarily belong to the object it is wrought upon. Throughout the poem, then, he rallies on behalf of the quotidian, but such rallying still reinforces his sense of the ease with which poetic fictions may bespeak even simple desires, and hence also reminds us of the dangers of his own more familiar form of fiction-making:

> I leave this notice on my door
> For each accustomed visitor—
> "I am gone into the fields
> To take what this sweet hour yields.
> Reflexion, you may come tomorrow,
> Sit by the fireside with Sorrow—
> You, with the unpaid bill, Despair,
> You, tiresome verse-reciter Care,
> I will pay you in the grave,
> Death will listen to your stave—
> Expectation too, be off!
> To-day is for itself enough—
> Hope, in pity mock not woe
> With smiles, nor follow where I go:
> Long having lived on thy sweet food,
> At length I find one moment's good
> After long pain—with all your love
> This you never told me of.   ("To Jane. The Invitation" 29–46)

We are initially reminded, perhaps, of familiar twentieth-century variations on this theme, of Auden's "find this mortal world enough," or Frost's "Earth's the best place for love." But the lines continue to cast doubt on the possibilities for living within the received fictions of harmony between human beings in their natural environment, and the seemingly inexorable pull toward devastation, the arbitrary force that seems always to thwart their potential and longing for tranquility. He may say that "To-day is for itself enough," but that is only because that particular day which is expected, invited, anticipated is a day designated to be unlike other days. Hope is joined to fear, as the sonnet had reminded us,[4] and the "sweet food" of hope feeds also the "tiresome verse-reciter Care." It is only because hope is the sign of impoverishment that he bids "Expectation" to "be off" as well, but we know that he continues to hope and continues to expect; at least in the fiction of this poem, he is inviting Jane because he expects her presence, he hopes for her company, and he expects fulfillment, of a sort, in her friendship. The old Shelleyan encroachment of the unfulfilled desire begins to rear its foreboding head: the overwhelming sense of imminence which is reinforced by the "invitation" context becomes one more fiction of hope, which over-burdens even expectation, and which reminds us that verse signals the pain of "Care." Insisting that he will leave care behind, he instead reinforces its inevitability.

But do verse and "care" really exist on the same level of regret? Is the matter as simple as one always implying the other? He is leaving despair and care and hope, he says, because he now seeks a temporary but real fulfillment; yet we know that these are lines of care-worn poetry as well, that the expectation for fulfillment in Jane's friendship in the woods is another form of hope, and we of course know that the invitation is itself a verse-reciter full of the Care of hope for human sympathy. There is an agony of unfulfilled but lurking desire, which reaches its climax in the final stanza, and which suggests that the withholding of anticipated fulfillment is the requisite of poetic creativity, even as it is the very trope of poetic creativity (recall the *Defence*'s "the mind in creation is as a fading coal"):

Radiant Sister of the day,
Awake, arise and come away
To the wild woods and the plains
And the pools where winter-rains
Image all their roof of leaves,
Where the pine its garland weaves

> Of sapless green and ivy dun
> Round stems that never kiss the Sun—
> Where the lawns and pastures be
> And the sandhills of the sea—
> Where the melting hoar-frost wets
> The daisy-star that never sets,
> And wind-flowers, and violets
> Which yet join not scent to hue
> Crown the pale year weak and new,
> When the night is left behind
> In the deep east dun and blind
> And the blue noon is over us,
> And the multitudinous
> Billows murmur at our feet
> Where the earth and ocean meet,
> And all things seem only one
> In the universal Sun.— (47–69)

There is an agony of awaiting, an urge to burst forth which yet is suspended by the historical Jane's inaccessibility to Percy Shelley as lover. The violets do not join scent to hue because the year is still pale, weak, and new, and the hoar-frost is only just melting and not yet gone. There is a great deal of hope and care in this instance of verse-reciting, and it may well be that the poet will only be able to discharge his debt to sorrow in the grave; that is, a sublimated sorrow is lurking even in the anticipated retreat. The seeming oneness in the "universal Sun" is the condition of this described scene only under a certain poetic rendering, only within this artistically rendered invitation to a real occasion, which yet resonates with hints, intimations, and ineffable longing beyond its superficial circumstance. But this is only the invitation, and therefore by nature as yet unfulfilled. Part 2 of the composition, "To Jane. The Recollection," corresponds to the fading part of the inspiration in creativity which necessarily wanes, even while it marks the successful trip that his invitation elicited.

The "Recollection" section is closer to the sentiments of *Adonais*, perhaps, than it is to *Epipsychidion*. For here we recall faded glory that yet can be inscribed—and therefore permanently enshrined—but the enshrining yields memory of happiness which is fleeting. It therefore yields also the despair of dissipation. The verse-preface sums up the central perspective of his recollection:

Now the last day of many days,
All beautiful and bright as thou,
The loveliest and the last, is dead.
Rise, Memory, and write its praise!
Up to thy wonted work! come, trace
The epitaph of glory fled;
For now the Earth has changed its face,
A frown is on the Heaven's brow.

("To Jane. The Recollection" 1–8)

The value of the quotidian, then, even in Shelley's final years, is still very qualified; his primary concern is finally our inability to determine for it a definitive worth distinct from its aesthetic rendering. This is not simply a poem which celebrates the successful day: it is the self-conscious assertion of its absence.

Indeed, it is only after the event, after the invitation has been acted on (somewhere in the interstices of the invitation and the recollection), that a more obtrusive fictionalizing process takes over. The first Jane poem indulges the fictionalizing habits of the poet only marginally, and there it at least tries to be no more than a concession to aesthetic necessity. But "The Recollection" slows down the rhythm, exhibits a high number of medial pauses, and follows an alternating—rather than a rapid couplet—rhyme scheme. The effect is to make us linger over the exegetical possibilities, over the manifold interpretations of the fictions which have intruded into the winter world:

There seemed from the remotest seat
    Of the white mountain-waste,
To the soft flower beneath our feet
    A magic circle traced,
A spirit interfused around
    A thrilling silent life,
To momentary peace it bound
    Our mortal nature's strife; —
And still I felt the centre of
    The magic circle there
Was one fair form that filled with love
    The lifeless atmosphere. (41–52)

If, as the verse-preface insists, the earth has changed its face, that is because the poet had fictionalized a "magic circle" to stand as the "sweet food" of hope of the first poem. He has, of necessity, stepped out of the magic circle and back into the normative world, but that is because the circle had been drawn *onto* the world; stepping out of it, then, would be tantamount to erasing it, not to going elsewhere: in the water they saw imaged "Sweet views, which in our world above / Can never well be seen" (69–70). He does not name a Power, but the "spirit interfused" echoes Wordsworth's "presence" in "Tintern Abbey," which disturbs him with the joy of elevated thoughts, the sense of "something far more deeply interfused" (97) whose dwelling is in the empirical world and in the mind of man. But Shelley is not claiming a benevolent force that sustains the universe; in fact, he is pointing out that his joy dissolves after a startlingly brief time. His "spirit interfused" is as transient as his day with Jane:

> We paused beside the pools that lie
>   Under the forest bough—
> Each seemed as 'twere, a little sky
>   Gulphed in a world below;
> A firmament of purple light
>   Which in the dark earth lay
> More boundless than the depth of night
>   And purer than the day,
> In which the lovely forests grew
>   As in the upper air,
> More perfect, both in shape and hue,
>   Than any spreading there. . . . (53–64)

Only in retrospect does the day begin to resemble the tone of his escape fantasy with Emily in *Epipsychidion*. Here he yearns for a supra-nature that contradicts "The Invitation" 's assertion that "To-day is for itself enough." The day he poetically *recalls* is "purer than the day," and the world in which he experiences it is a mock-heaven. William Keach offers a particularly insightful comment: "But the illogically extravagant comparative rhetoric—'More boundless' and especially 'More perfect'—destabilizes the activity of idealizing reflection by making it seem driven, 'leaning.' 'More boundless' even threatens to undo that binding of 'Our mortal nature's strife' to 'momentary peace' in the previous section" (*Shelley's Style* 214).

Furthermore, "The loveliest and the last" dead day of the verse-preface recalls the apostrophe to Urania in *Adonais*:

Thy extreme hope, the loveliest and the last,
The bloom, whose petals nipt before they blew
Died on the promise of the fruit, is waste;
The broken lily lies—the storm is overpast.   (*Adonais* 51–54)

The storm of Shelley's passions is overpast without ever having been entirely fulfilled: even in the first stanza of the recollection, he recalls a foreboding Nature that is to be harnessed now, in a despairing present that is the aftermath of the experience: "The lightest wind was in its nest, / The *Tempest* in its home" ("To Jane. The Recollection" 11–12; italics mine).

In the first Jane poem, the poet had promised to leave the verse-reciter behind, because his name is "Care." But after expectation, after ill-defined sense of imminence, after a fleeting moment of happiness that yet is full of foreboding, comes inevitably recollection, which follows a familiar Shelleyan pattern: recollection necessarily implies absence, or impoverishment, which leads to despair/hope, which is the very ground of poetry and its fictions of compensation and solace. The Jane poems are of this world, but we finally realize that for Shelley the poetry of this world can only amount to an intensely qualified and anxious deflection away from it. The first Jane poem had described the poet's expectations about the day. The second begins with expectation of enshrined memory ("Rise, memory, and write its praise!"), and then inscribes a day made occasion for poetic sorrow, because it is remembered as now lost. Its central feature, then, is its dissolution. With dissolution of the real joys of the quotidian comes the kind of obtrusive fictionalizing which we have come to mistrust, and which was not in full evidence when the poet was still anticipating it: "It seemed as if the hour were one / Sent from beyond the skies, / Which scattered from above the sun / A light of Paradise" (17–20). The poetry that praises it is also the poetry which perceives it as impossible to be re-lived in Shelley's quotidian circumstances. The memory which writes the day's praise is therefore finally occasion for further anguish: "Less oft is peace in S[helley]'s mind / Than calm in water seen" (87–88). His fiction of compensation ends, and he will return to Mary, who is conspicuously absent from the poem (even though she had been on the walk), but whose lurking shadow presumably motivates the poet's desire to take such large leaps of relief.[5]

For all of their attempted felicity, then, the two poems together anticipate "The Triumph of Life." We inexorably return to the quest which
obliterates the merely literal, even when that accidental obliteration is
offered precisely in the service of invigorating our perception of the literal:

> Like one beloved, the scene had lent
>   To the dark water's breast,
> Its every leaf and lineament
>   With more than truth exprest. . . .
>
> ("To Jane. The Recollection" 77–80)

The "more than truth exprest" may be the best that we can manage in the
service of truth.

"The Triumph of Life"

What, finally, does serve Truth? This is the question Shelley ends his career
on, resolute indeed in his need for the question, but always at a loss on the
issue of definitive answers. Such concerns are in evidence in virtually all the
poems of his last year: certainly in the other late lyrics, and in interesting
ways in *Hellas*, which was composed in October 1821 to celebrate the War
of Greek Independence. *Hellas* in particular illustrates Shelley at work on
the problems of the temporal moment, and still troubling over the possibilities for practicable solutions to real problems in the world. It thus bears
a few points of interesting comparison with the tenor of the poems of 1822:
the chorus is comprised of captured Greek women, and so we witness only
potential independence on the one hand (from the Greeks), and fear of
utter failure on the other (from the Turks). The hope is conceived in
impoverishment, and the tone of suspended imminence (the enslaved but
hopeful insist, "The world's great age begins anew") is conceived within
despair over specific historical circumstances. Though he is motivated primarily, as he insists in the Preface, "solely from the intense sympathy which
the Author feels with the cause he would celebrate" (Preface, *Hellas* 408),
the poem is necessarily an explicit probing of the interpretive strategies of
human beings in times of peril, which is the time of us all. We have in *Hellas*, then, the Wandering Jew who is summoned to interpret Mahmud's
dreams; we have proclamations about the transience of the phenomenal

world and the immortality of thought "and its quick elements"; and we have finally the dictum of the later Shelley: "Nought is but that which feels itself to be" *(Hellas* 785).

The tone of surging potential in *Hellas,* however, can be sustained only in response to a firm belief in its potential actualization; as far as unadulterated truth is concerned, Shelley simply does not know how to serve anymore, only that his poetry actualizes desire for apprehension of truth. Sometimes, of course, such actualization becomes the intimation of a truth by indirection, a stripping of the veils of illusion only to reveal another illusion which yet breaks us of the complacency of lazy, unconscious interpretation. This is where Shelley's final poem takes its place: unfinished, disjointed, and fragmented, and therefore utterly apt in its aspect of his darkest homage to truth.

Indeed, the title which Shelley gave to his final, unfinished poem is "The Triumph of Life," and the last question the narrator asks in that poem is "Then, What is Life?" One of the central scenes concerns the figurative car of life vanquishing those who come into contact with it. Many critics have nevertheless claimed that the poem's primary motivation is to evince the effects of epistemological uncertainty attendant on theistic investigation, or proto-theistic questing; and in the late 1970s and '80s, Paul de Man popularized a reading in which the figurality of signification borne out by the fragment is most emphasized.[6] But I would submit that "The Triumph of Life" takes both metaphysical dualism, and its inevitable epistemological doubt, as givens. Shelley is already fully convinced that the deep truth is imageless, is beyond even poetic imaging. Now, in his final year, he is preoccupied by poetry's relationship to quotidian existence, for he already acknowledges the inherent inefficacy of fiction and its tropes. Convinced that even a world of the hyper-quotidian is still a world without the comforts of definitively defined value, he despairs over the vacuity even of a heightened sensitivity to imminence—imminent meaning, imminent self-actualization, imminent spirituality. Finally he realizes that his relentless feeling of imminence feeds into the inexorability of fiction, of figure and of trope, which in turn affect his very (amorphous) feeling of imminence. The situation is a circular one, then, and ultimately—and as far as Shelley reached in the poem before his death—unactualized imminence is not enough for him.

Indeed, in the opening situation of the poem, we are presented with a description of a natural, temporal phenomenon (sunlight), which is interrupted by a vision, and then a vision within vision, until the sequence returns to the unanswerable question: not, what is transcendence, but what is life, the quotidian actuality which we continue to inhabit when our visionary quests have failed. The question could never have been successfully answered, because the poem is agonizingly aware of the triumph of life over poetic fiction; and the only forum for such exposure, of course, occurs within the confines of a poetic fiction, an original myth which self-destructs even as it destroys.

"The Triumph" picks up, then, where the Jane poems fear to travel and where *Adonais* ends, as Shelley determines to explore the means by which human beings not yet in a position to be with that which they seek (that is, dead), actually cope with the task of living. And, to his horror, he discovers that the concept of life, in the sense even of quotidian existence, is as amorphous an abstraction, as resistant to definition, as are his notions of transcendence. For the purposes of this poem, "life" is construed as a coping with images—themselves doomed always to inefficacy—or as our experience of subject-object relationship. This epistemological/phenomenological perspective sees myth, or fiction, as the center of both the subject-object dualism, and the quite different natural-transcendent one. The existence (and failure) of the latter use of myth involves the failure of the former. We shall further see that, since mythic structures make tropes out of objects, and since the visionary questor also appropriates objects as tropes of transcendence, life remains elusive, triumphant in its impenetrability. If troped objects can cease to exist as objects for the myth maker, and if we remain living anyway in a world progressively robbed by us, through our troping, of its components, then life ultimately overcomes us.

It is therefore entirely appropriate that the poem begins with a simile: "Swift as a spirit hastening to his task / Of glory and of good, the Sun sprang forth" ("Triumph" 1–2). Since "The Triumph" discloses Shelley's growing suspicion of the potential inefficacy and the danger of fiction and myth—or of fiction as hardened into myth—its initial association makes the associative leap, the conscious artifice, more obtrusive. The deconstructionists' Shelley is therefore truly related to my Shelley, except that I claim for him entirely different motivations, metaphysical conceptions, and concluding anxieties. I cite J. Hillis Miller as obvious example[7]:

> Light for Shelley is the condition of human seeing and naming, which means it is the principle of substitution and forgetting. Each thing is seen as anoth-

er thing and so forgotten. Each new light at once veils the old and affirms itself as a new source of illumination. This light is always a screen. It covers over as it illuminates, since it is a power of figuration that makes things be what they are not. (*The Linguistic Moment* 150–151)

To say that "it is a power of figuration," however, is already to fall into the trap Shelley decries: we ought to pause long enough to notice the light—to notice the physical presence of light—before we make an easy equation, one that can casually insist that light (or anything, for that matter) can absolutely equal anything. The instability of poetic powers of figuration is a given by this point in Shelley's career; here his primary anxiety, and his primary focus of attention, is the integrity precisely of those "things" which we make over, as Miller observes, into "what they are not."

Indeed, there is a vast number of epic-like similes throughout the entire poem, because Shelley is emphasizing the deferral of perception that mythmaking effects.[8] In the first stanza, for instance, we do note that the sun has risen, but not until the second line. Primacy is initially given, then, to a conception of a spirit hastening to his task, not to the sun: perception is hence immediately displaced from sun to the equivalent which Shelley provides. This is a perverse answer to, and virtual parody of, the Berkeleyan assertions he has been making in his later years, that "Nothing exists except as it is perceived."[9] Perverse as it may be, though, it possesses a brutal and unforgiving logic. For if things exist only as they are perceived, then the sun which Shelley perceives first as analogue of something else (a swift spirit), and then as basis for myth (all things "Rise as the Sun their father rose" 18) does not exist as sun in the mind of the percipient. Its status as object denied, its light dissipates and a transparent "shade" is spread over the scene as he engages in a fuller displacement of normative perception: that of allegorical, figurative vision.

This conditions the paradigmatic pattern of progressive light-usurpation, in which each image of light supersedes its predecessor. The first appearance of light in the poem is the sun, immediately obscured by an attempt to transcend, through a "trance of wondrous thought," the objective order which it represents. "Sun" at this stage is not an image for transcendental longing, for its initial appearance is intended to effect greater apprehension of our earthly existence: "and the mask / Of darkness fell from the awakened Earth" (3–4). We are invited, then, to expect the veil of light to unveil the earth, to lift the mist of familiarity which obscures from us the wonder of our being. But in "The Triumph of Life" it does not work. The second instance of light-usurpation is that of the narrator's vision, which at this early stage still resembles life as we know it:

> When a strange trance over my fancy grew
>   Which was not slumber, for the shade it spread
>
> Was so transparent that the scene came through
>   As clear as when a veil of light is drawn
> O'er evening hills they glimmer; and I knew
>
>   That I had felt the freshness of that dawn,
> Bathed in the same cold dew my brow and hair. (29–35)

We are herein led to believe that the vision may still be one of enhanced understanding of quotidian life, for the narrator thinks he "sate beside a *public* way" (43) while he observes the throngs of people "Numerous as gnats" (46), and then finally the figure of the car of life. But the juxtaposition of quotidian life and figurative vision is enhanced by Shelley's use of the state of reverie (a strange trance, not slumber), where we are both awake and dreaming at the same time. The vision is a kind of transparent veil through which the narrator still sees the literal scene before him, which is combined with a sense of déjà vu. The visionary public way is superimposed over the carefully placed private scene: witness such directions as "before," "behind," "at my feet," "above my head." By the time we reach the vision of Rousseau within the narrator's vision, in our privileged position of hindsight we may recall that the narrator's vision occurs during dawn, after "thoughts which must remain untold / Had kept [him] as wakeful as the stars" (21–22). Defying natural order, he turns night into his day because something, clearly, is wrong. But in this poem it is not simply a matter of poetic compensation for impoverishment; rather, the "thoughts which must remain untold" condition a vision which seems to catch itself at its own habit of metaphoric substitution. Rousseau's vision will occur at two removes from quotidian existence, then, and will yield knowledge neither of life itself nor of an ultimate spiritual meaning. Appropriately, he is laid to sleep in a trope of his own conception of the state of nature, under a mountain where soft grass and sweet flowers abound. When he wakes to "a gentle trace / Of light diviner than the common Sun" (337–38), we are at three removes from the sun of apparently objective perception which began the poem.

As I previously noted, the first scene which the narrator witnesses is one of a multitude of people, most of whom pursue "their serious folly as of old" (73). In his very own vision, which, it is crucial to observe, "was not slumber," he perceives individuals desperately attempting to find a means with which to invest life with meaning: "But more with motions which each other crost / Pursued or shunned the shadows the clouds threw" (62–63). Herein begins another recurrent pattern, for virtually all the defeated are associated in the poem with shadows, with the very impulse for mythography, then, which originates in the "forms" of absence. If life as we know it is divested of meaning prior to our personal impositions of order, then life qua life is necessarily posited as incomplete. When we try to "complete" it, though, we only further diminish it. For rather than seek definition of the clouds themselves, or the sun which the clouds obscure, in "The Triumph of Life" the multitude become obsessed with the "shadows the clouds threw" and hence, like the questor of *Alastor*, "Heard not the fountains whose melodious dew / Out of their mossy cells forever burst / Nor felt the breeze" (*Alastor* 67–69).

Lloyd Abbey voices the reader's initial and important response to such dilemmas: "The poem systematically posits image after image as potential analogue of ultimate reality and then, by submerging these images in life's natural cycle, poetically demonstrates their inadequacy" (*Destroyer and Preserver* 128). But if temporal metaphors are inadequate as vehicles to the transcendence of temporality, or even to the spiritualizing of temporality, what becomes of the external, empirical world from which those metaphors are drawn? The pursuit of shadows is analogous to the futile human pursuit of reality by way of fictions whose fictionality has been suppressed. In "The Triumph of Life" deferral of relationship with the sun obscures the sun and leaves clouds. Deferral of perception of the clouds—still objective objects—leaves the creator of tropes merely with shadows of clouds. But shadows are insubstantial stuff, and so after artifice obscures the sun and vision annihilates conscious perception of it, life makes its presence known by reasserting its own omnipresence—one that is forsaken by questors who seek a common denominator to existence. Since the narrator has already effectively diminished the sun, it is appropriate that it is the figurative light of life that makes him conscious of the sun's diminution: "And a cold glare, intenser than the noon / But icy cold, obscured with [ ] light / The Sun as he the stars" (77–79). Just when they thought they were transcending the concrete, life reappears to them in its full "light," reminding them that it is the light of common life in which they are bound to live.[10]

It is important to remember, however, that the poem's underlying premise is philosophical skepticism, and not an utter subversion of spiritual or meaningful ideals; the very existence of a metaphysical realm—so the truism goes—is not dependent on visionaries resolving their epistemological problems. But the question is implicitly asked yet again: if one finally realizes after all that Mont Blanc is only a mountain, how does one then, upon return to the world, cope with the mountain? In "The Triumph of Life" Shelley's cynicism reaches its nadir: those with the greatest potential, with the exception of the "sacred few," are not only overrun by the car of life, but even worse, are chained to it. For the victims in the following quotation, life had been lived as if it were a trope, and so they were inexorably defeated by life when the trope was removed, when they had no choice but to acknowledge the existence of the world which they inhabited:

> The Wise,
>
> The great, the unforgotten: they who wore
>   Mitres and helms and crowns, or wreaths of light,
> Signs of thought's empire over thought; their lore
>
>   Taught them not this—to know themselves; their might
> Could not repress the mutiny within,
>   And for the morn of truth they feigned, deep night
>
> Caught them ere evening. (208–15)

These are not the spiritually sterile, but the wise, indeed those who had mastered "thought." But human beings, like Rousseau and like the narrator, cannot ultimately give satisfactory answers to the "whence" of the world, to "the morn of truth," and so, in feigning an answer, mythologize and hence potentially dehumanize their existence. As Leslie Brisman observes in *Romantic Origins*, "each request for the 'whence' of origins invites mystification" (179). Even visionaries are human, but those who are conquered by life are individuals who cannot reconcile themselves to the paradox inherent in self-transcendence: sustained experience of the sublime requires the transcendence of familiar human contexts. Involved in a quest to obliterate consciousness of their merely human selves, they fail miserably when the self that inhabits life—the "mutiny within"—makes its presence known. Our humanity finally rebels, finally attempts, it would seem, to break out of its confinement in fiction. For these vanquished, life is not acknowledged as anything other than a privation of an ontological presence; but it inevitably catches up to them, and so "deep night" catches them "ere evening."

In "The Triumph of Life" the mythology of institutionalized forms of religion has hardened into the ideology that eclipses its originating moment in humanly constructed fiction. It also eclipses the deep truth that is extra-textual, beyond fiction, beyond any image we would offer in its place:

> And Gregory and John and men divine
>
> Who rose like shadows between Man and god
>   Till that eclipse, still hanging under Heaven,
> Was worshipped by the world o'er which they strode
>
>   For the true Sun it quenched. (288–92)

A remarkable overlay of possibilities is provided in these lines: Gregory and John themselves become tropes—"shadows"—who eclipse apprehension of a true metaphysical Absolute, and who substitute for it a false light of fictional illumination, one which quenches the "true Sun," but which is really a shadow. But the pattern of light-usurpation in the poem thus far has figured the eclipse of the sun as the attenuation of quotidian perception. Still, "the true Sun" puns on the true *Son* as incarnation, as incarnated image of the transcendent that is accessible to mortal perception. We have, then, a kind of double entendre: Gregory and John eclipse the quotidian light of common life by offering an ascetic mythology of institutionalized religion, but, since their ascetic mythology masquerades as the deep truth, their images become our standard of value for truth, become the images for a "true Sun" which is in fact imageless. The "true Sun" that is eclipsed by Gregory and John, though, is also a conventional image, and so Shelley too indulges in the double jeopardy of image-fixation.

The Norton editors remind us that Gregory VII established the pope's temporal power, and that John had been the name of choice for popes. The problems are clear, and we have met them before: as mythographers of an ideal held to be qualitatively distinct from temporality, Gregory and John attempt to concretize that which by its very nature is abstract, and which cannot be contextualized in the terms of a temporal lexicon. Instead of employing metaphor to draw troped objects into propinquity with "the true Sun" (which would be in accord with the prescriptions of *A Defence of Poetry*), they literalize the metaphor and hence figuratively "quench" the sun. It is also interesting that their work is referred to in terms that suggest substitution of one sun for another which is blinding. The deconstructionists' Shelley would have it that there is only infinite deferral to be offered in the first place. But Shelley, I think, is suggesting that such an assumption is precisely the mistake we are in danger of making if we stop at our realization that the "leap of faith" is a qualitative leap into willful absurdity; that is, if we fail to allow that the leap to absurdity is the necessary concomitant of the ascription of all human value, however it may be conceived, and that the recognition of gaps in the lexicon does not itself preclude the existence of anything at all. In this poem, the most troubling anxiety in a world of intuited lexical gaps is our comportment to the world of quotidian pathos. For the deluded, the literalization of metaphor, or the institutionalization of a transcendent reality, is conceived as a more powerful light—so luminous that it supersedes the sun it purports to be further illuminating. But like the delusions of those who are left only with shadows, this process displaces perception of ultimate reality by first displacing perception of temporal life.

The exemption from defeat of the "sacred few," "they of Athens and Jerusalem" (134), is therefore remarkably apt:

> All but the sacred few who could not tame
> Their spirits to the Conqueror, but as soon
> As they had touched the world with living flame
>
> Fled back like eagles to their native noon. (128–31)

J. Hillis Miller again provides a useful comment, but in the service of a conclusion I should like to dispute:

> They exist as personages in texts composed by others, not even in texts composed by themselves. The idea that they come from some transcendent light and return unstained to it is an affirmation of the texts that create their images, the Platonic dialogues, the New Testament Gospels. These texts are examples of those figures projected on the false and fragile glass [of *Adonais*]. Like all human fabrications they are without certain authenticity. (*The Linguistic Moment* 128)

The sacred few can fly back "like eagles to their native noon" only because a true Sun is being posited which yet is eclipsed by those who take a metaphor for a real being; that is, Shelley describes the sacred few in terms of conventional metaphors, indeed the very ones whose inefficacy he consistently exposes in the poem—but in order to emphasize even more strongly that the fictionalized, already established images do not call in question what is nevertheless their deep and truthful (and therefore imageless) destiny. Shelley indulges in the catachresis, certainly, but at a point in the poem where we recognize catachresis as the issue of the common quest for articulation. The deep truths themselves are imageless, and those closest to them are therefore silent. Since the silence of the sacred few is related to our struggle with the ineffable, and since we are not fulfilled by silence, we develop a reflexively trusting response to fictions about them, and to fictions that invoke them as sanctioning authorities. Indeed, this is one of the reasons they have no real place in the quotidian world: they too have degenerated to the various manifestations of the "equals" sign. Finally, however, we also remember that Shelley is working within another double construction: superimposed on this more complicated explication is the transparent sense of the lines; namely, that Jesus and Socrates subscribe to a view of transcendence which actually exists, and which we can only vaguely appreciate in the trope of "native noon."

Rousseau meets the narrator and tells him his story, the most crucial part of which is his encounter with the shape all light. Shelley may well have in mind Matilda, the presiding genius of Eden in Dante's *Purgatorio*, who bathes Dante in a stream that obliterates memory of sin from his consciousness. Eventually Dante is given a vision of the Car of the Church.[11] But the obliteration of consciousness that occurs in Shelley's poem is not finally redemptive.[12] When the "shape all light" appears before Rousseau, instead of seeking from her further illumination of the scene in which he finds himself, he immediately invites obliteration of conscious perception of that scene, as he exclaims:

> If, as it doth seem,
> Thou comest from the realm without a name,
>
> Into this valley of perpetual dream,
> Shew whence I came, and where I am, and why—
> Pass not away upon the passing stream. (395–99)

To be sure, he is curious about the strange context in which he finds himself ("where I am, and why"), but his questions are prefaced by an assumption ("Thou comest from the realm without a name") which would virtually prescribe a particular type of answer, one which would place him in a scene explicable only in terms of an unknown. There is, of course, nothing to sanction Rousseau's assumption that the shape comes "from the realm without a name." It seems more likely that she is a trope for the popularized version of the historical Rousseau's vision of an ideal state of nature, and so, like the tropes of the others in this poem, she is a light become shadow.[13] Life cannot sustain Rousseau's insatiable desire to deal only with an idealized vision of life. Hence, as we shall see, his trope blots "The thoughts of him who gazed on them"—he ceases to have conscious thought of that which exists—and when his trope is necessarily removed by the intrusion of life, "the fair shape waned in the coming light."[14]

Shelley is also playing against the first "Triumph" of Petrarch's *Trionfi*, in which Love triumphs over man: Petrarch falls asleep and dreams of a powerful light, in the midst of which is a car carrying Love. As Earl Schulze points out, Shelley is writing an "allegory against allegory," in which irony is the controlling feature:

> Shelley's relation to the allegorical tradition begins in his perception of its ambiguity, its "double face of false and true." Either ultimate reality cannot be known directly, or it cannot be communicated except by figurative means. We inherit from the past a veil of allegory which records simultaneously our nearest approximations to the divine and the idols of our common humanity. ("Allegory" 35)

Shelley exploits masterfully the tradition he works within; by evoking Love's triumph over man, he parodies his own formulation that "the great secret of morals is love, or a going out of our own nature" (*Defence* 487). In "The Triumph" going out of our nature in order to love leads to a variation on the problematic of *Epipsychidion*; that is, all things are potentially equal because all are potential victims of the fiction-maker's irresistible habits. Rousseau projects a figurative vision of transcendental meaning—one who is feminine, beautiful, and evocative of the long line of Shelley's beloved visionary females—but instead of imaginatively extending his nature, he subjugates himself to his very longing.[15]

The central tension in the poem's quest for answers is now beginning to assert itself most emphatically. Following *A Defence of Poetry*, we would assume that the unvanquished are to draw life into *propinquity* with their conception of their spirituality. This would presumably guard against the implicit denigration of life and of that conception of spirituality; but then how does one conceive of life itself without engaging in myth, indeed without creating fiction which functions as myth? And does not epistemological doubt cast a shadow on temporality also? Shelley offers no definitive answers. Life comes to assert its temporal presence, but it comes clothed, as it only can, in the guise of myth: taking his cue from the book of Ezekiel and from Petrarch's allegorical *Trionfi*, the poet conceives of life as a swiftly fleeting chariot guided by yet another "shadow" and drawn by blinded figures.

It should not surprise us, then, that Shelley's description of the chariot and its charioteer is rendered in terms of the obtrusive fictionalizing we have already encountered in such poems as *Epipsychidion*. But his avoidance of image-fixation in this case is extreme (if necessary), and we come away from it with a strong sense of what life is not, just as the earlier Shelley had only been able to manage the affirmations of a negative theology. Within the chariot sits an ill-defined shape:

> and a Shape
> So sate within as one whom years deform
>
> Beneath a dusky hood and double cape
>   Crouching within the shadow of a tomb,
> And o'er what seemed the head a cloud like crape
>
>   Was bent, a dun and faint etherial gloom
> Tempering the light; upon the chariot's beam
>   A Janus-visaged Shadow did assume
>
> The guidance of that wonder-winged team.
>   The shapes which drew it in thick lightnings
> Were lost. (87–97)

Life is a "shape," but of what? What kind of configurations are we to visualize? And what shape can be given to its charioteer the "Shadow," even if we do know that it is "Janus-faced"? Life herself is deformed, of course (though we do not know precisely in what fashion), from years of hard work, but she also wears a "crape" because she is in mourning. Life reminds us of death here because the life to which Shelley is granting victory is the one of mutable, mortal, quotidian existence. But Life reminds us of death also, perhaps, because in our perceptual sterility, in the recurrence of our impressions blunted by reiteration, and in the pathos of our quest to appropriate it as an image of Otherness, we are dead to Life. And even for Shelley to describe her he must gesture toward some shape, some outline of form; therefore the chariot of Life is initially introduced by a veil of light which is brighter than all discernible lights, but the figuration of Life itself within the chariot can only become a fainter "gloom / Tempering the light." For life to become an image, she must be defined, must be given a form we can (almost) see in contrast to her immediate—and initially presented—environment.

It is in view of such cruxes that Shelley's rendering of Rousseau becomes most interesting. In many respects, Rousseau fathered the Romantic conception of the state of nature, but his own vacillation on the matter, and his own consciousness of its fictional status, would not have been lost on Shelley or his immediate readers. The Preface to the *Second Discourse* is most telling:

> For it is by no means a light undertaking to distinguish properly between what is original and what is artificial in the actual nature of man, or to form a true idea of a state which no longer exists, perhaps never did exist, and probably never will exist; and of which it is, nevertheless, necessary to have true ideas, in order to form a proper judgment of our present state. (*Second Discourse* 44)

In a still famous essay on metaphor in Rousseau, Paul de Man takes up this very problem:

> As a genetic narrative in which the state of nature functions at the very least as a point of departure or as a point of reference (if no longer necessarily as a point of arrival), the *Second Discourse* seems to contradict the radical rejection of reality on which it bases its claim to free itself from the constraints of facts. Rousseau seems to want to have it both ways, giving himself the freedom of the fabulator but, at the same time, the authority of the responsible historian. (*Allegories of Reading* 137)

Even Shelley's decision simply to appropriate a historical personage and to fictionalize him within his own visionary narrative, suggests the double vision of the nature of figurative expression, and also of human understanding in terms of figures. He does not quite transform his characters into mythic embodiments, as he had done in *Epipsychidion*, but in some respects Shelley's appropriation of Rousseau makes him even more guilty of fabrication. Rousseau appears to us as a speaking human being, not as a planet, not as a tempest, not as a symbol of something immediately other than himself. Shelley is trying, in "The Triumph of Life," to tell the truth about something, as it were, to expose the ominous implications for temporality of our fictionalizing habits. But we find ourselves suspending disbelief, only so that we may understand, through our encounter of the fictionalized rendering of the historical Rousseau, the poet's implicit claims about the dangers of fiction. To see Mont Blanc and remark Power; to see a beautiful woman and remark Platonic Form; to see a burial ground and remark redeeming "Unapparent," is to live with—and within—a permanent suspension of disbelief. It may be, in any case, that reality cannot be fully negotiated through the mind whatever our vigilance for truth, but Shelley has always been at pains to distinguish the forms of belief from its object. His concern here is with the embellishment of the quotidian that is the inadvertent consequence of the embellishment of belief. Shelley's truth telling has been as elaborately fictional as the historical Rousseau's had been, and finally we have the poem, not Rousseau, not Shelley himself, and certainly no clear sense of what truth he ultimately wishes to tell. Whatever denouement Shelley could have found had he lived would still not have obviated the difficulty of sorting through an interpretation of the narrator's vision of Rousseau's vision, which itself is highly figurative. Having warned us of the embellishments of fiction as well as the limits of the "literal," what Truth could he have settled down to tell?

The chariot of life arrives immediately after the description of the failed quests of the misguided who vainly seek "shadows," just as Rousseau will first behold the chariot after vainly asking his trope for answers about that which is beyond life. How are we to live in a world where our tenors could as easily function as vehicles? The quotidian itself affords no answers to that which is beyond it, and so, in contrast to the ontologically defined "seeing eye" of Ezekiel, the eyes of Shelley's charioteer are "banded":

> little profit brings
>
> Speed in the van and blindness in the rear,
>   Nor then avail the beams that quench the Sun
>   Or that these banded eyes could pierce the sphere

>   Of all that is, has been or will be done. —
> So ill was the car guided, but it past
>   With solemn speed majestically on . . . (100–106)

Yet this very dismantling is still framed in myth. The chariot is still a trope. Rousseau explains that he had attempted to live in the world, but even he cannot escape destruction. Shelley by 1822 has long deemed the historical Rousseau's writings about a purely instinctive interaction with nature, and a natively given, passive belief in the existence of God, grossly inadequate. The naturalistic education Rousseau prescribes in *Emile*, for example, potentially leads, in Shelley's despairing perception, to a dehumanization of the self: the first appearance of Rousseau in "The Triumph" is of a rather humorous, fully "naturalized" vegetable-like man:

>   That what I thought was an old root which grew
> To strange distortion out of the hill side
>   Was indeed one of the deluded crew,
>
> And that the grass which methought hung so wide
>   And white, was but his thin discoloured hair. (182–86)

Rousseau later suggests that he did try to invest life with meaning, for he insists, "I / Am one of those who have created, even / If it be but a world of agony" (293–95). Even though he has already told us, "I / Have suffered what I wrote, or viler pain!" (278–79), the lines offer two distinct possibilities: he creates a world of agony and so at least is better than those who are uncreative, or, alternatively, even though the quotidian world is one of agony, he is still able to create from it. The latter meaning (which is subtly muted) would place him in the direct line of the speaker of "To a Sky-Lark." But in "The Triumph of Life" Shelley superimposes that "sky-lark" conception of poetic creation onto one which views the creative process as subtly and partly *responsible* for a kind of impoverishment itself; that is, two ideas are conflated in the lines, so that we think of a created world of agony as well as a quotidian world made more agonizing *because* of the creating. The poet never had any trouble in filling the abyss with temporal images. He is now concerned with filling the absence of meaning in temporality itself, and despairing over his suspicion that the process may lead only to further vacancy, indeed may condition the vacancy.

A *Defence of Poetry* counsels that poetry should create "anew the universe, after it has been annihilated in our minds by the recurrence of impressions blunted by reiteration." Note that the Shelley of the *Defence* desires to create the universe anew, in the service of what I have called the "hyper-quotidian," not create a different, delusionary one. Clearly, then, he is calling for a perpetual process of the discovery of meaning, in despite of our doubts. But in "The Triumph" Shelley is despairing even of the faith that he professes in the *Defence*. For in the *Defence* he knows what Blake knew: that the world can be confronted only if it is constructed in a definite form. But in "The Triumph" Shelley finally learns that saving the world from becoming an amorphous abstraction is a somewhat arbitrary process. Myth and metaphor, in this sense, are involved in a process of *naming* within a world of already problematized referents. Rousseau had indeed desired the perpetual creativity Shelley prescribes in the *Defence*, and since he is "one of those who have created," he had attempted to define his impressions. Of other artists, Rousseau maintains that "their living melody / Tempers its own contagion to the vein / Of those who are infected with it" (276–78). In Shelley's literary adaptation of the inoculation medicine of his time, classical poets rely on catharsis; they cure by infecting. But instead of creating the universe anew they "temper" their contagion, their passion, to the norms of their audience. Rousseau, on the other hand, has "suffered what he wrote, or viler pain": no physician, he has the virtue as well as the vice of creating an agony he cannot cure. He at least has made, then, an honest effort, but one no more sustaining for its integrity.[16]

Does the poem imply a path to self-actualization that finally does not destroy the self in the process? Rousseau insists that not life but his own heart overcame him. But if "neither age / Nor tears nor infamy nor now the tomb" (241–42) could, as he insists in the poem, temper his heart to "its object," then life could not sustain his infinite desire for his finite being's consummation of spiritual completion. This is indeed an example of how, as the narrator observes earlier, "God made irreconcilable / Good and the means of good" (230–31).[17] Rousseau had attempted to live in the world, even to create meaning from his impressions of it.[18] But those who would create anew the universe are necessarily endowed with heightened powers of imagination. We are recalled to the problems of the *Alastor* questor: when the temporally confined, finite being begins to experience insatiable desire for fulfillment in life of his heart's infinite desire, he is inexorably led to defeat, indeed to self-defeat. In this sense, then, "The Triumph of Life" truly is Shelley's palinode for *Alastor*. Desire for meaning and the means to attain meaning are, perhaps, irreconcilable. But Rousseau is defeated by life precisely because life cannot sustain his fictions about it. He is thus wrong when he insists that life did not defeat him, or at least he does not properly qualify the assertion. Ultimately, Rousseau's self-deprecation sounds very much like a refutation of the *Defence*'s "create anew the universe" ideals:

> Figures ever new
> Rise on the bubble, paint them as you may;
>   We have but thrown, as those before us threw,
>
> Our shadows on it as it past away. (248–51)

Life defeats our myths about it even when we are not engaged in quests for the sublime. Creating anew the universe ultimately amounts to throwing shadows/myths onto it in compensation for our sense of incompletion. Value and meaning, then, must reside somewhere between the myth of natural religion and the mystification of the "quest for origins." We persist in the quest for light—illumination—and then more and more light as each one fails, and becomes a shadow. In this world, "life" emits the only unvanquished light, because it is beyond our penetration.

  We are now in a position to evaluate further Rousseau's experience of the shape all light. The landscape in which he falls asleep prior to the encounter is sometimes identified as the canal of birth from which, like a maturing Wordsworthian character, he must "wake to weep."[19] But Rousseau the character in the poem goes to sleep in a scene of nature akin to the historical Rousseau's definition of an ideal state of nature. Since the poem implicitly scrutinizes fictional renderings as forms of potential defeat, it is appropriate that after his sleep he hears sounds from a rivulet,

> which all who hear must needs forget
>
> All pleasure and all pain, all hate and love,
>   Which they had known before that hour of rest:
> A sleeping mother then would dream not of
>
>   The only child who died upon her breast
> At eventide. (318–23)

After hearing the delightful sounds, a mother would forget such horror. But in fact, this is a very powerful, striking image of something which cannot be accommodated by a theory of perception.[20] If epistemological uncertainty must plague us in life, then consolation cannot be imparted to such a mother by asserting that perhaps her dead child has ascended all lofty stars and joined those who, in the language of *Adonais*, are "Far in the Unapparent." Rousseau quite properly falls asleep while attempting to live in his trope of nature, then, because real sensory, conscious experience is annihilated in the face of his fiction about life's potential. Even when relating his story to the narrator, he is still sufficiently deluded by his failed trope to wonder "Whether my life had been before that sleep / The Heaven which I imagine, or a Hell / Like this harsh world in which I wake to weep, / I know not" (332–35). There is no reason for him to "know not." Before that sleep he still knew of a world in which children die upon the breasts of their mothers at eventide. So he retreated from the world of harsh experience and substituted for it an Edenic, mythic world of "April prime" where he would not have to cope with the angst of epistemological doubt or with the agony necessarily inherent in quotidian life.

Rousseau awakens from his sleep of mythic life and is almost immediately confronted with the cold glare of the chariot, which dismantles his myth. The shape all light arrives with the nepenthe just after he awakens, however, when he still has not yet encountered anything to invalidate his "April prime" beliefs. Recall that he had deemed the forgetfulness which the rivulet offered a "Heaven." When he wakes up he is still not willing to relinquish his fiction, and so appropriately encounters another "light" of false illumination, which then substitutes a nepenthe in place of his sleep of forgetfulness. Just as his trope of nature, in his sleep of oblivion, enabled him to "forget thus vainly to deplore / Ills," so the shape all light sustains, temporarily, his fictions:

> And still her feet, no less than the sweet tune
> To which they moved, seemed as they moved, to blot
>   The thoughts of him who gazed on them, and soon
>
> All that was, seemed as if it had been not,
>   As if the gazer's mind was strewn beneath
> Her feet like embers, and she, thought by thought
>
>   Trampled its sparks into the dust of death. (382–88)

It follows logically that Rousseau immediately deems this a beneficent process. The reader may well be horrified by the malevolence of such destructiveness, but Rousseau, grateful that perception of his fictional structure—the shape all light, false illumination—has replaced conscious perception, or thought, of life, assumes that the shape is the embodiment of ultimate reality, straight "from the realm without a name." His myth, which looks like the very vehicle to invest life with meaning, actually annihilates perception of the quotidian, and then ultimately becomes an impotent attempt to transcend concrete reality. He drinks the nepenthe, and so instead of being informed about the whence of origins, life comes to annihilate myth, his hope to discover the whence of origins, and the self-possession which had provided him with a confident basis for self-delusion.

Nevertheless, the lessons of life do afford him at least some knowledge, as, describing the manner in which he then plunged into the throng that had gathered around the chariot, he attempts to affirm his status as an individual human being stripped of fictions:

> me sweetest flowers delayed not long,
> Me not the shadow nor the solitude,
>
> Me not the falling stream's Lethean song,
> Me, not the phantom of that early Form
> Which moved upon its motion. . . . (461–65)

Here, sweetest flowers do not delay him because life has dismantled his natural religion fictions. Rousseau, not "the shadow"—mythic creation—of himself, desires to confront the light of demythologized life. But the circularity of the very quest defeats him again. Precisely at the point when Rousseau would bare his bosom to unadulterated life, "The grove / Grew dense with shadows to its inmost covers, / The earth was grey with phantoms, and the air / Was peopled with dim forms" (480–83). Bereft of myth, Rousseau discovers that it is myth which invigorates human beings, that our response to life's swift advance is to fling yet more and more shadows onto the bubble in an ill-wrought attempt to fill the absence of perceptible meaning. Hence are born the myths wrought of avarice, "arrayed in which those worms did monarchize / Who made this earth their charnel" (504–5). The corrupt, attempting to fill their emptiness, construct images of plenitude, never to understand that the meaning and value they have imposed actually proceed from the "Phantoms diffused around." But we too are the corrupt, in our own fashion. Just as Rousseau's quest ended in myth and its debilitating consequences, so here myth consumes all: "lawyers, statesman, priest, and theorist" (510). Whether we attempt to transcend life or to live within it, the plenitude we find relies on our fictions.

Had Shelley lived to complete the poem, it is doubtful that the conclusion could have escaped the circularity of "The Triumph"'s patterns. Rousseau observes individuals clothed with shadows, and then sees, in the final existing lines, an unmasking of shadows. Yet the unveiling process is not a voluntary one; these are still individuals who know only a world of tropes, not a world of objects. Just as life could not be defined within a fiction, within the terms of a humanly constructed lexicon, so the poem could never have progressed far beyond the final cry, "Then, what is life?" once myth and metaphor had been effectively eliminated. Indeed, the poem's personae languish because they can find nothing to replace the veils:

From every form the beauty slowly waned,

>   From every firmest limb and fairest face
> The strength and freshness fell like dust, and left
>   The action and the shape without the grace

Of life. . . . (519–23)

Fictions had sustained these vanquished, and so they are left "without the grace of life" when the fictions are removed. "Mask after mask fell from the countenance / And form of all," but instead of finally unveiling a deep truth about life, the deep truth remains, in Shelley's final poem, not only imageless, but also unfelt. Finally, nothing substantial remains when the light of life obliterates the shadows:

>   each one
> Of that great crowd sent forth incessantly
>   These shadows, numerous as the dead leaves blown
>
> In Autumn evening from a poplar tree—
>   Each, like himself and like each other were,
> At first, but soon distorted, seemed to be
>
>   Obscure clouds moulded by the casual air;
> And of this stuff the car's creative ray
>   Wrought all the busy phantoms that were there   (526–34)

As shadows depart from the deluded, that is, as life obliterates myths about it, the shadows are further distorted into "obscure clouds"—thus enabling the cycle to perpetuate itself—or are reformed even by life, as she calls troped objects back unto herself. Just as "the sun shapes the clouds," so the car's "ray" is "creative": it re-shapes and transforms our perception of the myths we employ to define it.

The poem finally approaches its climax, then, but it is one which could never have been properly achieved. For indeed, if tropes deflect perception of life, and life itself is shown to resist definition, we may well ask, "Then, what *is* life?"

Left with a world of absences and of failed tropes, though, "The Triumph" ultimately bears testimony, perhaps, to the limitations of our apprehensions, and hence by extension, to the possibilities for new discovery in a world not yet comprehended. In "The Triumph of Life," Shelley could only point to the absences, and perhaps for a poem—and finally for a poetic canon—which knows that "what is life" can never be answered satisfactorily, this may well be enough.

Notes

Introduction

1. I use the term "fiction" in a very broad sense throughout this book, one which is sensitive to—though not strictly defined by—its appropriation in current critical theory. My working definition has elements in common with that of Michael O'Neill, who, in *The Human Mind's Imaginings: Conflict and Achievement in Shelley's Poetry*, defines it in the context of his discussion of *The Sensitive Plant* and *The Witch of Atlas*: ". . . it suggests not only the imagination's products but also the process which results in these products. . . . Moreover, in both poems, 'fictions' often betray or assert in various ways an awareness of their fictional status, swinging between the seeming confession that they are 'only' fictions, made-up, fabricated, and the implicit claim that their kind of feigning offers a more valuable experience than didactic or realistic alternatives" (126). Frank Kermode's *The Sense of an Ending: Studies in the Theory of Fiction* is also relevant, particularly its discrimination between the self-consciousness of fiction and the encrustations of myth: "Fictions can degenerate into myths whenever they are not consciously held to be fictive" (39).

2. See, for example, Part Two (65–88) of James Engell's *The Creative Imagination: Enlightenment to Romanticism,* which provides a survey of eighteenth-century approbations of the associative powers of imagination.

3. I have already cited Engell, above. For Aarsleff, I am thinking of *The Study of Language in England 1780–1860* and *From Locke to Saussure: Essays on the Study of Language and Intellectual History*. In the latter, see especially the essays "Locke's Reputation in Nineteenth-Century England," and "Wordsworth, Language, and Romanticism," which challenges Abrams by insisting on the importance of French thought.

4. I generally cite the 1800 text of the Preface; in this instance, I quote from the 1850 text, from *The Prose Works of William Wordsworth*, as edited by Owen and Smyser.

Chapter One

1. *Queen Mab* was composed between June 1812 and February 1813.

2. Much as I hold to the poetic inadequacies of *Queen Mab*, I describe

it as an "introduction" because it is the first of Shelley's long poetic efforts that does not properly belong to the juvenilia.

3. For an illuminating discussion of the Romantic interest in the epic (allegorical, didactic, political, and autobiographical), see Stuart Curran's chapter on "The Epic" (158–179) in *Poetic Form and British Romanticism*.

4. In fact, in *Shelley's Major Poetry* Carlos Baker complains that "*Queen Mab* is a somewhat belated example of the eighteenth-century moral allegory" (23), and he cites a number of "collateral descendants of *The Faerie Queene* and first cousins to *Queen Mab*," claiming that "reading some of these might have been painful to Spenser; it was evidently not so with the youthful Shelley" (24). As far as *Queen Mab* is concerned, critical opinion has changed little since Baker.

5. In the light of various important discussions about the cultural constructions of the "Romantic ideology," one talks about imagination in these terms only with reluctance, and with a keen sense of the dangers of reflexively assenting to generalizations. Nonetheless, my aim is briefly to lay down the parameters of Shelley's early education in some of the generalizations of his age, precisely because, as I claim, he comes to know them as constructs to be feared.

6. Many members of the Locke school, however, were likely to see words as necessary and useful, if limited and cheat-prone, tools. They would therefore save their strongest ammunition for "lying" tropes. For elaboration, see Hans Aarsleff's *From Locke to Saussure*, 372–77.

7. In the course of giving printing directions to Hookham, his publisher at the time, Shelley asked that *Queen Mab* be printed "on fine paper & so as to catch the aristocrats: They will not read it, but their sons & daughters may" (March 1813; *Letters* 1: 361). Stephen Behrendt, in *Shelley and His Audiences*, comments: "Shelley's strategy is to make the book attractive enough to sell, even if the readership he seeks is not the purchasers themselves—the wealthy but nonreading collectors of fine editions—but rather their more inquisitive offspring, whom Shelley might enlist in his army of young reformers" (83).

8. The notes to "There is no God," for example, are heavily indebted to his early pamphlet, *The Necessity of Atheism*.

9. Not everyone has found this to be disturbing. Ross Woodman, for example, sees Mab as that "pure intelligence" which can comprehend all things (*Apocalyptic Vision in the Poetry of Shelley* 75), and Carlos Baker, who finds almost nothing redeeming in the entire poem, sums her up as "the usual hierophant, the revealer of wonderful secrets" (24).

10. Stuart Curran claims that she takes Ianthe's soul up and out of the world not to escape the earth, but because Ianthe is to confront the world's realities "directly and whole" (*Poetic Form* 172). I would contend that Ianthe must become a disembodied soul—the process is described as the release of "The chains of earth's immurement" (1.188)—and that she must leave the known world with Mab, because Shelley is far more enamoured of his fictions than he is with things as they are, or even with things as they could realistically become.

11. Since the Norton editors excise the notes, I quote from the Oxford Hutchinson/Matthews edition of *Shelley's Poetical Works* for *Notes on Queen Mab*.

12. See Desmond King-Hele's *Erasmus Darwin and the Romantic Poets*, 194–200, for a discussion of the similarities between both *The Temple of Nature* and *The Botanic Garden* and *Queen Mab*. King-Hele's discussion is confined mainly to noting similarities; he does not deal with how and why Shelley also departed from Darwin's practice.

13. I offer this explanation as a qualification to, not a rejection of, Stephen Behrendt's analysis, which discusses the notes in terms of the standard rhetorical "argument by testimony": "Shelley's copious use of these diverse sources constitutes an implicit claim to authority, demonstrating not only the depth and breadth of his own reading but also the degree to which he had digested this wide-ranging reading and brought it to bear on his own formulations. His careful citation of his sources serves at least in part also to soften the radicalism of many of his arguments by linking them to the writings of more thoroughly established thinkers" (*Shelley and His Audiences* 89–90).

14. The irreducibility to literal paraphrase of the "*cognitive* content" of metaphor is, of course, a much discussed topic among current theorists, both philosophical and literary. One of the finest discussions of this problem is still Paul Ricoeur's "The Metaphorical Process as Cognition, Imagination, and Feeling." *Critical Inquiry* 5 (1978): 143–59.

15. See Joseph Barrell's *Shelley and the Thought of His Time*, pages 64–79 passim, for a very early but still representative analysis of these inconsistencies. Barrell notes, for example, that Necessity is not qualified sufficiently in relation to individual will, and is furthermore not mentioned once in Mab's projection for the future.

16. In *Destroyer and Preserver: Shelley's Poetic Skepticism*, Lloyd Abbey also notes that metaphors throughout *Queen Mab* are "self-explicating" (29).

17. I realize, of course, that it would be asking too much to expect Shelley to provide a definitive solution to the free will/determinism dilemma. My concern here is the ease with which he marshals his nascent ideas into an elaborate fiction, one that holds out the promise of a revelation of absolute truth. At this stage in his development, Shelley's views on the matter have most in common with those of Godwin, who in *An Enquiry Concerning Political Justice* holds to a highly qualified and complex view of free will. Godwin claims that the individual is strongly *influenced* by (a sort of determinism) his evaluation of the future. See F. E. L. Priestley's account of the subject in volume 3 of his edition of *Political Justice*, 17–19, and 98–99.

18. In *Radical Shelley* Michael Henry Scrivener suggests that the "cyclical transformation of matter"—Shelley's "There's not one atom of yon earth," and so on—serves "to emphasize a common humanity, and demystify the artificial distinctions of social hierarchy" (69). I would claim that this animation of matter, inimical to hierarchy though it may be, is just a different kind of mystification.

19. The most famous English (literary) dialogue before Shelley would be Dryden's *An Essay of Dramatic Poesy*, with four sharply distinguished speakers. Volume IV of Lord Monboddo's *Of the Origin and Progress of Language* has a long section on dialogue, and David Hume, who did not usually employ dialogue, did write *Dialogues Concerning Natural Religion*.

20. Earl Wasserman, of course, offers many insights into the importance of dialogue and dialectic in Shelley's work, and he discusses *A Refutation of Deism* partly to prepare the ground for his main arguments: "Shelley's seizure here on irreconcilable polarities is a fundamental characteristic of his bent of mind; and his unresolved, skeptical way of proceeding in this prose dialogue, in accordance with the established ironic conventions of that genre, is the normative structure which he then shaped into a variety of complex poetic modes in *Alastor* and other poems that similarly involve a dramatic conflict of characters" (*Shelley: A Critical Reading* 15).

21. See especially pages 25–46. Wasserman, for example, sees the Narrator as "the same as the author of *Queen Mab*, who conceived of man and nature as of essentially the same category because both are imbued with, and defined by, the 'Soul of the Universe'" (*Critical Reading* 15). Stephen Behrendt is typical of more recent variations on Wasserman's thesis: "The narrator in *Alastor*, who fails adequately to understand the Visionary because of his own conditioned Wordsworthianism, mirrors the public

generally, who too often unthinkingly equate public position with reliabil-ity of opinion" (100).

22. I offer this explanation also with an eye to answering Earl Wasser-man, who claims that there is nothing properly to explain the turn to despair and cynicism which Shelley underwent after *Queen Mab* (*Critical Reading* 5).

23. Shelley takes the phrase "obstinate questionings" from Words-worth's "Immortality Ode":

> Not for these I raise
> The song of thanks and praise;
> But for those obstinate questionings
> Of sense and outward things,
> Fallings from us, vanishings;
> Blank misgivings of a Creature
> Moving about in worlds not realised. . . .
>
> ("Ode: Intimations of Immortality" 140–46)

In *Alastor* Shelley gives a different, more disturbing interpretation to the idea of "worlds not realised," one which suggests a guilty rejection of and lack of attention to the world. His questor does not question sense; he evades it.

24. Harold Bloom, in his essay "The Unpastured Sea," asserts that it is the natural world that finally fails the questor: "Shelley's poet longs to realize a vision, and this intense and overconstant yearning destroys natu-ral existence, for nature cannot contain the infinite energy demanded by the vision" (*Romanticism and Consciousness: Essays in Criticism* 379). I would add that nature fails the questor only because the natural world cannot become other than the natural world; for it is not nature for its own sake that the questor pursues.

25. In *The Supplement of Reading: Figures of Understanding in Roman-tic Theory and Practice*, Tilottama Rajan makes a related observation I find very helpful in this context: "[The Poet's] journey through regions that are culturally and temporally distant draws our attention to a hermeneutic problem, while also putting the Poet in the space of the auratic. Scattered through the poem are references to the Orient that try to make the vacan-cy repeatedly alluded to in the poem into an occultation of meaning" (300).

26. This is the terminology of Max Black, whose book *Models and*

Metaphors was one of the first in the explosion of studies of metaphor. Other terms of a host of other theorists would not be inappropriate here, but I find Black's the most self-explanatory.

27. There has always been a great deal of difficulty in dating "Speculations on Metaphysics." The date used to be given as 1815, but in more recent years, and according to some scholars, it has moved up (P. M. S. Dawson's dating in the appendix to *The Unacknowledged Legislator: Shelley and Politics*, for example). Despite this tendency to assign "Speculations" to early 1817, I find the ideas and even the subtle nuances of style to be closer to Shelley's 1815 work; in any case, the ideas expressed in the fragment correspond in important ways to his earlier speculations, and I therefore discuss "Speculations on Metaphysics" as if it were *conceived*, at least, in 1815. Any conclusions drawn from this fragment must be tentative.

28. For a wide-ranging discussion of the role of Aristotle and analogy, see Paul Ricoeur's *The Rule of Metaphor*, especially Chapter 8 (257–313). Ricoeur traces Aristotle's importance in this regard, from Aquinas and on through Heidegger to Derrida.

29. The real problem, however, is the use of a particular kind of name for an abstract Thing. For some pre-Shelleyan etymological theorists, all abstractions, without exception, were in fact derived from concrete nouns (notably Horne Tooke's opinion), and in the Lockean tradition it was indeed names that made possible abstractions, even general terms. The reliance on names in the process of conceptualization, then, would not have been lost on Shelley, but indeed would have made it all the more important for him to guard against the predilection for collapsing mere names into "things," or into the exclusive objects of thought.

30. In *The Excursion* the Wanderer insists that he has been cured of the defect of limitless desires:

> Oh! no, the innocent Sufferer often sees
> Too clearly; feels too vividly; and longs
> To realize the vision, with intense
> And over-constant yearning; — there — there lies
> The excess, by which the balance is destroyed.
> Too, too contracted are these walls of flesh,
> This vital warmth too cold, these visual orbs,
> Though inconceivably endowed, too dim
> For any passion of the soul that leads
> To ecstasy; and all the crooked paths

Of time and change disdaining, takes its course
Along the line of limitless desires.
I, speaking now from such disorder free. . . .

(The Excursion 4.174–86)

Shelley had read *The Excursion* in 1814 with Mary, who remarked in her journal of the occasion that Wordsworth "is a slave" (15). *The Excursion* is an important source for *Alastor*, but by indirection; Wordsworth's Wanderer is still (like Shelley's) very much *wandering* in search of novel experiences. Shelley would never have allowed his hero to resolve his impulses by becoming the moralizing, God-fearing individual of the Wanderer's variety.

31. In *Shelleyan Eros: The Rhetoric of Romantic Love*, William Ulmer rejects the view that makes, as he elegantly puts it, "solipsism the scapegoat for the text's most disturbing implications" (26). Unlike Ulmer, I see no reason to rescue the status of solipsism in this context, although I am sympathetic to his implicit warnings against reducing the entire poem to a mere moral lesson about the dangers of selfishness. He instead locates the poem's central tension in a rhetoric of repression. Noting the physical signs in the visible universe that the questor encounters during his frantic search for the veiled maiden, Ulmer insists that the questor's "search for absolute love returns him, by antithetical reflex, to sensuous images with a force proportionate to his original desire for unmediated ecstasy. The return of the repressed means the return of the body, which renews repression, and, in so doing, renews the entire cycle" (32). I am claiming, obviously, that the effacement of body takes place on an uninterrupted continuum.

32. Chapter 3 of Keach's *Shelley's Style* is devoted to a brilliant elucidation of Shelley's use of reflexive imagery.

33. I am thinking not only of the novels, *St. Irvyne* and *Zastrozzi*, but also the short lyrics published in the *Alastor* volume of 1816.

34. In the "Immortality Ode" (as in many of Wordsworth's poems), it is the independent identity of nature that allows the individual to become an integrated and social being. But compare the questor's shunning of nature with the following stanza from Wordsworth's poem:

Earth fills her lap with pleasures of her own;
Yearnings she hath in her own natural kind,
   And, even with something of a Mother's mind,
      And no unworthy aim,

> The homely Nurse doth all she can
> To make her Foster-child, her Inmate Man,
>   Forget the glories he hath known,
> And that imperial palace whence he came. (78–85)

35. Stuart Sperry offers a more optimistic interpretation of the swan scene, one in which the Poet's privilege is affirmed: "Yet one cannot read the passage without realizing that what raises the Poet in dignity and power above the bird and its song is precisely his isolation from the kind of natural community the swan enjoys. The distinguishing quality of the Poet's humanity, his very voice and timbre, are rooted in his solitude, in his unappeasable desire and despair, which find no echo or reflection in the 'deaf air' or 'blind earth' " (*Shelley's Major Verse: The Narrative and Dramatic Poetry* 34). One *can*, I think, read the passage and realize that our Poet is isolated not only from human community, but also from human audience. The Poet is on his way to death, and in despair, and he is isolated because he is hot in pursuit of a dream-phantom.

36. In *Shelley's Process*, Jerrold Hogle suggests that the logic on which the narrator closes *Alastor* aligns him with the side of Shelley's early writing years, one which "demands one source and center for all 'subordinate' relationships." Thus, Hogle continues, the narrator's conclusion refuses "to recognize what he has done with Mother Nature and what the Poet has attempted with his dream-maiden and death" (57). I would add that Shelley is slowly coming to recognize his affinity with the narrator, but that his treatment of him betrays a guilty consciousness of his uncertainty over how to remedy the matter.

Chapter Two

1. William Shelley was born on January 24, but died three years later.

2. *Reveries of a Solitary Walker* is on Mary Shelley's reading list of Shelley's reading for 1815.

3. (I quote *Julie ou La Nouvelle Héloïse* in the French for lack of a good widely available English translation.) In *Blindness and Insight: Essays in the Rhetoric of Contemporary Criticism* Paul de Man cites this and other passages from Rousseau, cautioning that they are uttered by a fictional character, and do not contradict his own thesis that "It is always against the explicit

assertion of the writer that readers degrade the fiction by confusing it with a reality from which it has forever taken leave" (17). It is, however, Shelley's primary anxiety that both he and his readers tend to degrade reality by confusing it with their own fictions.

4. Such approbation of faith, however, is not without ulterior (rhetorical) motives. On the issue of Hume's vacillation in matters of religion, and its relationship to Shelley's skepticism, see C.E. Pulos's *The Deep Truth: A Study of Shelley's Skepticism*, especially 23ff.

5. Shelley's views differ radically from those of the skeptics on many points; it is their influence on his thought which is to the point, not a wholesale extrapolation of skeptical thought onto Shelleyan views. As a myriad of critics have pointed out, one is always faced with balancing Shelley's skepticism with his idealism. More recently, Andrew J. Welburn, in *Power and Self-Consciousness in the Poetry of Shelley*, has suggested that for Shelley "Individual consciousness is sustained only in the dynamic tension between them [skepticism and idealism], where the boundaries of the self and the world remain to be drawn and defended by the individual mind" (22).

6. I am, however, fully conscious of the difficulty in locating true "poetic forebears" for Shelley. As a "second generation" Romantic, he would have seen Wordsworth, Coleridge, and Southey more as elder brothers than as genuine forebears, even as his approach to eighteenth-century formal considerations would have been partly influenced by his reading of his elder contemporaries. For Shelley, *ut pictura poesis* was still the received orthodoxy.

7. Stuart Curran clarifies an important context for English Romantic hymnody: "The congregational assumptions of the hymn, for instance, are controverted by the intense privacy of most literary hymns in the English tradition and by the tendency of Protestant sects to emphasize the solitary, individualistic nature of religious experience. . . . By the time of the English Romantics, indeed, hymn writing was all but identified in the popular mind with Protestant Dissent" (*Poetic Form* 57).

8. See also Harold Bloom's *Shelley's Mythmaking*, in which (the early) Bloom claims that "Mont Blanc" and "Hymn to Intellectual Beauty" mark the beginning of "Shelley's mature mythopoeia," of "a primal vision; that is, a strictly poetic attempt to compete with religion and philosophy as a coherent presenter of ultimate realities" (24). It is my claim, of course, that particularly in his self-conscious uses of hymnic form Shelley is engaging in

dialogue with religion and philosophy, but that his difficulties with expression and with assured comprehension of the ineffable, render him both unable and unwilling to make of poetry a "coherent presenter of ultimate realities."

9. Earl Wasserman also notes the importance to Shelley of preserving potentially useful elements of Christianity, although Wasserman is not as interested in Shelley's self-consciousness with respect to his fictions: "For part of the poem's art consists in purging Christianity of its superstitions without destroying its abstract framework, or in revealing the irony that Christian terminology and conceptions can be transvalued by translation into the true religious framework" (*Critical Reading* 193).

10. See especially pages 77–88 of *Principles of Human Knowledge*, in which Berkeley expounds his notion of "signs" and their relationship to God. For Berkeley, the "natural philosopher" ought to engage in a search for and effort to understand "those signs instituted by the Author of Nature." This represents one version of the Adamic theory of language-origin, rejected by Locke and many others. Although rejected also by Shelley, it forms an important backdrop to his evolving understanding of language and tropes: if all language is man-made, how does one encode an idea of that which transcends humanity and language?

11. The essay is dated tentatively as 1817, and is therefore roughly within the time span of the philosophical framework of the hymns.

12. "Wordsworth's Poems" are on the Shelley Reading List for 1815 in Mary's *Journal*, and it is likely that the entry refers to Wordsworth's collection of that year.

13. This observation may serve as a correction to Roland Duerksen's claim, in *Shelley's Poetry of Involvement*, that the "light" of Intellectual Beauty shines "upon the mind's potentiality and upon real things perceived by the mind" (16).

14. The number of critics who have claimed an atheistic view for Shelley is too great to be enumerated here. It is always difficult to draw a line, of course, between a deconstruction of belief in an ineffable concept, and a deconstruction of the means which a poet has at his disposal for expression of a concept which he deems finally to be ineffable. It is my contention that Shelley's anxieties proceed upon the latter hypothesis.

15. See William Collins' "Ode to Peace," for example, which immediately personifies the abstract concept by giving it very physical characteristics: "O Thou, who bad'st thy Turtles bear / Swift from his Grasp thy golden Hair" (1–2). Charles Wesley's famous hymn for children, "Gentle

Jesus, Meek and Mild," would be an obvious example of the confident religious hymn.

16. It is important to remember, however, that Shelley first began reading Plato at college, and so was familiar with the philosopher's principal tenets long before his more mature reading of him was under way. See Joseph Barrell, *Shelley and the Thought of His Time*, 21. Furthermore, as many critics have pointed out, in 1817, in his translation of *The Symposium*, Shelley translated Plato's "Beauty" as "Intellectual Beauty."

17. Plato's elaboration of the problems of mimetic art can be most fruitfully explored in *The Protagoras*, *The Ion*, *The Phaedrus*, and of course *The Republic*.

18. There are certainly exceptions to this rule, and many eighteenth-century poetic challenges to the value of generalization. But the idea of generalization in eighteenth-century uses of language in general and of rhetorical tropes in particular was a standard against which all deviations were considered. On the various complexities of this issue, see especially Earl Wasserman, "The Inherent Values of Eighteenth-Century Personification," or Bertrand H. Bronson's article, "Personification Reconsidered," in *Facets of the Enlightenment*. In the latter paper, Bronson insists that for eighteenth-century authors, generalization "was one of the chief ways in which man transcended his private experience and became adult" (147).

19. For a brief discussion of public taste, see J. R. de J. Jackson: "During the Romantic period the reading public seems to have forgotten about the vein of poetry in the English tradition that conveyed unfamiliar ideas or expressed common ones in an unfamiliar way. . . . If the Romantics had confined their poems to a coterie of adepts, a larger audience might gradually have been cultivated, but the assumption that poetry should be accessible to all had taken such a hold that this possibility seems hardly to have been considered" (*Poetry of the Romantic Period* 187).

20. Angela Leighton and Kenneth Cameron, on the other hand, hold that Power and Intellectual Beauty are presented in the poem as two qualitatively distinct concepts. See Cameron, *Shelley: The Golden Years*, 242. Leighton suggests that "in spite of the poem's inspired celebration of the manifestation of Intellectual Beauty in the natural world, it nonetheless strains after knowledge of a different and more remote Power" (*Shelley and the Sublime* 53).

21. In *The Transforming Image*, Jean Hall takes a different view, for she claims that the hymn provides a good example of Shelley's progress toward seeing the "poem as an imaginary equivalent of the world—as a poetic

world that might be transformed by his poetic powers" (32). What it would mean to transform a poetic world with poetic powers is never sufficiently clarified by Hall.

22. In clarifying Jesus' assertion that one must not serve two masters, Shelley insists: "If we would profit by the wisdom of a sublime and poetical mind, we must beware of the vulgar error of interpreting literally. Nothing can well be more remote from truth than the literal and strict construction of such expressions as Jesus Christ delivers" ("Essay on Christianity" 209).

23. The word is also used in fascinating ways by Wordsworth, from "rolls through all things" in "Tintern Abbey," to "She was a thing" in the last Lucy poem, and even to his note to "The Thorn," where, drawing on a long established philosophical tradition, he insists that words can be viewed *as* things. As I have already noted in Chapter One, Shelley was intimately familiar with the claims about language made by such authors. He would have perhaps counted on the reader's more immediate association of "thing" with the idea of empirical object, but it is important to bear in mind that he also implicitly sets such associations against the more complicated history of "thing."

24. It has long been a famous story that, opposing Coleridge in playful fashion, in the hotel register at Chamonix and at other locations during the trip, Shelley signed himself, in Greek, "Democrat, Philanthropist and Atheist." Under the "destination" column, he indicated "L'Enfer." For further details, see Richard Holmes, *Shelley: The Pursuit*, 342. Shelley, as we have seen, consistently uses the term "atheist" to oppose himself to institutionalized forms of religion, especially Christianity; in any case, his opposition to the received orthodoxy expressed by Coleridge in his hymn is unmistakable. Harold Bloom, one of the first critics to elucidate the relationship between "Mont Blanc" and "Hymn Before Sun-Rise," goes so far as to suggest that "the posture of servility with which Coleridge proceeds to worship the Creator of this white leviathan" would likely have been offensive to many readers, "Shelley as a hypothetical one among them" (*Shelley's Mythmaking* 17).

25. In our sense-making efforts, it can be tempting to overlook such problematizations. In *Shelley's Mythmaking*, even a high-pitched Harold Bloom suggests that "Shelley is not content to describe the second term of his metaphor in its own particulars, but rather alternates its presentation by extensively looting the components of the suppressed first term. The justification for this mingling is that it enables the poet to write simultane-

ously on two levels of apprehension which can be understood on one level of meaning" (23). My argument proceeds on the assumption that Shelley knew it could never have been that easy.

26. In identifying "the everlasting universe of things" with "the source of human thought" I am arguing against a common (and I believe mistaken) critical assumption, one which originates in Earl Wasserman's attempt to see the poem in terms of a "One Mind" versus individual human mind distinction. Wasserman separates what he sees as the One Mind of line one from the tributary human thought of line five. The first is composed of rapidly flowing waves but the other is just a feeble brook, coming from secret springs. In this view, the "such as" simile applies to the source which joins the main flow of the river, but not to the river itself, which includes but goes far beyond merely human thought. See *A Critical Reading*, especially 222-25. More recently, in *Shelley's Process* Jerrold Hogle has offered a deconstructive reading, but where Wasserman sees "One Mind," Hogle sees "linguistic play of differences": "The individual psyche in 'Mont Blanc' arises out of, and is a differentiation within, an earlier, larger, centerless, and essentially linguistic play of differences and similarities. The 'source of human thought' does not bring 'its tribute' to larger cascades from outside the general confusion; it is formed 'Of water' too and so shares the basis of every emergence from the 'everlasting' flow. It is both a part of the flow and a particular riverbed or avenue carved out by the torrent in a particular direction" (75).

27. I am thinking in particular of discussions by J. Hillis Miller and Paul de Man, who treat especially "The Triumph of Life" in terms of the poem's use of metaphor to efface the possibilities of definitive meaning. See Paul de Man, "Shelley Disfigured," *The Rhetoric of Romanticism*, and J. Hillis Miller's chapter on Shelley in *The Linguistic Moment*. I have chosen to cite the Simpson quotation here because it is more useful and more suggestive than most mainstream deconstructionist readings. I by no means intend to suggest that Jerrold Hogle's weighty discussion of "Mont Blanc" is inconsiderable or unimportant, only that it ranges far beyond the strict confines of deconstruction as it has principally come down to us. But Hogle does offer readings which do correlate with, and enhance, Simpson's; for example, in *Shelley's Process* he reminds us that "any focal point temporarily chosen by the speaker of 'Mont Blanc' must always be, first, a reference to another one impinging on its space. Then, since each figure seeks itself inside the other and finds only the seeking-outside-itself already there, the interplay, still needing an 'other' to help define it, defers to a third

point (or even a fourth) that seems to ground the others while also depending on them for its status as a ground" (76).

28. See M. H. Abrams, "Structure and Style in the Greater Romantic Lyric," in Harold Bloom's *Romanticism and Consciousness*.

Chapter Three

1. The details of the various changes Shelley was forced to make to the poem form a fascinating story, but are beyond the scope of this discussion. (For a comprehensive discussion, see *Shelley and His Circle V*, 141–67.) It must be remembered, however, that Shelley had initially described the lovers as biological brother and sister, not brother and adoptive sister. So while we examine his attempt in the poem to reach a true "public," we ought also to remember that he also meant to shock them, perhaps even unconsciously wished to be *less* accessible to the uninitiated multitude (those for whom mountains are only mountains). His disclaimer to Thomas Moore, in a letter of 16 December 1817, is not very convincing: "The truth is, that the seclusion of my habits has confined me so much within the circle of my own thoughts, that I have formed to myself a very different measure of approbation or disapprobation for actions than that which is in use among mankind; and the result of that peculiarity, contrary to my intention, revolts and shocks many who might be inclined to sympathise with me in my general views" (*Letters* 1: 582). Shelley's need to put himself above the normative moral standards of the rest of humanity, and his wish that his own mind could truly insulate him from the horrors he was facing at the hands of an unsympathetic external world, are resonant of the kind of ambiguities and moral difficulties that are manifested in Laon himself.

2. Michael Henry Scrivener suggests that Shelley alludes to the French Revolution mainly as a convenient vehicle, one that enables him to deal with something else: "The principal obstacle to comprehending the poem historically is to see it only in relation to the French Revolution, which is actually a symbol for the English situation of 1816–1817" (*Radical Shelley* 128). If this is so, then we have allegory translating into literal truth which itself becomes an allegory of another literal truth. This suggests the same kind of predicament that Shelley encountered in "Mont Blanc."

3. In *Shelley's Theory of Poetry*, Earl J. Schulze points to the incest motif in the poem, and concludes that "Shelley deliberately inverts traditional

symbols to stress the anti-utopian or sinister potential in social institutions which, through restrictive, artificial codes, are incompatible with natural human desire" (51). I do not disagree with this interpretation, but I think Shelley is also on the alert to the sometimes inadvertent sinister potential of traditional symbols themselves, and not only as they reflect on the sinister aspects of particular institutions.

4. One must also remember, of course, that Shelley would have been disinclined to abandon such motifs for reasons that also take into account the literary climate for poetic narratives with supernatural and fantastic plots. The rage for the Gothic novel in the 1790s bore issue in a rage for the fantastic poetic romance in the early nineteenth century: Southey's *Curse of Kehama* (1810), an Indian tale of supernatural action, and *Thalaba the Destroyer* (1801), an Arabian romance full of magical happenings, had been great favorites of Shelley in his youth. Certainly such poems as Walter Scott's *The Lay of the Last Minstrel* (1805) and *Marmion* (1808) are what we would today refer to as escapist fiction, and are replete with extravagant and supernatural events; in fact *Marmion* even makes explicit political and didactic points—projections for England's future, praise for her political heroes of past—by including verse epistles to introduce each canto. I am claiming, however, that precisely because such conventions were part of the normative climate of taste, of which Shelley was throughout his life suspicious, he would have been aware of the ominous implications of supernatural tale-telling in a poem that seeks to remedy the potentially sterile complacency of his audience's consciousness.

5. In *Allegory: The Theory of a Symbolic Mode*, Angus Fletcher clarifies the value and intention of anagogy as distinct from allegory, in ways that are suggestive of the kind of issues Shelley was exploiting. Employing *The Faerie Queen* as his point of departure, Fletcher asserts: "It is the peculiar character of true myth, we may say, to enforce acceptance of a totally ambivalent imagery, whereas true allegory would achieve a rigid displacement of one aspect of the ambivalence. . . . anagogy implies a mythic, visionary structure that goes beyond the poetry of strict correspondences which we normally call 'allegory'" (321–22). Shelley is aiming for some form of mythical, anagogic vision; the problem is that in *The Revolt of Islam* he does not successfully distinguish between his impulse for allegory and his impulse for anagogic epic. It is of the utmost significance, however, that he embarks on *The Revolt* in an attempt to reach a larger vision within a more comprehensive structure.

6. Shelley's lifelong preoccupation with skeptical thought may yet

again be discerned, although his continuing struggle here for some sort of affirmation of faith signals an ever increasing need to qualify the skeptics. Hume's *A Treatise of Human Nature* treats belief in the afterlife in a manner that might have struck resonant chords in Shelley:

> The strongest figures are infinitely inferior to the subject. . . . A future state is so far remov'd from our comprehension, and we have so obscure an idea of the manner, in which we shall exist after the dissolution of the body, that all the reasons we can invent, however strong in themselves, and however much assisted by education, are never able with slow imaginations to surmount this difficulty, or bestow a sufficient authority and force on the idea. I rather choose to ascribe this incredulity to the faint idea we form of our future condition, deriv'd from its want of resemblance to the present life, than to that deriv'd from its remoteness. (114)

Hume's "want of resemblance to the present life" describes exactly one of Shelley's anxieties.

7. The pamphlets are entitled *A Proposal For Putting Reform to the Vote Throughout the Kingdom* and *We Pity the Plumage, But Forget the Dying Bird. An Address to the People on the Death of Princess Charlotte.* See Michael Henry Scrivener's *Radical Shelley* 108–39, for a full description and analysis of Shelley's 1817 political concerns and their manifestations in his writing.

8. It is with such facts in mind that Stuart Curran suggests that, while *Queen Mab* "relates a finished vision," *The Revolt of Islam* is concerned with how that vision is to be attained (*Annus Mirabilis* 26). Though doubtless Shelley is sincerely calling for a liberation of human consciousness, in ways that can pave the way for reform, I think that the plethora of impracticalities and impossibilities described in the poem preclude the possibility of its use as a manual for effective revolution. I will cite only a few examples here: Laon's unlikely rescue by the kindly hermit in Canto Three; the success of Laon's speech about pacifism in Canto Five in preventing a riotous, blood-hungry multitude from killing Othman; the eagle that brings Cythna food in her under water cave in Canto Seven. I am not trying to suggest that Shelley (or Professor Curran) holds up such instances as examples of what is possible, but I would claim that Shelley himself sometimes loses sight of whatever desire he may have had to give concrete guidance to those with revolutionary potential.

9. See the *Apology* for the most illuminating illustration of Plato's view on this matter. Poetic inspiration is often a sign of at least temporary madness. In any case, in the *Apology* in particular Socrates insists that because

poets write under a divine influence, they do not, under normal circumstances, understand their own work.

10. That Shelley is writing under the burden of Plato's indictments is evident even in this respect, for the *Republic*'s invective against poetry also reminds us of the political and social inefficacy of the artist. Socrates' "apostrophe" to Homer speaks to Shelley's anxiety over his political efficacy: "'Friend Homer,' then we say to him, 'if you are only in the second remove from truth in what you say of virtue, and not in the third—not an image maker, that is, by our definition, an imitator—and if you are able to discern what pursuits make men better or worse in private or public life, tell us what State was ever better governed by your help? . . . but who says that you have been a good legislator to them and have done them any good?'" (*The Republic* 473)

11. This idea bears a qualified consonance with the thought of the period, at least among Shelley's immediate circle. William Hazlitt's 1818 introductory lecture in the *Lectures on the English Poets* series shares much in common with Wordsworth's essays, and also reminds us of the framework Shelley was both working within and rebelling against. In fact, Mary's *Journal* records that they became personally acquainted with Hazlitt in February 1817. By 1818 Shelley was of course in Italy, but Hazlitt's notions are very much a part of their common inheritance. In the lecture Hazlitt asserts that even if poetry "is a fiction, made up of what we wish things to be, and fancy that they are, because we wish them so, there is no other nor better reality" (*Lectures on the English Poets* 5: 3). Having established this, he goes on to speak more directly to the exclusivity of poetry's domain, in ways that also anticipate Eliot's "objective correlative": "It is the perfect coincidence of the image and the words with the feeling we have, and of which we cannot get rid in any other way, that gives an instant 'satisfaction to the thought'" (*Lectures on the English Poets* 5: 7). Shelley's understanding of the process also extends to *thoughts* which—adapting the language of Hazlitt's essay—we cannot bring into being in any other way.

12. Few critics have given an *exclusively* political reading; I am referring to the reading perspective or organizing bias. In *The Unacknowledged Legislator*, for example, P. M. S. Dawson claims that "The deliberate overturning of all limitation in *Prometheus Unbound* has a political rather than a personal relevance" (121); Angela Leighton claims that the poem is a "grand political reworking of the Prometheus myth," that "in *Prometheus Unbound* the desire to meet hidden powers and voices in the sublime landscape is linked to a political idealism which is new, and which makes of this work

Shelley's most consistently optimistic expression of the revolutionary purpose of writing" (*Shelley and the Sublime* 73); Michael Henry Scrivener reads the poem in its contemporary political context, and in the context of the explicitly political poems, unpublished in Shelley's lifetime, which were written during the *Prometheus Unbound* period. He is especially interested in the effect that "Peterloo" had on the writing of Act Four, which he reads as "a positive vision of realized idealism to inspire the post-Peterloo reform movement" (*Radical Shelley* 240).

13. In "Unsaying His High Language: The Problem of Voice in *Prometheus Unbound*," Susan Hawk Brisman offers a view of language and poetry in the poem which is important, useful, and interesting, but which, as will become clear, I take issue with on many counts. Her basic thesis is that the "Promethean voice" moves "from defiance to sympathy and love" (52), and that the "Promethean principle . . . denies that thoughts have sense and shape without words" (57–58). Thus she concludes that "the claim made for Promethean language is ontological as well as formal" (58). While I do not disagree that Shelley is wary of separating thought from words, I shall be arguing here that his skepticism denies him such glowing reports about the possibilities of language, even in a regenerated world.

14. This notion was axiomatic long before Shelley's career, and certainly in various contexts Locke, Rousseau, and others frequently refer to language as a system of "arbitrary signs" (see, for example, Rousseau's "A Discourse on the Origin of Inequality," in *The Social Contract and Discourses* 64).

15. See also Tilottama Rajan's interesting analysis of the relationship between reader and personae: "Panthea's attempt to voice her dream is an invitation to Asia as implied reader to re-cognize the dream she herself has had. As such, the dialogue between the two sisters serves as a model for the dialogue intended to occur between author and reader" (*Supplement of Reading* 308).

16. See *Shelley and His Circle VI*, 633–47, for a discussion of the date and text of the essay.

17. There are many more examples, I think, to support my view that the "clear knowledge" correlates with the nature and effect of communication. In addition to the passage in II.iv.72–77, cited above, there is also the qualification which the furies themselves offer. Hoping to firmly convince Prometheus that the "clear knowledge" he awakened leads to ruin, the furies cite first the example of Jesus: "His words outlived him like swift poi-

son / Withering up truth, peace, and pity" (*Prometheus Unbound*   I. 548–49). First the furies tell Prometheus that he provides "clear knowledge"; then to mock it, to show it in its worst possible distortion, they insist on the explanation that Jesus' "*words*" did live, but lived to destroy truth, peace and pity. Also, when Prometheus (and humankind) are freed, "Language is a perpetual Orphic song" (IV.415), partly because to free Prometheus is to liberate language from its enslaving role.

18. Similar sentiments are expressed in *Julian and Maddalo*, which was begun early in 1819, and which draws on conversations Shelley and Lord Byron had in Venice in the summer of 1818. Maddalo, the Byron figure and the more cynical of the two, laments: "Most wretched men / Are cradled into poetry by wrong, / They learn in suffering what they teach in song" (544–46).

19. Especially in the *Anatomy of Criticism*. See, for example, pages 105–6: "The efficient cause of civilization is work, and poetry in its social aspect has the function of expressing, as a verbal hypothesis, a vision of the goal of work and the forms of desire" (106).

20. Loosely following Northrop Frye, in "Intentional Structure of the Romantic Image" Paul de Man points to the paradox of the poetic image which derives from nostalgia for the natural object, which yet can only exist when its "transcendental presence is forgotten." He thus concludes: "The existence of the poetic image is itself a sign of divine absence, and the conscious use of poetic imagery an admission of this absence" (*Rhetoric of Romanticism* 6).

21. And tautology, as David Simpson remarks in the Introduction to his *Wordsworth and the Figurings of the Real*, "is the mode of narcissism" (xiii). The treatment of Jupiter suggests again the degree to which Shelley's later poetry is so deeply responsive to (and revisionary of) his own earlier efforts; *Alastor*, after all, virtually abandons the Poet-questor precisely at the point of his death-by-(qualified)-narcissism.

22. In *The Supplement of Reading*, Tilottama Rajan suggests that reading *Prometheus Unbound* in the context of Shelley's implied prescriptions for reading obviates the difficulties inherent in its self-conscious semiotic fractures: "The fourth act, in which Shelley stages an objectively unverifiable outcome in the theatre of his own mind, invites us to stage Shelley's vision in the theatre of *our* minds and thus bridge the gulf between intention and actuality conceded in the notion of lyrical drama" (308). This is a powerful and important insight, but one which, as I shall argue, must be

qualified by the still-tragic overtones even of Shelley's poetic triumphs. The triumph which the poem salvages from the ruins of failed vision cannot, I claim, fully bridge intention with actuality.

23. I will provide a selection of examples. Carlos Baker sees Demogorgon as "Necessity—an enigmatic amoral law in terms of which the struggle between the powers of good and those of evil has been carried on since the beginning" (*Shelley's Major Poetry* 94). Milton Wilson also sees him as a version of Necessity, but qualified by Humean skepticism, particularly over causation (*Shelley's Later Poetry* 138). In *Red Shelley*, an enthusiastic Paul Foot reads Demogorgon as representative of the unawakened masses, because "Demos in Greek means the people; Gorgon, the monster. Demogorgon is the 'people-monster'" (194). In *Shelley: The Golden Years* Kenneth Neill Cameron asserts: "Demogorgon's 'mighty law' is clearly the law of necessity, which controls events and actions that individuals believe are matters of personal decision or 'desires within'" (514); in *The Mutiny Within* James Rieger maintains: "Demogorgon is the product of Platonic and Gnostic syncretism and by virtue of that ancestry an exact emblem of the Shelleyan Imagination" (17); Richard Cronin, in *Shelley's Poetic Thoughts*, reads Demogorgon as an echo, as a shapeless mass who "can only articulate the thoughts of those who address him" (152).

24. For purposes of convenience, my pagination for the Hughes article refers to the Norton Critical Shelley edition.

25. Richard Cronin suggests that this seems to be "a classic expression of Platonic pathos, of the refusal to admire beauty, however glorious, unless it shadows Beauty" (*Shelley's Poetic Thoughts* 147). But Cronin goes on to cite the rest of Asia's apotheosis ("Though evil stain its work, and it should be / Like its creation, weak yet beautiful, / I could fall down and worship that and thee." 14–16), and then takes the initial interpretation farther, claiming that for Asia, "the two earths collapse into one another, for Asia realises that if evil is present in the actual earth then this must betoken a flaw in the ideal earth of which it is a shadow; evil in the creation can derive only from evil in the creator" (147). I must disagree with this interesting interpretation, first because Plato's realm of Ideal Forms does not participate in the world of becoming—the world of becoming imitates the Ideal because it is qualitatively different from it, and so by nature flawed. It would be the a priori assumption of virtually any variety of Platonist, in fact, that evil in the shadow betokens the inevitable result of mere imitation of the Ideal. But my main claim is that the emphasis in the lines is on the predilection for displacement of the actual, on the virtually unconscious act

of valuation of the actual exclusively in terms of the projected form we give to the Ideal.

26. See also *Lines Written Among the Euganean Hills*, written in the autumn of 1818:

> And my spirit which so long
> Darkened this swift stream of song,—
> Interpenetrated lie
> By the glory of the sky:
> Be it love, light, harmony,
> Odour, or the soul of all
> Which from heaven like dew doth fall,
> Or the mind which feeds this verse
> Peopling the lone universe. (311–19)

The poet's felicitous indecision about the source of his relief is a healthy sign for him. It may be the temporal world by which he is "interpenetrated," but it may also be the mind's capacity to create fictions. Either way, and most importantly, the deep "glory of the sky" cannot be fixed in any particular image.

27. Michael O'Neill also offers a useful analysis:

> What Shelley dramatizes throughout is the unavoidability of interpretation. Characters are shown choosing to see or read reality in a certain light and, as a consequence, shaping reality. The same burden and the same freedom are proffered to the reader by a text that is endlessly generous in possibilities of interpretation. It is, then, the ability of the shadow world to resist our desire for unequivocal meaning which makes it an apt emblem of the imaginative openness of mind that Shelley wishes to encourage. (95)

28. See Albert J. Kuhn, "English Deism and the Development of Romantic Mythological Syncretism" and Earl Wasserman, *Shelley: A Critical Reading*, 271–72. Wasserman goes so far as to claim that syncretism "is at the heart of *Prometheus Unbound*" (271). I disagree with Wasserman's assertion that "it is Shelley's assumption that if all creeds, or their mythic embodiments, were shaped into the highest form they admit, they would be precisely translatable into each other" (271). I would claim that the only translation Shelley would apply to all myths is that they are all unanswerable to epistemological doubt.

29. I therefore subscribe to a view directly contrary to that of Jean Hall,

who offers instead that "As with Shelley's other poems, *Prometheus Unbound* converts the universe into a poetic universe—it is an imaginary world that indirectly mirrors the poet's self" (88). Shelley is instead showing the dangers of such conversions. A far more formidable thesis which I also take issue with is advanced by Paul Fry in his magisterial book, *The Reach of Criticism*. Fry contends that "the deep truth is not imageless but an image," because the poetic process, in defamiliarizing objects, works thus: "something specific, concrete, and quotidian is torn aside to reveal something specific, concrete, and unusual"; he thus concludes that "the similarity between surface and subsurface is greater than the contrast" (140). I claim, of course, a more theistic Shelley than does Professor Fry.

30. Shelley in fact was very disappointed with most of the canto, and he seems, among other things, to be alluding to the cynicism and virtual misanthropy of Byron's lines about "the beings of the mind," when he writes to Peacock: "The spirit in which it is written is, if insane, the most wicked & mischievous insanity that ever was given forth. It is a kind of obstinate & selfwilled folly in which he hardens himself" (17 or 18 December 1818; *Letters* 2: 58). I cite one further stanza as example of the kind of posture Shelley struggles against:

> The beings of the mind are not of clay;
> Essentially immortal, they create
> And multiply in us a brighter ray
> And more beloved existence: that which Fate
> Prohibits to dull life, in this our state
> Of mortal bondage, by these spirits supplied
> First exiles, then replaces what we hate;
> Watering the heart whose early flowers have died,
> And with a fresher growth replenishing the void.
> (*Childe Harold's Pilgrimage* 4–5)

The "beings of the mind" referred to are literary images, mythic figures (Shylock, Othello, Pierre) like the Jupiter I have been discussing. See Charles Robinson, *Shelley and Byron: The Snake and Eagle Wreathed in Fight*, 68–80, for an interesting and more comprehensive discussion of Shelley and Canto Four.

31. I am not dismissing the political poems of 1819, especially not *The Mask of Anarchy*, which does employ an obtrusively allegorical structure to make an almost entirely political point. Most of these are occasional poems,

though, especially the *Mask*, written in response to the "Peterloo" massacre on 16 August 1819 in St. Peter's Field, Manchester. Given Shelley's abiding interest in poetry's political inefficacy, it is not surprising that he should continue to try his hand at such endeavors. A poem that makes a fairly simple political statement is inoffensive enough, and would not have given rise to the kind of angst I have been discussing; my interest has been with those poems which attempt a larger vision of humanity, or of ultimate meaning, and how such poems can comport themselves toward political and social issues.

32. This was a deliberately radical notion for Shelley, even given the climate of generic experimentation among his contemporaries. He would have been well familiar with Samuel Johnson's statement, in his *Life of Cowley*, that writers concerned only with novelty will not produce greatness, "for great things cannot have escaped former observation" (1: 21). Not only is Shelley searching for new "things," he is hoping that one day we will have an entirely new art for observing them.

33. Milton Wilson also finds this puzzling, suggesting that "it is difficult to decide exactly what is meant by 'ruling them like slaves,' unless it simply means the application of scientific discoveries which control disease, and thereby prolong life, but do not finally destroy mutability" (*Shelley's Later Poetry* 174).

34. In *The Prelude*, which Shelley could not have read, Wordsworth's epiphanic moments are "spots *of* time," and they renovate a mind which is coming to terms with its consciousness of progression through time.

35. In *A Study of English Romanticism*, Northrop Frye comments on the common Shelleyan situation: "If man could lose his specifically human consciousness, he would also lose his specifically human pain and misery; but it would be a poor exchange" (96).

36. In "Speech and Silence in *The Cenci*," Michael Worton cites this and other passages to advance an interesting thesis, which, though somewhat different in approach from my own, provides a more comprehensive discussion of this central motif.

Chapter Four

1. See Holmes, *Shelley: The Pursuit* 629–31, for a brief discussion of Shelley's infatuation.

2. Paul Fry claims that only religious allegory refers to ineffable concepts. I disagree with this formulation, as I shall be illustrating in my dis-

cussion of *A Defence of Poetry*; but in discussing the *Defence*'s notion of the allegory of religion Fry does, in passing, make an important observation about *Epipsychidion*: "in any less purely theistic allegory, when interpretation is a matter of finding parallels for certain figures, then plainly the hidden sense is not ineffable but a *paraphrase* that has its own definite shape and purport" (*The Reach of Criticism* 139). I shall be claiming that there can be no paraphrase for abstract concepts, and that this is one of the primary motivating anxieties for Shelley in the poem.

3. In his discussion of *Epipsychidion* in *Shelleyan Eros*, William Ulmer explores the importance of the poem's Dantean legacy, which stresses, he reminds us, "the inability of language to represent or actualize referents" (133). As such, Ulmer's basic thesis is that "In *Epipsychidion* the interdependence of language and desire in the Shelleyan imagination achieves definitive illustration" (131). In my own reading, I would factor in the anxiety over the quotidian which is one effect of the language-desire dialectic.

4. See Shelley's letter to William Gifford, Editor of *The Quarterly Review*, which had published a very hostile review of *Endymion*. Although Shelley concedes that the poem is in many ways defective, he insists on the promise that it shows, and cites a few passages as particularly worthy. Shelley's strong feelings about the review hint that the ungenerous reception of Keats's poetic romance struck him, perhaps unconsciously, as a warning he might have better heeded himself (Letters, November 1820; 2: 251–53).

5. See *The Phaedrus* for the most comprehensive of Plato's discussions of this issue. I will cite one representative example:

> Thus far I have been speaking of the fourth and last kind of madness, which is imputed to him who, when he sees the beauty of earth, is transported with the recollection of the true beauty; he would like to fly away, but he cannot; he is like a bird fluttering and looking upward and careless of the world below; and he is therefore thought to be mad. And I have shown this of all inspirations to be the noblest and highest and the offspring of the highest to him who has or shares in it, and that he who loves the beautiful is called a lover because he partakes of it. (*Phaedrus* 156)

6. In *Shelley: A Critical Reading*, Earl Wasserman offers a comparison with the Song of Solomon which sees the biblical text as a more important influence than I grant it here. See 419–30, passim.

7. On lines 25–32, see also Michael O'Neill: "Each image represents a new attempt and a new failure to define completely. The passage yields a paradoxically double sense that words are inadequate and that they manage adequately to tell us this. They convince us of the 'splendour' of their subject. The final image suggests a reciprocity between poem and woman" (*The Human Mind's Imaginings* 158). It is just this supposed reciprocity between poem and woman that I am querying.

8. Michael Henry Scrivener does not see such renderings as a problem: "The soul that loves transcends actuality and creates in another sphere a 'world' lacking the restrictions of the imprisoning world. . . . For Shelley 'Emily' is not just a beautiful young woman he is attracted to, but the vessel in which he perceives the Ideal he has been searching for his entire life" (*Radical Shelley* 269).

9. It is for this reason that Emily has sometimes been seen exclusively as a refined Idea: Carlos Baker asserts: " 'Epipsychidion' was not in its deeper movements a love-poem to a particular Italian girl, though it masqueraded as one. It was Shelley's attempt to arrest and to project an apparition with which his imagination had always been haunted. . . . The Idea which bears the name of Emilia in 'Epipsychidion' may be defined as that part of the inmost soul which participates in the world-soul" (*Shelley's Major Poetry* 219). I am claiming, however, that it is not as simple even as this.

10. Webb does qualify his observation by claiming that "Shelley could never conceive of a poem as autotelic. . . . It was possible, desirable and cathartic even, to compose verses which were personal and which relieved one's own feelings, but the essential aim of poetry was grander and higher" (*Shelley: A Voice Not Understood* 85). I acknowledge that Webb and critics like him do offer these qualifications, but they still neglect the problematic posed by Shelley's contrary impulses, and the anxiety attendant upon belief in poetry's higher value.

11. Here there is a subtle evocation of Spenser's Bower of Bliss in Book Two of *The Faerie Queen*, where nature is ominously presented as pre-lapsarian but also indistinguishable from art.

12. Michael O'Neill cites lines 470–76, and suggests an interesting conclusion which bears upon my own: "The writing 'concedes' the presence of fictionalizing through its use of simile and through images which bring about a revelation of the 'isle's beauty.' In evoking this revelation it lays claim to offer more than fictionalizing" (*The Human*

Mind's Imaginings 175). I would suggest that the poem finally offers very little other than fictionalizing. Becoming aware of one's own fictions is not tantamount to offering something beyond them.

13. Stuart Sperry offers a useful interpretation of the passage, which relates it to the basic problematic of the ineffable: "The fact is that language, even the symbolic language of verse, depends ultimately on nature, and can only approach those idealizations conceived within the self" (*Shelley's Major Verse: The Narrative and Dramatic Poetry* 180).

14. See Shelley's affectionate letter to Peacock of 15 February 1821 (*Letters* 2: 261), in which he gives a very brief, initial, and indeed untroubled response to *The Four Ages of Poetry*. In the letter he urges Peacock to reconsider the *Ion*, probably because he had in mind its insistence upon the divine inspiration of poets.

15. I again find myself in disagreement with Paul Fry's important account of Shelley's premises: "His most profound contribution to a philosophical basis for poetics, a contribution that can be found also in Longinus and Dryden, is his having questioned the dualism at the heart of most accounts of knowledge and creation: content and form, thought and expression, truth and verification, and so on" (*The Reach of Criticism* 159).

16. Two assertions of Sidney's are particularly apposite here: "And the metaphysic, though it be in the second and abstract notions, and therefore be counted supernatural, yet doth he indeed build upon the depth of nature. . . . Nature never set forth the earth in so rich tapestry as divers poets have done, neither with pleasant rivers, fruitful trees, sweet smelling flowers, nor whatsoever else may make the too much loved earth more lovely" (*An Apology for Poetry* 14–15).

17. See also Earl J. Schulze, who discusses the relationship between imagination and world in the *Defence* in ways that bear some consonance with my own analysis: "Imagination produces a type of belief, but a type for which there is no evidence or demonstration beyond its own presence, its own vivid experience, here and now. Imaginative belief is, therefore, distinct from belief in nature, without which, he feels, mind could not exist, consciousness would cease. Imaginative belief arises out of consciousness, out of 'an intense and vivid apprehension of life,'; the belief in nature gives rise to consciousness itself" (*Theory of Poetry* 76).

18. See John W. Wright's *Shelley's Myth of Metaphor*, especially pages 29–32, for a concise discussion of Shelley's understanding of relational apprehension.

19. William Keach also notes that Shelley's view of language becomes increasingly troubled in the *Defence*: "Yet the more specific he becomes in examining its unique resources, the more likely he is to reveal an underlying linguistic skepticism that runs throughout the *Defence* like a counterplot" (*Shelley's Style* 22).

20. For a full discussion of the nature of the relationship between the two poets, and its bearing on *Adonais*, see Donald Reiman's essay in *Shelley and His Circle V*, 399–427.

21. But see Angela Leighton, who notes Shelley's psychological detachment from the "facts" of Keats's death while he was writing (*Shelley and the Sublime* 129). That he did not know the actual details of the death is of minimal importance compared to the fact that a human being whom Shelley had known, had liked, and had admired was dead at so young an age.

22. Shelley's letter to Horace Smith underlines this obsession, even though he is less than genuine about his interest in metaphysics: "I am glad you like 'Adonais,' and, particularly, that you do not think it metaphysical, which I was afraid it was. I was resolved to pay some tribute of sympathy to the unhonoured dead, but I wrote, as usual, with a total ignorance of the effect that I should produce" (14 September 1821; *Letters* 2: 349). To be "afraid" that it is metaphysical is to be afraid that its clear gestures towards metaphysics deflect attention from the empirical world.

23. Edwin Silverman's *Poetic Synthesis in Shelley's Adonais* provides a full account of sources for the poem and of the pastoral elegy convention. He cites Spenser's *Astrophel*, the elegy for Sidney, as Shelley's primary influence.

24. Critics have been very divided on this issue, though. Earl Wasserman (*Critical Reading* 462–502, passim) and Kenneth Neill Cameron (*Golden Years* 422–44, passim) reject the standard New Critical view that the poem is basically Platonic in orientation, in favour of advancing a perspective of radical skepticism for the poem.

25. In a well-known letter to Charles Ollier of 25 September 1821, Shelley insists that his elegy "is the least imperfect of my compositions" (*Letters* 2: 355).

26. See, for example, lines 64–66 of "Lycidas": "Alas! What boots it with uncessant care / To tend the homely slighted Shepherd's trade, / And strictly meditate the thankless Muse?"

27. One must, however, note Ross Woodman's excellent account of

the poem's anagogical vision which, he argues, motivates the entire poem: "The anagogical dimension of *Adonais* provides the focus of the entire poem. It is the energizing principle which compels the poet to press on towards the object of knowledge as distinct from the mythical account which defines the limits of his art. Shelley's goal is the 'deep truth' which is 'imageless.' The dialectic of sacred passion drives the poet, as it drives Dante in the *Paradiso*, beyond imagery to its primal source" (*Apocalyptic Vision* 158–59). Shelley, I have been arguing, does try to push on to the imageless truth, but he is never certain as to what the "primal source" of his imagery might be. In the later Shelley, it is precisely this drive towards anagogy which prescribes his emphatic attention to the quotidian.

Chapter Five

1. See William Keach's valuable discussion of the poem as "a subtly muted variation on the *carpe diem* invitation genre that includes poems like Herrick's 'Corinna's going a Maying'" (*Shelley's Style* 209).

2. Again, Wordsworth's "To My Sister" is apposite, for that poem marks "the first mild day of March," and in exhorting Dorothy to "Come forth and feel the sun," Wordsworth also allegorizes a meaning to the mild weather:

> Love, now a universal birth,
> From heart to heart is stealing,
> From earth to man, from man to earth:
> —It is the hour of feeling.
>
> One moment now may give us more
> Than years of toiling reason:
> Our minds shall drink at every pore
> The spirit of the season. ("To My Sister" 21–28)

Wordsworth's "heart to heart" is uttered from within an entirely different syntactical context, but given the consonance of subject matter, the evocation may still stand. In any case, it is significant that Wordsworth envisions in his invitation poem a cyclical pattern of renewal that Shelley denies himself. Shelley's answer to Wordsworth's "One moment" is, in the Jane poems (and in spite of "Ode to the West Wind"), truly just *one* moment.

3. Judith Chernaik sees this as less of a problem, offering a useful reading of Nature in the poem with which I take issue:

> The account of wintry woods and sea is the kind of natural description at which Shelley is unsurpassed, in which physical life, and the meaning it embodies and evokes, effortlessly pass one into the other. The whole of nature—land, sea, and sky—seems to have a life of its own, whose secrets are bare to the eye of the poet. It is as if nature, in its multiplicity and continual process, revealed to him the secret of unity and timelessness—in the "wild woods" where nature is not bound or limited, where day and night, winter and summer, earth and ocean, meet and appear to be merged into one. (*The Lyrics of Shelley* 171)

I am claiming that the poem offers such sentimentality only superficially.

4. The sonnet, dated by the Norton editors as probably before the end of 1819 (*Shelley's Poetry and Prose* 312n4), bears obvious similarities with lines from *Prometheus Unbound* (especially III.ii.190–92). I quote the first five lines: "Lift not the painted veil which those who live / Call Life; though unreal shapes be pictured there / And it but mimic all we would believe / With colours idly spread,—behind, lurk Fear / And Hope, twin Destinies" (1–5).

5. See especially William Keach, *Shelley's Style* 202–8, who provides brief but important biographical details to help substantiate his claim that other characters haunt the Jane poems. Judith Chernaik's chapter, "The Magic Circle," in her *The Lyrics of Shelley* also provides important details and claims about Mary's absented presence in the poems. See pages 162–75 passim.

6. The effects of the canonization of deconstructive readings of "The Triumph of Life" are still very much with us. In fact, in the "Afterword" to *The Supplement of Reading*, Tilottama Rajan reminds us that "since the publication of *Deconstruction and Criticism*, the poem has become a synecdoche for the self-effacement of language and of romanticism as a cultural project that continues to mobilize the economy of criticism" (351).

7. But the single most influential reading, of course, has been Paul de Man's "Shelley Disfigured." Jerrold Hogle and Tilottama Rajan, among others, have also provided penetrating and important deconstructive readings of "The Triumph of Life," though I would qualify them in the same manner in which I hope to qualify Miller.

8. See also Donald Reiman's *Shelley's "The Triumph of Life": A Critical*

Study, 100–109. Reiman approaches the issue of metaphor and simile in related (though ultimately different) ways. For example, he states of the simile: "He wanted to make quite clear, in many cases, that he was not *equating* two things but merely suggesting a *likeness* at one specific point of comparison or—as in extended, 'epic' similes—at several specific points. He was, in other words, attempting to avoid the vagueness and impressionism that some critics seem determined to find in his poetry" (101).

9. This is the well-known quotation from "On Life" that leads into Shelley's discussion of the "intellectual philosophy." See especially pages 477–78.

10. Angela Leighton, however, offers the most optimistic reading to date of "The Triumph of Life." Although she acknowledges that "much of the poem is a grotesque allegory of Life as a living death," her chapter also makes a claim for "the other sense of Life as an intense imaginative 'apprehension'" (*Shelley and the Sublime* 160). Therefore, of the chariot, she suggests: "It offers the onlooker a choice of interpretation, in being cold but like the noon, repellent yet fascinating, glaring yet blind. The description of the chariot presents the possibility both of inevitable destruction and of strange beauty" (161).

11. The best discussion of the influence of Dante's *Purgatorio* is by Earl Schulze, in his article "Allegory Against Allegory: 'The Triumph of Life.'" See especially pages 36–53 passim. I grant the precise details of Shelley's revisions of Dante (and of Petrarch) a less central role than does Professor Schulze, although I do acknowledge that the points of alleged departure identified by him are interesting and useful.

12. Here I am in strong disagreement with Earl Schulze, who sees the effacement of Rousseau's thoughts, and the subsequent fading of the shape all light, as indicative of a potential for re-creation and self-revelation which Rousseau does not grasp: "contingencies are erased not to encourage self-oblivion but to produce the freedom of self-reflection" ("Allegory" 53).

13. Paul de Man's view in "Shelley Disfigured" is again consonant with my own, but with the important qualifications that I have been offering: "We now understand the shape to be the figure for the figurality of all signification. The specular structure of the scene as a visual plot of light and water is not the determining factor but merely an illustration (*hypotyposis*) of a plural structure that involves natural entities only as principles of articulation among others. It follows that the figure is not naturally given or produced but that it is posited by an arbitrary act of language" (116). I am claiming that Shelley took the arbitrariness of such symbols for granted by

this stage in his career, and that his concern now is with the implications for the natural world. Shelley is striving towards a mode of signification whose attendant figurations at least do not *overly* embellish, or overly mislead.

14. I say *"this* Rousseau's" because Shelley is responding to those elements in Rousseau which he could most conveniently appropriate for his particular ends. Rousseau's own attitude to nature and to fictions is deeply ambivalent, and so when Shelley recalls us to his presumed nature-worship, he is also reminding us that things are not always as simple as they appear. He is, then, the perfect surrogate for Shelley, who yet prefers not to render *himself* as one so defeated. *Reveries of the Solitary Walker* provides a good example of Shelley's own ambivalent appropriation of Rousseau, for in the "Second Walk," he describes an encounter with a Great Dane that knocked him unconscious. The scene recalls the poem's description of his loss of consciousness at the hands of the "shape all light":

> Night was coming on. I saw the sky, some stars, and a few leaves. This first sensation was a moment of delight. I was conscious of nothing else. In this instant I was being born again, and it seemed as if all I perceived was filled with my frail existence. Entirely taken up by the present, I could remember nothing; I had no distinct notion of myself as a person, nor had I the least idea of what had just happened to me. I did not know who I was, nor where I was; I felt neither pain, fear, nor anxiety. I watched my blood flowing as I might have watched a stream, without even thinking that the blood had anything to do with me. (39)

The fact that Shelley seems to recall the effects of a Great Dane when rendering the effects of the shape all light is a tremendous parody. The dog is absolutely of the quotidian world, and the real Rousseau loses memory because he has had a great collision. In the light of such information, to lose consciousness because of a self-projected fiction seems all the more pathetic, even grimly humorous.

15. In *Shelley's Process* Jerrold Hogle reads more potential for optimism into the "shape all light" than I grant it here, although I must acknowledge the relevance and importance of his claims. He suggests that if we take a "more fluid, relational, unselfish, and transfer-based" understanding of the situation,

> The "shape all light" seen as a form of the One can then be read as an eternal motion both entering into and reconfigured by the imagination, as in fact a

motion interrelating and altering several eternal drives that helps generate but finally shifts beyond the Ones of Dante and Petrarch. . . . The incompleteness in signs can be seen and then used as renewal and extension of hope rather than its limit, denial, or death. The imagination, too, can happily come to see its function not as the worship of its own objectified power but as the release, realization, and extension of such renewals in 'vitally metaphorical' reveilings of existence as currently perceived. (337)

As my current chapter in particular makes clear, I believe that Shelley came to hold even the "vitally metaphorical" function of imagination as potentially suspect.

16. Tilottama Rajan's discussion of Rousseau's relationship to the reader and to the persona "Shelley" are relevant here:

Paradoxically, it is because 'Shelley' does not let him rest but deconstructs him that he comes to life, for to be deconstructed is to be read, and Rousseau is at least read, where 'Adonais' in some sense is killed with reverence. But more importantly it is through the power of speech that Rousseau returns to life, because until he speaks, he is simply a root in the hillside. The dialectic of author and reader, as Shelley dramatizes it here, is a complex one, which transforms writing into speech through a process in which the reader deconstructs the writer, but in which the writer also speaks back and in some sense deconstructs the reader. (*Supplement of Reading* 338–39)

Both reading and writing are problematized, then, but I would still claim that whatever the reader recuperates with respect to him, the entire scene of Rousseau's humiliation remains deeply disturbing, quite outside the bounds of any redeeming supplement.

17. See also Rousseau's *A Discourse on the Moral Effects of the Arts and Sciences*: "But so long as power alone is on one side, and knowledge and understanding alone on the other, the learned will seldom make great objects their study, princes will still more rarely do great actions, and the peoples will continue to be, as they are, mean, corrupt, and miserable" (28)

18. At this point it is instructive to remark Michael Henry Scrivener's analysis:

From "The Triumph of Life" one can extrapolate the following analysis: the failure of the French Revolution was due to the inability of true wisdom to emerge from the Enlightenment, in which power and knowledge were too closely linked, and adequate scope was not given to imagination; the failure of Rousseau was not the result of an excess of lust for political or economic power, but of an idealism that overreaches itself. Rousseau was creative, if also imperfect, and left a valuable heritage of libertarian "beacons," the truly use-ful results of the Enlightenment and French Revolution. (*Radical Shelley* 309–10)

I take, clearly, a less strictly political approach to the poem, but, since I am emphasizing the quotidian concerns of Shelley, his struggle to maintain consciousness of his temporal reality, I am very sympathetic to Scrivener's analysis.

19. In *Shelley's Mythmaking* Harold Bloom sees the scene as the begin-ning of Rousseau's *re*birth, "a symbolic representation of that process of rebirth described by Wordsworth in the 'Intimations' ode, in which a poet passes from his initial vision into a time when vision ceases in its original sense, and another kind of vision may or may not succeed it" (263).

20. Shelley may well have had in mind Mary's (and his own) traumas in coping with the deaths of Clara and William. A comment that Shelley offers in a letter to Claire Clairmont, who had been suffering from ill health, is highly suggestive in this matter of the failure of refined perception to obviate real ills: "How is your Health? . . . I am positive and most anxious on this subject,—for ill-health is one of the evils that is not a dream, and the reality of which every year, if you neglect it, will make more impressive" (31 March 1822; *Letters* 2: 403).

Bibliography

Aarsleff, Hans. *The Study of Language in England 1780–1860*. Princeton, NJ: Princeton University Press, 1967.

——. *From Locke to Saussure: Essays on the Study of Language and Intellectual History*. Minneapolis: University of Minnesota Press, 1982.

Abbey, Lloyd. *Destroyer and Preserver: Shelley's Poetic Skepticism*. Lincoln: University of Nebraska Press, 1979.

Abrams, M. H. *The Mirror and the Lamp: Romantic Theory and the Critical Tradition*. London: Oxford University Press, 1953.

——. *Natural Supernaturalism: Tradition and Revolution in Romantic Literature*. New York: Norton, 1971.

——. "Structure and Style in the Greater Romantic Lyric." In Bloom, *Romanticism and Consciousness*, 201–29.

Addison, Joseph and Richard Steele. *The Spectator*. 4 vols. London: J. M. Dent; New York: E. P. Dutton, 1951.

Allott, Miriam, ed. *Essays on Shelley*. Totowa, NJ: Barnes and Noble, 1982.

Armstrong, Isobel. *Language as Living Form in Nineteenth-Century Poetry*. Sussex: Harvester Press, 1982.

Baker, Carlos Heard. *Shelley's Major Poetry: The Fabric of a Vision*. Princeton, NJ: Princeton University Press, 1948.

Baker, John Ross. "Poetry and Language in Shelley's 'Defence of Poetry.'" *Journal of Aesthetics and Art Criticism* 39 (1981): 437–49.

Baker, Joseph Ellis. *Shelley's Platonic Answer to a Platonic Attack on Poetry*. Iowa City: Iowa University Press, 1965.

Barcus, James E, ed. *Shelley: The Critical Heritage*. London: Routledge and Kegan Paul, 1975.

Barrell, Joseph. *Shelley and the Thought of his Time*. New Haven, CT: Yale University Press, 1947.

Barzun, Jaques. *Romanticism and the Modern Ego*. Boston: Little, Brown, 1943.

Becht, Ronald E. "Shelley's *Adonais*: Formal Design and the Lyric Speaker's Crisis of Imagination." *Studies in Philology* 78 (1981): 194–210.

Behrendt, Stephen. *Shelley and His Audiences*. Lincoln: University of Nebraska Press, 1989.

Berkeley, George. *Principles of Human Knowledge and Three Dialogues Between Hylas and Philonous*. Ed. Roger Woolhouse. London: Penguin, 1988.

——. *Three Dialogues Between Hylas and Philonous*. Ed. Colin M. Turbayne. New York: Liberal Arts Press, 1954.

Black, Max. *Models and Metaphors: Studies in Language and Philosophy*. Ithaca, NY: Cornell University Press, 1962.

Blank, G. Kim. *Wordsworth's Influence on Shelley: A Study in Poetic Authority*. New York: St. Martin's Press, 1988.

Bloom, Harold. *The Anxiety of Influence: A Theory of Poetry*. London: Oxford University Press, 1973.

———. *Poetry and Repression: Revisionism from Blake to Stevens*. New Haven, CT: Yale University Press, 1976.

———. *The Ringers in the Tower: Studies in Romantic Tradition*. Chicago: University of Chicago Press, 1971.

———, ed. *Romanticism and Consciousness: Essays in Criticism*. New York: W.W. Norton, 1970.

———. *Shelley's Mythmaking*. Ithaca, NY: Cornell University Press, 1959; 1969.

———. *The Visionary Company: A Reading of English Romantic Poetry*. London: Faber, 1962; Ithaca, NY: Cornell University Press, 1971.

Bloom, Harold et al. *Deconstruction and Criticism*. New York: Seabury, 1979.

Bostetter, Edward E. *The Romantic Ventriloquists: Wordsworth, Coleridge, Keats, Shelley and Byron*. Seattle: Washington University Press, 1963.

Brisman, Leslie. "Mysterious Tongue: Shelley and the Language of Christianity." *Texas Studies in Literature and Language*, 23 (1981): 389–417.

———. *Romantic Origins*. Ithaca, NY: Cornell University Press, 1978.

Brisman, Susan Hawk. "'Unsaying His High Language': The Problem of Voice in *Prometheus Unbound*." *Studies in Romanticism* 16 (1977): 51–86.

Bronson, Bertrand H. "Personification Reconsidered." In *Facets of the Enlightenment: Studies in English Literature and Its Contexts*. Berkeley: University of California Press, 1968.

Brown, Nathaniel. *Sexuality and Feminism in Shelley*. Cambridge, MA: Harvard University Press, 1979.

Burnet, James (Lord Monboddo). *Of the Origin and Progress of Language*. 6 vols. Menston, England: Scolar Press, 1967.

Burwick, Frederick. "The Language of Casuality in *Prometheus Unbound*." *Keats-Shelley Journal* 31 (1982): 136–58

Bush, Douglas. *Mythology and the Romantic Tradition in English Poetry*. 1937; New York: Norton, 1963.

Butter, Peter H. *Shelley's Idols of the Cave*. Edinburgh: Edinburgh University Press, 1964.

———. "Sun and Shape in Shelley's 'The Triumph of Life.'" *Review of English Studies* n.s. 13 (1962): 40–51.

Byron, Lord George Gordon. *Childe Harold's Pilgrimage*. Ed. Jerome J. McGann. vol. 2 of *The Complete Poetical Works*. Oxford: Clarendon Press, 1980.

Cameron, Kenneth Neill. *Shelley: The Golden Years*. Cambridge, MA: Harvard University Press, 1974.

———. "*Rasselas* and 'Alastor': A Study in Transmutation." *Studies in Philology* 15, 1 (1943): 58–78.

———, ed. *Romantic Rebels: Essays on Shelley and His Circle*. Cambridge, MA: Harvard University Press, 1973.

———. *The Young Shelley: Genesis of a Radical*. New York: Macmillan, 1950.

Cameron, Kenneth Neill and Donald H. Reiman, eds. *Shelley and His Circle,*

1773–1822. 8 vols. to date. Cambridge, MA: Harvard University Press, 1961 – .

Cantor, Paul A. *Creature and Creator: Myth-Making and English Romanticism.* Cambridge: Cambridge University Press, 1984.

Chernaik, Judith. *The Lyrics of Shelley.* Cleveland: Case Western Reserve University Press, 1972.

Clark, David Lee. "The Dates and Sources of Shelley's Metaphysical, Moral, and Religious Essays." *University of Texas Studies in English* 28 (1949): 160–94.

Clark, Timothy. *Embodying Revolution: The Figure of the Poet in Shelley.* Oxford: Clarendon Press, 1989.

Coleridge, Samuel Taylor. *Biographia Literaria: Or Biographical Sketches of My Life and Work.* Ed. James Engell and W. Jackson Bate. Princeton, NJ: Princeton University Press, 1983.

———. *Lay Sermons.* Ed. R. J. White. Princeton, NJ: Princeton University Press, 1972.

———. *The Complete Poetical Works of Samuel Taylor Coleridge.* Ed. Ernst Hartley Coleridge. 2 vols. Oxford: Clarendon Press, 1912.

Collins, William. *Thomas Gray and William Collins: Poetical Works.* Ed. Roger Lonsdale. Oxford: Oxford University Press, 1977.

Cowper, William. *Poetical Works.* Ed. H. S. Milford. 4th ed. rev. Norma Russell. London: Oxford University Press, 1967.

Crompton, Margaret. *Shelley's Dream Women.* London: Cassell, 1967.

Cronin, Richard. *Shelley's Poetic Thoughts.* New York: St. Martin's Press, 1981.

Curran, Stuart. *Poetic Form and British Romanticism.* New York: Oxford University Press, 1986.

———. *Shelley's Annus Mirabilis: The Maturing of an Epic Vision.* San Marino, CA: Huntington Library, 1975.

———. *Shelley's Cenci: Scorpions Ringed with Fire.* Princeton, NJ: Princeton University Press, 1970.

Dante Alighieri. *The Divine Comedy of Dante.* Ed. John D. Sinclair. London: Bodley Head, 1958.

Darwin, Erasmus. *The Botanic Garden, Or, The Origin of Society.* Menston, England: Scolar Press, 1973.

———. *The Temple of Nature.* Menston, England: Scolar Press, 1973.

Dawson, P. M. S. *The Unacknowledged Legislator: Shelley and Politics.* Oxford: Oxford University Press, 1980.

DeLuca, V. A. "The Style of Millenial Announcement in *Prometheus Unbound.*" *Keats-Shelley Journal* 28 (1979): 78-101.

De Man, Paul. *Allegories of Reading: Figural Language in Rousseau, Nietzsche, Rilke, and Proust.* New Haven, CT: Yale University Press, 1979.

———. *Blindness and Insight: Essays in the Rhetoric of Contemporary Criticism.* 2nd ed., revised. Minneapolis: University of Minnesota Press, 1983.

———. *The Rhetoric of Romanticism.* New York: Columbia University Press, 1984.

Drummond, Sir Willam. *Academical Questions.* Delmar, NY: Scholars' Facsimiles and Reprints, 1984.

Dryden, John. *An Essay of Dramatic Poesy: A Defence of an Essay of Dramatic Poesy, Preface to the Fables*. Ed. John L. Mahoney. Indianapolis: Bobbs-Merrill, 1965.

Duerksen, Roland A. *Shelley's Poetry of Involvement*. Basingstoke: Macmillan, 1988.

Duffy, Edward. *Rousseau in England: The Context for Shelley's Critique of the Enlightenment*. Berkeley: University of California Press, 1979.

Engell, James. *The Creative Imagination: Enlightenment to Romanticism*. Cambridge, MA: Harvard University Press, 1981.

Enscoe, Gerald E. *Eros and the Romantics: Sexual Love as a Theme in Coleridge, Shelley and Keats*. The Hague: Mouton, 1968.

Everest, Kelvin, ed. *Shelley Revalued: Essays from the Gregynog Conference*. Leicester: Leicester University Press, 1983.

Fletcher, Angus. *Allegory: The Theory of a Symbolic Mode*. Ithaca, NY: Cornell University Press, 1964.

Fogle, Richard Harter. "The Abstractness of Shelley." *Philological Quarterly* 24 (1945): 362–79.

———. "Empathic Imagery in Keats and Shelley." *PMLA* 61 (1946): 163–91.

———. "Image and Imagelessness: A Limited Reading of *Prometheus Unbound*." *Keats-Shelley Journal* 1 (1952): 23–36.

———. *The Imagery of Keats and Shelley: A Comparative Study*. Hamden, CT: Archon Books, 1962.

———. *The Permanent Pleasure: Essays on Classics of Romanticism*. Athens: University of Georgia Press, 1974.

Foot, Paul. *Red Shelley*. London: Sidgwick and Jackson, 1980.

Frye, Northrop. *Anatomy of Criticism*. 1957. Princeton, NJ: Princeton University Press, 1973.

———. *A Study of English Romanticism*. Chicago: University of Chicago Press, 1968.

Fry, Paul. *The Reach of Criticism: Method and Reception in Literary Theory*. New Haven, CT: Yale University Press, 1983.

Fussell, Paul. *The Rhetorical World of Augustan Humanism: Ethics and Imagery from Swift to Burke*. Oxford: Clarendon Press, 1965.

Godwin, William. *An Enquiry Concerning Political Justice and Its Influence on General Virtue and Happiness*. Ed. F. E. L. Priestley. 3 vols. Toronto: University of Toronto Press, 1946.

Grabo, Carl Henry. *The Magic Plant: The Growth of Shelley's Thought*. Chapel Hill: University of North Carolina Press, 1936.

———. *A Newton Among Poets: Shelley's Use of Science in Prometheus Unbound*. Chapel Hill: University of North Carolina Press, 1930.

———. *Shelley's Eccentricities*. Albuquerque: University of New Mexico Press, 1950.

Hall, Jean. *The Transforming Image: A Study of Shelley's Major Poetry*. Urbana: University of Illinois Press, 1980.

Hall, Spencer. "Shelley's 'Mont Blanc.'" *Studies in Philology* 70 (1973): 199–221.

Hartman, Geoffrey H. *Beyond Formalism: Literary Essays 1958–1970*. New Haven, CT: Yale University Press, 1970.

Hawkins, Peter S. and Anne Howland Schotter, eds. *Ineffability: Naming the*

Unnamable, from Dante to Beckett. New York: AMS Press, 1984.

Hazlitt, William. *The Complete Works of William Hazlitt.* Ed. P. P. Howe. 21 vols. London: J. M. Dent, 1930-34.

Hildebrand, W. H. "Shelley's Early Vision Poems." *Studies in Romanticism* 8 (1969): 198–215.

Hoagwood, Terence Allan. *Skepticism and Ideology: Shelley's Political Prose and Its Philosophical Context From Bacon to Marx.* Iowa City: University of Iowa Press, 1988.

Hodgson, John A. "'The World's Mysterious Doom': Shelley's 'The Triumph of Life.'" *ELH* 42 (1975): 595–622.

Hogle, Jerrold. "Metaphor and Metamorphosis in Shelley's 'The Witch of Atlas.'" *Studies in Romanticism* 19 (1980): 327–353.

———. "Shelley's Fictions: The 'Stream of Fate.'" *Keats-Shelley Journal* 30 (1981): 78–99.

———. "Shelley's Poetics: The Power as Metaphor." *Keats-Shelley Journal* 31 (1982): 159–97.

———. *Shelley's Process: Radical Transference and the Development of His Major Works.* New York: Oxford University Press, 1988.

Holmes, Richard. *Shelley: The Pursuit.* New York: E.P. Dutton, 1975; reprint Elizabeth Sifton-Penguin, 1987.

Horne Tooke, John. *Diversions of Purley.* 2 vols. Menston, England: Scolar Press, 1968.

Hughes, D. J. "Coherence and Collapse in Shelley, with Particular Reference to 'Epipsychidion.'" *ELH* 28 (1961): 260–83.

———. "Kindling and Dwindling: The Poetic Process in Shelley." *Keats-Shelley Journal* 13 (1964): 13–28.

———. "Potentiality in *Prometheus Unbound.*" *Studies in Romanticism* 2 (1963): 107–126. Rpt. in *Shelley's Poetry and Prose.* Ed. Donald H. Reiman and Sharon B. Powers. New York: Norton, 1977. 603–20.

———. "Prometheus Made Capable Poet in Act One of *Prometheus Unbound.*" *Studies in Romanticism* 17 (1978): 3–11.

Hume, David. *Dialogues Concerning Natural Religion.* Ed. Norman Kemp Smith. 2nd ed. Indianapolis: Bobbs-Merrill, 1947.

———. *A Treatise of Human Nature.* Ed. L. A. Selby-Bigge. Oxford: Clarendon Press, 1967.

———. *Essays: Moral, Political and Literary.* Oxford: Oxford University Press, 1963

———. *An Enquiry Concerning Human Understanding.* Ed. Charles W. Hendel. Indianapolis: Bobbs-Merrill, 1955.

Hunt, Leigh. *The Poetical Works of Leigh Hunt.* Ed. H. S. Milford. London: Oxford University Press, 1923.

Jackson, J. R. de J. *Poetry of the Romantic Period.* Vol. 4 of The Routledge History of English Poetry. London: Routledge and Kegan Paul, 1980.

Johnson, Samuel. *The History of Rasselas Prince of Abissinia.* Ed. Geoffrey Tillotson and Brian Jenkins. London: Oxford University Press, 1977.

———. *Lives of the English Poets.* Ed. George Birkbeck Hill. 3 vols. Oxford: Clarendon Press, 1905.

Jones, F. L. "Shelley and Spenser." *Studies in Philology* 39 (1942): 662–69.

———. "Canto One of *The Revolt of Islam*." *Keats-Shelley Journal* 9 (1960): 27-33.

Kames, Henry Home, Lord. *Elements of Criticism*. 7th ed. 2 vols. Edinburgh, 1788.

Kapstein, Israel. "The Meaning of Shelley's 'Mont Blanc.'" *PMLA* 62 (1947): 1046–60.

Keach, William. *Shelley's Style*. New York: Methuen, 1984.

Kelley, Theresa M. "Proteus and Romantic Allegory." *ELH* 49 (1982): 623–52.

Keats, John. *Complete Poems*. Ed. Jack Stillinger. Cambridge, MA: Belknap-Harvard University Press, 1982.

Kermode, Frank. *The Sense of an Ending: Studies in the Theory of Fiction*. London: Oxford University Press, 1967.

King-Hele, Desmond. "Erasmus Darwin's Influence on Shelley's Early Poems." *Keats-Shelley Memorial Bulletin* 16 (1965): 26–28.

———. *Erasmus Darwin and the Romantic Poets*. London: Macmillan, 1986.

———. *Shelley: The Man and the Poet*. London: Macmillan, 1960.

Knight, G. Wilson. *The Starlit Dome: Studies in the Poetry of Vision*. London: Oxford University Press, 1960.

Kroeber, Karl. *Romantic Narrative Art*. Madison: University of Wisconsin Press, 1960.

Kuhn, Albert J. "English Deism and the Development of Romantic Mythological Syncretism." *PMLA* 71 (1956): 1094–1116.

———. "Shelley's Demogorgon and Eternal Necessity." *Modern Language Notes* 74 (1959): 596–99.

Leavis, F. R. *Revaluation: Tradition and Development in English Poetry*. 1936. Reprint Harmondsworth: Peregrine-Penguin, 1983.

Leighton, Angela. *Shelley and the Sublime: An Interpretation of the Major Poems*. Cambridge: Cambridge University Press, 1984.

Levin, Samuel. *Metaphoric Worlds: Conceptions of a Romantic Nature*. New Haven, CT: Yale University Press, 1988.

Locke, John. *An Essay Concerning Human Understanding*. Ed. Peter H. Nidditch. Oxford: Clarendon Press, 1979.

Maclean, Norman. "From Action to Image: Theories of the Lyric in the Eighteenth Century." *Critics and Criticism: Ancient and Modern*. Eds. R. S. Crane. Chicago: University of Chicago Press, 1952.

Mahoney, John L. "The Idea of Mimesis in Shelley's 'A Defence of Poetry.'" *British Journal of Aesthetics* 24 (1984): 59–64.

Marshall, William Harvey. *Byron, Shelley, Hunt, and The Liberal*. Philadelphia: University of Pennsylvania Press, 1960.

Massey, Irving. *The Uncreating World: Romanticism and the Object*. Bloomington: Indiana University Press, 1970.

Mawer, Noel Dorman. "Shelley, Metaphor, and the Romantic Quest for Unity." *Prose Studies* 7 (1984): 209–24.

Matthews, G. M. "Shelley's Grasp upon the Actual." *Essays in Criticism* 4 (1954): 328–31.

———. "On Shelley's 'The Triumph of Life.'" *Studia Neophilologica* 34 (1962): 104–34.

———. "Shelley's Use of 'Recall.'" *Times Literary Supplement* 20 Jan. 1956: 37.

———. "A Volcano's Voice in Shelley." *ELH* 24 (1957): 191–228.

McConnell, Frank D. "Shelleyan Allegory: 'Epipsychidion.'" *Keats-Shelley Journal* 20 (1971): 100–112.

McCormick, Peter J. *Fictions, Philosophies, and the Problems of Poetics.* Ithaca, NY: Cornell University Press, 1988.

McGann, Jerome J. *The Romantic Ideology.* Chicago: University of Chicago Press, 1983.

———. "The Secrets of an Elder Day: Shelley After *Hellas.*" *Keats-Shelley Journal* (1966): 25–41.

———. "Shelley's Veils: A Thousand Images of Loveliness." In *Romantic and Victorian: Studies in Memory of William H. Marshall,* ed. W. Paul Elledge and Richard L. Hoffman. Rutherford, NJ: Fairleigh Dickinson University Press, 1971. 195–218.

McNiece, Gerald. "The Poet as Ironist in 'Mont Blanc' and 'Hymn to Intellectual Beauty.'" *Studies in Romanticism* 14 (1975): 311–36.

Miller, J. Hillis. *The Linguistic Moment: From Wordsworth to Stevens.* Princeton, NJ: Princeton University Press, 1985.

Milne, Fred L. "The Eclipsed Imagination in Shelley's 'The Triumph of Life.'" *Studies in English Literature* 21 (1981): 681-702.

———. "Shelley on Keats: A Notebook Dialogue." *English Language Notes* 13 (1976): 278–84.

Milton, John. *Complete Poems and Major Prose.* Ed. Merritt Y. Hughes. Indianapolis: Odyssey-Bobbs-Merrill, 1957.

Mortenson, Peter. "Image and Structure in Shelley's Longer Lyrics." *Studies in Romanticism* 4 (1965): 104–10.

Murphy, John. *The Dark Angel: Gothic Elements in Shelley's Work.* Lewisburg, PA: Bucknell University Press, 1975.

Murray, E. B. "Annotated Manuscript Corrections of Shelley's Prose Essays." *Keats-Shelley Journal* 26 (1977): 10–21.

———. "'Mont Blanc''s Unfuled Veil." *Keats-Shelley Journal* 18 (1969): 39–48.

Nicolson, Marjorie Hope. *Mountain Gloom and Mountain Glory: the Development of the Aesthetics of the Infinite.* Ithaca, NY: Cornell University Press, 1959.

Notopoulos, James A. "The Dating of Shelley's Prose." *PMLA* 58 (1943): 477–98.

———. *The Platonism of Shelley.* Durham, NC: Duke University Press, 1949.

O'Malley, Glenn. *Shelley and Synesthesia.* Evanston: Northwestern University Press, 1964.

O'Neill, Michael. *The Human Mind's Imaginings: Conflict and Achievement in Shelley's Poetry.* Oxford: Clarendon Press, 1989.

Peacock, Thomas Love. *The Four Ages of Poetry.* In *The Works of Thomas Love Peacock.* Vol. 8 of *The Works of Thomas Love Peacock.* New York: Gabriel Wells, 1934

Perkins, David. *The Quest for Permanence: The Symbolism of Wordsworth, Shelley and Keats.* Cambridge, MA: Harvard University Press, 1959.

Petrarca, Francesco. *Triumphs.* Trans. E. H. Wilkins. Chicago: University of Chicago Press, 1962.

Plato. *The Dialogues of Plato*. Trans. Benjamin Jowett. 4 vols. 4th ed. Oxford: Clarendon Press, 1953.

Pope, Alexander. *The Poems of Alexander Pope: A One Volume Edition of the Twickenham Pope*. Ed. John Butt. London: Methuen, 1968.

Pulos, C. E. *The Deep Truth: A Study of Shelley's Scepticism*. Lincoln: University of Nebraska Press, 1962.

Quin, Mary A. "'The Daemon of the World': Shelley's Antidote to the Skepticism of *Alastor*." *Studies in English Literature* 25 (1985) 755–74.

Rajan, Tilottama. *Dark Interpreter: The Discourse of Romanticism*. Ithaca, NY: Cornell University Press, 1980.

———. *The Supplement of Reading: Figures of Understanding in Romantic Theory and Practice*. Ithaca, NY: Cornell University Press, 1990.

Reed, Arden, ed. *Romanticism and Language*. Ithaca, NY: Cornell University Press, 1984.

Rees, Joan. "'But for such faith': A Shelley Crux." *Review of English Studies* n.s 15 (1964): 185–86.

Reiman, Donald H. et al. *The Evidence of the Imagination: Studies of Interaction Between Life and Art in English Romantic Literature*. New York: New York University Press, 1978.

Reiman, Donald H. *Percy Bysshe Shelley*. New York: Twayne, 1969.

———. "Roman Scenes in *Prometheus Unbound* III.iv." *Philological Quarterly* 46 (1967): 69–78.

———, ed. *The Romantics Reviewed: Contemporary Reviews of British Romantic Writers*. New York: Garland, 1972.

———. *Romantic Texts and Contexts*. Columbia: University of Missouri Press, 1987.

———. "Shelley's 'The Triumph of Life': The Biographical Problem." *PMLA* 78 (1963): 536–50.

———. *Shelley's "The Triumph of Life": A Critical Study*. Urbana: University of Illinois Press, 1965.

Reiter, Seymour. *A Study of Shelley's Poetry*. Albuquerque: University of New Mexico Press, 1967.

Ricoeur, Paul. *The Rule of Metaphor*. Trans. R. Czerny et al. Toronto: University of Toronto Press, 1977.

———. "The Metaphorical Process as Cognition, Imagination, and Feeling." *Critical Inquiry* 5 (1978): 143–59.

Ridenour, George M. *Shelley: A Collection of Critical Essays*. Englewood Cliffs, NJ: Prentice-Hall, 1965.

Rieger, James. *The Mutiny Within: The Heresies of Percy Bysshe Shelley*. New York: Braziller, 1967.

Robinson, Charles. *Shelley and Byron: The Snake and Eagle Wreathed in Fight*. Baltimore: Johns Hopkins University Press, 1976.

Rogers, Neville. *Shelley at Work: A Critical Inquiry*. Oxford: Clarendon Press, 1967.

Rousseau, Jean-Jacques. *Julie ou La Nouvelle Héloïse*. 2 vols. Lausanne: Éditions Rencontre, 1970.

———. *The Social Contract and Discourses*. Ed. G. D. H. Cole, J. H. Brumfitt, and

John C. Hall. London: J. M. Dent, 1973.

——. *Reveries of the Solitary Walker*. Trans. Peter France. Harmondsworth: Penguin, 1979.

Sacks, Peter, *The English Elegy: Studies in the Genre from Spenser to Yeats*. Baltimore: Johns Hopkins University Press, 1985.

Schulze, Earl J. *Shelley's Theory of Poetry: A Reappraisal*. The Hague: Mouton, 1966.

——. "Allegory Against Allegory: 'The Triumph of Life.'" *Studies in Romanticism* 27 (1988): 31–62.

Scott, Sir Walter. *Poetical Works*. London: Oxford University Press, 1964.

Scrivener, Michael Henry. *Radical Shelley: The Philosophical Anarchism and Utopian Thought of Percy Bysshe Shelley*. Princeton, NJ: Princeton University Press, 1982.

Shakespeare, William. *The Complete Works*. Ed. Alfred Harbage. New York: Viking-Penguin, 1977.

Shealy, Anne E. *Journey Through the Unapparent: A Reading of Shelley's "The Triumph of Life."* Hicksville, NY: Exposition Press, 1974.

Shelley, Mary Wollstonecraft. *Journal*. Ed. F. L. Jones. Norman: University of Oklahoma Press, 1944.

——. *The Letters of Mary Wollstonecraft Shelley*. Ed. Betty T. Bennett. 2 vols. Baltimore: Johns Hopkins University Press, 1980–83.

Shelley, Percy Bysshe. *The Complete Works of Percy Bysshe Shelley*. 10 vols. (Julian Edition) Ed. Roger Ingpen and Walter E. Peck. London: Ernest Benn, 1926–30.

——. *The Esdaile Notebook*. Ed. Kenneth Neill Cameron. London: Faber, 1964.

——. *The Letters of Percy Bysshe Shelley*. Ed. F. L. Jones. 2 vols. Oxford: Clarendon Press, 1964.

——. *Prometheus Unbound: The Text and the Drafts—Toward a Modern Definitive Edition*. Ed. Lawrence Zillman. New Haven, CT: Yale University Press, 1968.

——. *Shelley's Adonais: A Critical Edition*. Ed. Anthony D. Knerr. New York: Columbia University Press, 1984.

——. *Shelley's Prose: The Trumpet of a Prophecy*. Ed. David Lee Clark. New York: New Amsterdam Books, 1988.

——. *Shelley: Poetical Works*. Ed. Thomas Hutchinson. Corrected, G. M. Matthews. Oxford: Oxford University Press, 1983.

——. *Shelley's Poetry and Prose*. Ed. Donald H. Reiman and Sharon B. Powers. New York: Norton, 1977.

——. *Zastrozzi and St Irvyne*. Ed. Stephen Behrendt. Oxford: Oxford University Press, 1986.

Sidney, Sir Philip. *An Apology for Poetry*. Ed. Forrest G. Robinson. Indianapolis: Bobbs-Merrill, 1970.

Simpson, David. *Irony and Authority in Romantic Poetry*. London: Macmillan, 1979.

——. *Wordsworth and the Figurings of the Real*. London: Macmillan, 1982.

Southey, Robert. *Poems of Robert Southey*. London: Oxford University Press, 1909.

Spacks, Patricia Meyer. *The Poetry of Vision: Five Eighteenth-Century Poets*. Cambridge, MA: Harvard University Press, 1967.

Spenser, Edmund. *The Faerie Queen*. Ed. A. C. Hamilton. London: Longman, 1977.

Sperry, Stuart. *Shelley's Major Verse: The Narrative and Dramatic Poetry*. Cambridge, MA: Harvard University Press, 1988.

Steinman, Lisa M. "Shelley's Skepticism: Allegory in *Alastor*." *ELH* 45 (1978): 255–69.

Tetreault, Ronald. *The Poetry of Life: Shelley and Literary Form*. Toronto: University of Toronto Press, 1987.

Thurston, Norman. "The Second Language of *Prometheus Unbound*." *Philological Quarterly* 55 (1976): 126–33.

———. "Author, Narrator, and Hero in Shelley's *Alastor*." *Studies in Romanticism* 64 (1975): 119–31.

Ulmer, William A. *Shelleyan Eros: The Rhetoric of Romantic Love*. Princeton, NJ: Princeton University Press, 1990.

Ward, William S. "Some Aspects of the Conservative Attitude Toward Poetry in English Criticism, 1798–1820." *PMLA* 60 (1945): 386–98.

Warton, Joseph. *An Essay on the Genius and Writings of Pope*. 2 vols. London, 1806.

Wasserman, Earl. "The Inherent Values of Eighteenth-Century Personification." *PMLA* 65 (1950): 435–63.

———. *Shelley: A Critical Reading*. Baltimore: Johns Hopkins University Press, 1971.

Webb, Timothy. *Shelley: A Voice Not Understood*. Manchester: Manchester University Press, 1977.

Weiskel, Thomas. *The Romantic Sublime: Studies in the Structure and Psychology of Transcendence*. Baltimore: Johns Hopkins University Press, 1976.

Welburn, Andrew J. *Power and Self-Consciousness in the Poetry of Shelley*. New York: St. Martin's Press, 1986.

Weller, Barry. "Shakespeare, Shelley and the Binding of the Lyric." *Modern Language Notes* 93 (1978): 912–37.

White, N. I. *The Unextinguished Hearth: Shelley and his Contemporary Critics*. Durham, NC: Duke University Press, 1938.

White, Newman I., Frederick L. Jones and Kenneth Neill Cameron. *An Examination of the Shelley Legend*. Philadelphia: University of Pennsylvania Press, 1951.

White, Newman I. *Shelley*. 2 vols. New York: Knopf, 1940.

Wilson, Milton. *Shelley's Later Poetry: A Study of his Prophetic Imagination*. New York: Columbia University Press, 1959.

Woodman, Ross. *The Apocalyptic Vision in the Poetry of Shelley*. Toronto: University of Toronto Press, 1964.

———. "Shelley's 'Void Circumference': The Aesthetic of Nihilism." *English Studies in Canada* 9 (1983): 272–93.

Wordsworth, William. *The Poetical Works of William Wordsworth*. Ed. F. de Selincourt and Helen Darbishire. rev. Helen Darbishire, 5 vols. Oxford: Oxford University Press, 1952–59.

———. *The Prose Works of William Wordsworth*. Ed. W. J. B. Owen and J. W. Smyser. 3 Vols. Oxford: Clarendon Press, 1974.

———. *The Prelude: 1799, 1805, 1850*. Ed. Jonathan Wordsworth, M. H. Abrams, and Stephen Gill. New York: W.W. Norton, 1979.

Worton, Michael. "Speech and Silence in *The Cenci*." In Allott, *Essays on Shelley*. Totowa, NJ: Barnes and Noble, 1982. 105–24.

Wright, John Williams. *Shelley's Myth of Metaphor*. Athens: University of Georgia Press, 1970.

Index

This book has beeen set in Carter and Cone ITC Galliard.
Galliard was designed for Merganthaler in 1978 by
Matthew Carter. Galliard retains many of the features of a
sixteenth-century typeface cut by Robert Granjon but has
some modifications that give it a more contemporary look.

Printed on acid-free paper.

Imageless Truths